The Wolves
of
North America

By

STANLEY P. YOUNG *and* EDWARD A. GOLDMAN

*Senior Biologists, Section of Biological Surveys, Division of Wildlife
Research, Fish and Wildlife Service, Department of the Interior.*

PART II

Classification of Wolves

By

EDWARD A. GOLDMAN

DOVER PUBLICATIONS, INC.

NEW YORK

International Standard Book Number: 0-486-21194-0
Library of Congress Catalog Card Number: 64-15510

Manufactured in the United States of America

Dover Publications, Inc.
180 Varick Street
New York, N. Y. 10014

PART II

Classification of Wolves
by
Edward A. Goldman

CONTENTS

vi

ILLUSTRATIONS

Plates

Text Figures

Tables

PART II

Classification of Wolves
by
Edward A. Goldman

VIII

INTRODUCTION

THE WOLVES of the genus *Canis* belong to the carnivorous family Canidae, which is nearly world-wide in distribution. The present revision includes the larger wolves, *Canis lupus*, and the red wolves, *Canis niger*, of North America, but excludes the coyotes, *Canis latrans*, which are somewhat wolf-like North American members of the same genus. Much evidence indicates that *Canis lupus*, the true wolf, as it may be called to distinguish it from other wolf-like species, is the progenitor of the domestic dog, *Canis familiaris*, the animal selected by Linné to typify the genus.

The true wolf (*Canis lupus*) is a living species formerly circumpolar in the Arctic land areas. From the Far North it extended south in the Old World to southern Eurasia, and in America from northern Greenland to the southern end of the interior plateau of Mexico, south of the 20th parallel of north latitude. It seems doubtful whether any other species of land mammal has exceeded this geographic range, and this wolf may, therefore, be regarded as the most highly developed living representative of an extraordinarily successful mammalian family.

The species *Canis lupus* forms a compact assemblage of closely allied geographic races. Complete intergradation is evident in numerous cases, and the relative values and combinations of characters presented indicate such close relationships that intergradation can be safely assumed where lack of material for study leaves gaps in the known ranges of continental forms. The wolf populations of Newfoundland, now extinct, and of Vancouver Island, still living, represent geographic detachment, but agree so closely with mainland races in their combinations of essential characters that sub-specific treatment seems fully warranted.

In America, the races of *Canis lupus* have received various colloquial names. Some of these are regional in application but are used to distinguish representatives of *Canis lupus* from the red wolves, *Canis niger*, and from the coyotes, *Canis latrans*, which are overlapped in geographic range. Perhaps most widely used is the common name "gray wolf" in reference to the grayish color tones that tend to prevail in the larger wolves; but colors vary from white through numerous shades of gray, buff, tawny, and brown to black. The term "brown wolf" was appropriately applied by Lewis and Clark to the dark-colored wolves of the forested region of western Oregon and Washington. The appellation "buffalo wolf" became extensively used for the wolves that were known to prey on the buffalo in the Great Plains region of the West. In the Southwest the Spanish name "lobo" is commonly used to designate the gray wolf. Gray wolves far exceed the coyotes in size, and as a rule contrast strongly with the red wolves also in this respect; but small gray wolves may be equaled by large red wolves in general dimensions.

The living red wolf, *Canis niger*, is much more restricted in distribution than the gray wolf. At the time of exploration and early settlement of the country, it inhabited the Mississippi River Valley and affluents from the Gulf of Mexico north at least to Warsaw, Ill., and Wabash, Ind., and from the Pecos River Valley, Tex., on the west to the Atlantic coast in Georgia and Florida on the east. The species is divisible into three subspecies. The reddish or tawny coloration tends to be distinctive, but owing to the range of individual variation, cranial features afford more reliable indices in making specific determination. West of the Mississippi River, the range of the red wolf is overlapped by that of the coyote. These two species are normally quite distinct, but small red wolves, especially in parts of central Texas, resemble coyotes very closely, and some specimens appear to be hybrids.

In revising the wolves of North America, twenty-three subspecies of *Canis lupus* are accorded recognition. *Canis niger* is subdivided into three geographic races. The revision is based mainly on a study of the extensive wolf material brought together especially in connection with the predatory animal control work conducted since 1915 by the Fish and Wildlife Service (formerly the Biological Survey), and other collections in the United States National Museum, now numbering 1,190 specimens. Many of these are skulls without skins, and in some cases skins without skulls. These specimens have been augmented by 178 from other American museums, making a total of 1,368 examined. (See "Acknowledgments," p. vii.) The assemblage has included the type or topotypes of most of the described forms. This unparalleled wealth of material has afforded a basis for accurate appraisal of the range of individual and geographic variation, and has led to satisfactory conclusions in most cases.

When the manuscript was about to go to press the descriptions of three new Arctic races were published (Anderson, 1943). These were added to the list of recognized forms on the basis of representations made by their describer who is well known as an eminent authority in his field. No opportunity was afforded, however, to obtain illustrations or to include cranial measurements in tables that had been prepared.

IX

HISTORY

The history of the Canidae, or dog family, as shown by the fossil record, extends, with many ramifications, far back in geologic time. The phylogeny of the family has been clearly traced by Matthew (1930, p. 133) to common ancestry with other carnivora in the Miacid family of Creodonts or Primitive Carnivora of the early Tertiary. The Canidae are primarily a group of carnivora, with long slender limbs and non-retractile claws, that became adapted for speed on open ground and acquired long jaws for snapping and slashing at prey. Development of hunting methods led to association in groups, teamwork, and finally to the highly complex social instincts and intelligence shown in modern dogs, wild and domestic. The dog family thus presents a wide contrast with the Felidae, or cat family, which represents another and even more exclusively carnivorous offshoot of Miacid ancestry. Unlike the dogs, the cats as a group developed shorter limbs with retractile claws and short jaws adapted to seizing and holding prey. Along with this physical equipment came the habits of concealment and lying in wait to pounce on a victim that could be quickly overpowered and killed. The cats evolved with similar success but as a group more solitary in habits and lacking the social behavior exhibited by the dogs. From the genus *Cynodictis*, a Miacid derivative of Oligocene time in both the Old and New Worlds, slow evolution brought the typical line of the dog family through the Miocene period to the genus *Canis* in the upper Pliocene or lower Pleistocene period. Originating in the northern hemisphere, the family became nearly world-wide in dispersal, but was absent from Australasia until the introduction of the dingo, probably by man.

Pleistocene deposits reveal the occurrence of wolves closely allied to the gray and red wolves of today that were transcontinental in distribution, as shown by finds in Cumberland Cave, Maryland, the Rancho Le Brea tar pits, California, and elsewhere. Apparently contemporaneous were wolves of the somewhat aberrant *Canis* (*Aenocyon*) *dirus* group which ranged from Alaska to the Valley of Mexico and from California east to Indiana and Florida.

Colonial settlers along the Atlantic coast of North America soon came in contact with the wolf. Perhaps the earliest reference to an American wolf in literature is that of Captain John Smith (1608-1631, p. CVI). In describing the animals of Virginia about 1609-1610, he wrote: "Ther be in this cuntry Lions, Beares, woulues, foxes, muske catts, Hares, fleinge squirells, and other squirels." Other early references to the animal were by William Wood (1635, p. 17) and by Thomas Morton (1637, p. 79), who dealt with its occurrence in New England. The first use of a distinctive name for an American wolf was by Schreber (1775), who entered the name *Canis lycaon* on plate 89 of his great work on the *Saugthiere*. The name was further validated by its appearance in the index, p. 585, of a section published in 1778. *Canis lycaon* was based by Schreber on Buffon's description and figure (1761, pp. 362-370, pl. 41) of a "loup noir," a female, captured in Canada when very young, kept chained, and taken alive to Paris by a French naval officer. In considering the names of North American wolves, Miller (1912, p. 95) showed that *Canis lycaon* Schreber must stand for the animal occurring in eastern Canada.

A very early name for the Florida wolf is *Lupus niger*, which was applied by Bartram (1791, p. 199) to the animal met with on the Alachua Savanna, Florida, in 1774. This name had been generally overlooked by authors until Harper (1942, p. 339) directed attention to it. Many years later the Florida wolf was described as

Canis floridanus by Miller (1912, p. 95). The name was based on a single specimen which proved to be of the so-called "red wolf" group. Previous to Harper's detection of an earlier name the red wolf was regarded as typified by *Canis lupus* var. *rufus* of Audubon and Bachman (1851, p. 240), from Texas. In this combination Audubon and Bachman erroneously linked the true wolf with the red wolf. In treating the mammals of Texas, Bailey (1905, p. 174) employed a full specific name, *Canis rufus*, for the red wolf which he distinguished from both the true wolf, *Canis lupus*, and the coyote, *Canis latrans*. Since no true wolf is known to have occurred in Florida in recent time it is reasonable to assume, as pointed out by Harper, that the specific name *niger* of Bartram must displace the more appropriate specific name *rufus* of Audubon and Bachman for the red wolf group. Black individuals of the red wolf group are very common, however, and it was evidently one of these that Bartram had in mind in bestowing the name *niger* to the Florida animal.

The close resemblance of the American gray wolf to *Canis lupus* of the Old World was noted by Richardson (1829, p. 60) in describing *Canis lupus occidentalis*, and in characterizing forms that he regarded as varieties, including *Canis lupus* var. *nubilus*, which Say (1823, p. 169) had treated as specifically distinct. Ten years later Richardson (1839, p. 5) published *Canis lupus* var. *fusca*. Many subsequent authors, however, in dealing with American true wolves, used names implying specific separation from the wolves of the Old World, and in the unrevised condition of the group, nominal specific names multiplied. *Canis pambasileus* was described by Elliot in 1905, and *Canis tundrarum* by Miller in 1912. *Canis nubilus baileyi* was added by Nelson and Goldman (1929, p. 165), and *Canis occidentalis crassodon* by Hall (1932, p. 420).

In "The Races of Canis Lupus," Pocock (1935), reverting to the usage of some earlier authors, treated the true wolves of the world, including the North American geographic races with the exception of *Canis lycaon* Schreber, as subspecies of *Canis lupus* Linné of Sweden. Comparison of Old World and New World material, and geographic considerations, seem to warrant this intercontinental linkage of subspecies. Specimens from the Anadyr region, northeastern Siberia, perhaps representing *Canis lupus dybowskii* Domanieski of Kamchatka, appear to be smaller, but in cranial features and dental details are very similar to the wolves of Alaska. Evidence of the near relationship of Asiatic and American wolves is not surprising in view of the close approach of the two continents, and the probability that animals venturing out on the ice would become marooned on detached ice fields and, under favorable wind conditions, be carried across Bering Strait.

Six subspecies of *Canis lupus* and one of *Canis rufus* (= *C. niger*) were described and the forms assignable to the two species were listed by the writer in 1937; and three additional subspecies have been published in connection with preparation of the present revision. In "The Names of the Large Wolves of Northern and Western North America," the nomenclature of the group was given comprehensive consideration by Miller (1912a). His paper afforded a very satisfactory basis for the work of subsequent authors.

Several names have erroneously been applied to wolves or may require clarification of status: The name *Canis mexicanus* Linné (1766, p. 60) was based on the *Xoloitzcuintli* of Hernandez (1651, p. 479) and was generally assumed by authors to refer to a Mexican true wolf until shown by G. M. Allen (1920, p. 478) to apply to the Mexican "hairless" dog. The early name *Canis lupus griseus* was proposed by Sabine (1823, p. 654) for the wolf of the vicinity of Cumberland House, Saskatchewan, Canada. Commonly treated as of full specific rank, it was accepted by authors for many years to designate wolves from regions as far south as Texas. However, as pointed out by Rhoads (Amer. Nat. 28: 524, 1894), by Bangs (Amer. Nat. 32: 505, July 1898), and by Miller (1912a, p. 2), the name is preoccupied by *Canis griseus* Boddaert (Elench. Anim., p. 97, 1784), a synonym of *Urocyon cinereoargenteus*. *Canis lycaon* B *americana*, applied by Hamilton Smith (Griffith's Cuvier, Anim. King. 5: 144, 1827) to the Florida wolf, was antedated by *Canis americanus* of Gmelin (Syst. Nat. 1 (13th ed.): 69, 1788) for an American Indian dog. Apparently combining the names *Canis (Lupus) griseus* and *Canis (Lupus) albus* of Sabine (Franklin's Journ., 1823, pp. 654 and 655 respectively) as *Canis occidentalis* var. *griseo-albus*, Baird (1857, p. 104) seems to have entertained a somewhat composite concept of a widely ranging race varying in color from "pure white to grizzled gray." No type was mentioned, and the name does not appear to be valid or clearly assignable to the synonymy of any particular race.

Reference is made by Baird (1859, p. 15) to the "lobo wolf, described in the Berlandiere MSS. as *Canis torquatus*," and he says: "The skull of Dr. Berlandiere's specimen (1379) is smaller than 2193, but similar in all essential features." No. 2193 was a specimen from Santa Cruz, Sonora, collected by C. B. Kennerly. Recourse to the U. S. National Museum catalog shows the entry dated January 26, 1855, as follows: "1379/*Lupus* young/ skull/7-3/4 in./Lt. D. N. Couch/Coll. L. Berlandiere/'*Lupus torquatus*.' " The unpublished Berlandiere manuscript, in the library of the U. S. National Museum, contains a very full description in Berlandiere's handwriting of an animal regarded by him as a wolf. Under the name *Canis torquatus* he placed *Canis mexicanus* Desmarest in synonymy. The species was assigned to a range on the coastal plains along the Gulf of Mexico in Tamaulipas. In the description reference is made to a nuchal band commonly discernible in both wolves and coyotes. The dimensions given of the young animal might be of either wolf or coyote. It seems clear that Baird (l.c.) in effect fixed on skull No. 1379, from Saltillo, Coahuila, as lectotype of the animal named *Canis torquatus*. As this skull cannot be found, its determination by Baird as that of a wolf is uncertain. It may be pointed out that the skull came from territory from which there appear to be no other authentic wolf records. The name *Canis torquatus* is not, therefore, satisfactorily assignable.

Canis frustror Woodhouse (Proc. Acad. Nat. Sci. Phila. 5: 147, 1851) from Cimarron River, about 100 miles west of Fort Gibson, Okla., was described as the American jackal believed to have been previously confounded with *Canis latrans*. In his Revision of the Coyotes or Prairie Wolves, Merriam (1897, p. 26) regarded *frustror* as a coyote, full specific rank being retained for it in accordance with his treatment of the other coyotes. On the basis of specimens collected later at Redfork, Okla., Bailey (1905, p. 175) concluded that *frustror*, instead of being a coyote, is more nearly related to the red wolf, *Canis rufus* (= *C. niger rufus*). This opinion was later shared by others, including the writer. The specimen regarded as the type in the U. S. National Museum is the stuffed skin without skull of an animal that was very young when collected. More critical comparison of this skin with those of red wolves and coyotes of similar age has convinced me that it is that of a coyote.

X

GENERAL CHARACTERS

The present revision includes the so-called true wolves, *Canis lupus*, and the red wolves, *Canis niger*, of North America. It excludes the coyotes, *Canis latrans*, the only other North American species currently assigned to the genus *Canis*. The species of the genus *Canis* are all larger and more robust than those of the foxes of the genera *Vulpes*, *Urocyon*, and *Alopex*, which are the other living representatives of the family Canidae in North America. In general structural characters, including the possession of glands on the upper basal part of the tail, all of the genera are very similar, but they differ in important details. In the wolves the normal number of mammae is ten. In *Canis*, in contrast with other North American canids, the pelage is elongated in a mane, erectile and conspicuous in anger, extending along the median line from the nape to a point behind the shoulders where it ends abruptly; the tail is more pointed than in *Vulpes* and *Alopex*, and more rounded, less crested than in *Urocyon*. The non-retractile claws are more blunt than in the foxes. As in the foxes, there are four toes on each hind foot and five on each front foot, the first short and rudimentary but bearing a well-developed claw, and a prominent callosity is present near the outer side on the posterior surface of the lower part of the forearm. In the wolves the tail gland is usually marked by a narrow patch of black-tipped hairs which are somewhat shorter and more bristly than those of surrounding areas. Even in Arctic wolves, in nearly pure white pelages, a few black-tipped hairs usually persist over this gland.

In the wolves, much as in the foxes, the cranium is elongated and tapered anteriorly, the jaws are very long, and the postorbital processes of the frontals and the zygomata are short, leaving a wide opening between them. Cranial characters distinguishing the wolves and coyotes of the genus *Canis* from the foxes of the genera *Vulpes*, *Urocyon*, and *Alopex* are presented by the frontals and adjoining bones. In *Canis* the postorbital processes are smoothly rounded above and evenly decurved, without depressions behind elevated edges, the posterior borders turning more obliquely inward and backward to form a sagittal crest than in the foxes. In addition, the median groove of the frontals ends farther forward, and the inion projects farther posteriorly than in the foxes. Compared with *Urocyon*, the genus *Canis* also differs notably in the union of the temporal ridges to form a long sagittal crest instead of their wide separation in a shield-shaped design, and in the absence of the prominent keel present in *Urocyon* on the under side of the lower jaw. Another differential cranial feature in *Alopex* compared with *Canis*, and in fact with the other foxes, is the encroachment of the squamosal arm of the zygoma over the jugal, so that the short postorbital process of the zygomatic arch is formed by the squamosal instead of by the jugal.

The dental formula in *Canis* is usually I. $\frac{3\text{-}3}{3\text{-}3}$; C. $\frac{1\text{-}1}{1\text{-}1}$; P. $\frac{4\text{-}4}{4\text{-}4}$; M. $\frac{2\text{-}2}{2\text{-}2}$ = 42, as in *Vulpes*, *Urocyon*, and *Alopex*, the other genera of North American Canidae. In dental sculpture, only minor details distinguish *Canis* from the other living Canids of the region. The upper carnassial (P.^{4}) is elongated antero-posteriorly, the crown partially cleft behind the middle consists of two main elements, an anterior lobe with a high conical point (paracone) directed backward, and a posterior lobe (metastyle) forming a laterally compressed shearing ridge; the protocone is variable but usually present as a small, blunt, antero-internal cusp in the red wolves and coyotes, and usually absent or rudimentary in the true wolves. The first upper molar is a large tooth transverse to the cranial axis in greatest diameter; the higher outer part is divided into two large conical cusps (protocone and hypocone), of which the anterior, the protocone, is the larger: the inner lobe is lower, with two small variable cusps, the posterior one obsolescent in the true wolves, and a low, crescentic ridge extends along the inner border. The lower carnassial (M.1) is longer (antero-posterior diameter) than the upper, with a laterally compressed paraconid-protoconid blade, the protoconid being much the higher of these two main divisions of the crown; the metaconid is a small but prominent conical cusp standing against the postero-internal base of the protoconid; a broad, low, posterior heel normally bearing two small cusps occupies about one-third of the crown surface. The posterior lower molars are very small, and not infrequently absent on one or both sides.

It is not surprising that some of the wolves of the recent past should be closely allied to living representatives of the gray and red species. *Canis armbrusteri* Gidley (Proc. U. S. Nat. Mus. 46: 98, 1913) from Pleistocene deposits in Cumberland Cave, Maryland, appears to have been allied to the red wolf, *Canis niger*, and other material from the same deposits indicates the occurrence of a close relative of the gray wolf. *Canis occidentalis furlongi* J. C. Merriam (Univ. Calif. Publ. Bull. Dept. Geol. 5: 393, 1910), from the Rancho La Brea tar pits, southern California, had many cranial characters in common with the gray wolves of today. Other remains from the tar pits suggest relationship to *Canis niger*. It may be of interest to point out that neither gray nor red wolves have been known in that region in recent time.

Associated with the material already mentioned from Rancho La Brea were the much more abundant remains of the widely ranging, somewhat aberrant, so-called Dire wolf, *Canis (Aenocyon) dirus* Leidy. The characteristics of this species have been fully described by J. C. Merriam (1912, pp. 218-246). The similarity in dentition and other general cranial features suggest that *Canis dirus* stood not far from the trunk line of evolution that led to *Canis lupus*. The skull exceeded that of *Canis lupus* in maximum size and massiveness, but some skulls of *dirus* are approached in general dimensions by *C. l. pambasileus* and some of the other large races of northern wolves. *Canis dirus* differs notably from *Canis lupus* in the shortness of the basicranial region behind the glenoid fossae. The posterior palatine foramina are situated farther back, near the posterior plane of the upper carnassials, instead of near or in front of a line drawn across the palate near the middle of these teeth. The lateral borders of the squamosals behind the zygomata slope slightly downward, instead of curving backward and upward to a point over the mastoids. The supraoccipital shield is narrower, and the inion is more prominent and projects farther posteriorly than usual in *Canis lupus;* these features are, however, approached in *Canis lupus nubilus*. In dentition, *C. dirus* is very similar to *C. lupus*. Points of general agreement in dental sculpture are the absence or rudimentary condition of the protocone in the upper carnassial, and the simple crown of the first upper molar. In the latter tooth the cingulum on the outer side is reduced to an inconspicuous line as in *lupus,* but the inner border of the inner lobe is distinctly lower than in the modern wolf. Despite the resemblance to *Canis lupus,* the departure in important cranial and dental details seems to warrant the recognition of the name *Aenocyon* as a genus or subgenus to include the wolves of the *dirus* group.

The gray wolves, *C. lupus,* red wolves, *C. niger,* and coyotes, *C. latrans,* form a compact group in North America, the three species differing from one another in characters that are usually distinctive, but quantitative rather than qualitative in value. The greater gross size is one of the best distinguishing characteristics of the gray wolf in contrast with the red wolf and the coyote; and in the same way the red wolf may usually be known from the coyote. Owing to geographic and individual variation, however, size alone is not always a safe index to specific determination. Large individuals of large subspecies of the red wolf about equal in size small examples of small races of the gray, and small red wolves closely approach large specimens of the coyote. And the resemblances are not confined to size, as is pointed out in describing the species. (Pls. 130-131.)

In the wolves, most of the sutures of the skull are clearly discernible at birth. The supraoccipital and interparietal become fused at a very early age. Soon to follow is closure of the sutures of the basicranial segment surrounding the foramen magnum. The supraoccipital, exoccipitals, and basioccipital are all firmly united, and the sutures have disappeared before the permanent dentition is fully in place. The union between most of these bones and the remainder of the skull, however, remains visible until finally closed with advancing age. The fusion of the interparietal and parietals is irregular, as it may come early or somewhat late in life. The jugals unite with the maxillae earlier than with the squamosals. Some of the sutures, however, remain distinct until extreme old age. Among the last to fuse are those between the nasals, maxillae, and premaxillae, forming the anterior segment of the skull, and the zygomatic union of the jugals and squamosals. The suture between the two halves of the lower jaw remains open. The temporal ridges unite to form a sagittal crest in both sexes early in life. The crest is usually more prominent in the males, than in the females, and reaches its highest development on the median line of the interparietal. The height of the crest and extent of closure of sutures are indices of age.

In the wolves, as in many other widely-ranging species, subspecific distinctions rest upon combinations of relatively slight characters indicating close relationships. The characters do not stand out very conspicuously as a rule, and allowance should be made for wide range of individual variation, but they are maintained with a fair degree of conotuncy over areas often of considerable extent. Individual variation in the color of both gray and red wolves is extraordinary. It ranges in some of the northern races of gray wolves from nearly pure white through mixtures of gray and buff to nearly pure black; and in the red wolves from grayish through more or less distinctly tawny to nearly pure black. Cranial characters are also variable, but within narrower limits, and are therefore more reliable than color in determining systematic relationships. The gray wolves, *Canis lupus*, and the red wolves, *Canis niger*, present specific patterns in dental sculpture, but the subspecies differ only in minor dental details.

In tracing the relationships of the subspecies or geographic races in the gray and the red wolves, the principal characters of taxonomic value are the following: Gross average size; general color, whether light or dark, plain grayish overlaid with black, or mixed with varying shades from pinkish buff to tawny; general form and massiveness of the skull, including height of brain case, frontal profile, posterior extension of inion, length of rostrum, and size of auditory bullae; size and relative length and breadth of molariform teeth. The males are usually decidedly larger than the females in all dimensions, with more prominent sagittal crests, but large females sometimes exceed small males, and females of a large race may exceed in size males of a smaller race.

Cranial abnormalities in the large number of specimens examined are few. In the skull of a young *C. l. irremotus* (No. 224445, U. S. Nat. Mus.) from Ingomar, Mont., in which the teeth of the permanent series were being acquired, the crowns were uncovered with enamel, leaving the dentine fully exposed. The small posterior lower molars may be absent, and the small anterior premolars may be lacking in either jaw. In a skull of *C. l. occidentalis* (No. 34447, Amer. Mus. Nat. Hist.) from Great Bear Lake, Mackenzie, a small additional upper premolar is present on the left side. In *C. l. lycaon* (No. 77344, Mus. Vert. Zool.) from Whitney, Ontario, three upper molars are present on each side. The supernumerary teeth are small, rounded, and very similar to the small corresponding molars normally present in the lower jaw. They are partially opposed to the lower molars and appear to have been functional to some extent.

XI

PELAGE AND MOLT

The pelage in the gray and red wolves is very similar in general character. In both species it consists of long guard hairs and much shorter and softer under-fur. The pelage is much longer and denser in the northern, than in the southern, races of gray wolves, in obvious response to climatic conditions. In the southern wolves the pads on the feet are entirely naked, and the hairs between the toes relatively short. In Arctic wolves, on the contrary, the edges of the pads are encroached upon by hairs to some extent, and long tufts between the toes doubtless afford additional support in passing over soft snow.

The annual molt seems to be somewhat irregular but, in the gray wolves at least, extends over a lengthy period during the summer. The new pelage, rather short in early fall, becomes longer in winter. The color is modified by wear of the tips of the guard hairs, or the complete removal of these hairs over large patches in some cases, thus exposing more of the under tone. This commonly results in a reduction of the black on the upper parts in the pelages of both gray and red wolves. In the red wolves the rufescent tone is most vivid in prime winter pelage, becoming duller through wear at other seasons. In the gray wolves, very old individuals tend to be somewhat grayer than those of younger age. Owing to greater length and density, the fur of northern wolves is much more valuable than that of the races inhabiting more southern territory.

XII

VARIATION

Variation in the wolves is assignable to several categories, of which perhaps the most obvious are geographic and individual.

GEOGRAPHIC

The gray wolves, *Canis lupus*, are all very similar in the more essential features and are believed to intergrade through the vast range of the species on the North American mainland. The component subspecies are the expressions of geographic variation in size, weight, color, and minor details of structure in response to environmental and genetic influences. The subspecies of wolves are based mainly on characteristic patterns of cranial structure, in which the gross size is combined with general agreement in certain proportions, and details that prevail with a fair degree of constancy over a geographic unit or area. Such areas may be either of limited or of vast extent. Some of the insular forms, such as *C. l. crassodon* from Vancouver Island and *C. l. beothucus* from Newfoundland, may present a somewhat greater degree of differentiation owing to isolation; but, as the trinomial names indicate, are not regarded as distinct species. The largest geographic races, *C. l. pambasileus*, *C. l. alces*, and *C. l. occidentalis*, inhabit Alaska, Yukon, and Mackenzie, and large wolves range south along the continental backbone to include

C. l. youngi of Utah, Colorado, and northern New Mexico. The gray wolves of the Arctic islands and eastern North America are somewhat reduced in size; and the smallest, *C. l. baileyi,* is from the Sierra Madre of Mexico. This small race was connected with the much larger subspecies *C. l. youngi* by *C. l. mogollonensis,* a rather compact form intermediate in geographic range, size, and detailed characters. The evidence presented by ample material shows that while there was intergradation, *C. l. baileyi* passed into the distinctly larger form *C. l. mogollonensis* within a restricted area in southeastern Arizona and southwestern New Mexico. This abrupt transition is probably due to the circumstance that the Sierra Madre and the Mogollon Mountain region were centers of wolf population not far apart, separated by a belt of less attractive desert or semi-desert terrain, entered by wolves only in small numbers. The contrast between the two races occupying such closely adjoining ranges seems most remarkable in view of the fact that wolves are known to include points 100 miles or more apart in the course of their regular movements.

Other geographic races, as *C. l. ligoni* of the Alexander Archipelago, and *C. l. alces* of the Kenai Peninsula, Alaska, appear to pass through narrow transitional areas into forms inhabiting adjoining territory. On the other hand, *C. l. occidentalis,* which ranges over an area of very great extent, apparently merges more gradually with the related forms. The boundaries of the ranges of such subspecies can only arbitrarily be fixed along lines representing the nearest apparent approach to scientific accuracy, as shown by specimens examined.

Geographic variation in color in *C. lupus* is shown in the lighter, less buffy tones in the normal grizzled grayish color phase, and the prevalence of nearly white or black individuals. Plain grayish colors tend to prevail in the wolves inhabiting the northern lowlands and the Great Plains east of the Rocky Mountains as far south as Oklahoma. From the Rocky Mountains to the Pacific Coast in the Northwest, the grizzled gray is usually more or less suffused with buff or cinnamon, and the muzzle, ears, and limbs are more vividly colored, the tones becoming more intense to the southward, and varying to tawny in *C. l. baileyi* of Mexico. Perhaps the most distinctively colored geographic race is *C. l. fuscus* of the forested region mainly west of the Cascade Range in Washington and Oregon. This race is dark "cinnamon" or "cinnamon buff" in general tone, with the back profusely overlaid with black. In Arctic wolves, white, usually with a varying admixture of thinly distributed dark hairs, prevails. Nearly white wolves, interspersed with those normally colored, are common east of the continental divide, and along the Rocky Mountains as far south as New Mexico and extreme eastern Arizona where individuals in this phase are referable to *C. l. mogollonensis*.

In *C. niger* the subspecies are based in part on geographic variation in size. Subspecies *rufus* of central Texas is small and closely resembles the coyote of the region. Increase in size is rapid toward the east, and some of the larger individuals of *C. n. gregoryi* from the Mississippi River Valley about equal small examples of *C. l. lycaon* of eastern Canada. The species was evidently based on the observation of individuals in the black phase such as are numerous in *C. n. gregoryi*, but appear to be rare in *C. n. rufus* of Texas.

INDIVIDUAL

Individual variation refers to the extent of divergence from the mean exhibited in a series of specimens from any given locality. In the wolves the range of this variation in size, color, and cranial details is very wide and should be carefully considered in the identification of specimens. While subspecies with confluent ranges may differ considerably in size, an unusually large individual of a small form may be similar in size to an unusually small individual of a large form.

Individual variation in color in most of the races of *C. lupus* is extraordinary, as it may extend through several color phases from nearly pure white to nearly pure black. Between these extremes are the grizzled grayish phase, which may be regarded as normal; a plain, more uniform gray phase in which the white and black are reduced and the buff eliminated; and a rufescent phase. While it is often convenient to refer to these color variations as color phases, there is no sharp line of demarcation between them. The races of the red wolf, *C. niger*, present two principal color phases. In one of these, the normal phase, "cinnamon buff," "cinnamon," or "tawny" tends to predominate, and the muzzle, ears, and outer surfaces of limbs, especially, exhibit the rufescent tones that led to the name for the species. Variation of this phase extends to individuals that are quite plain grayish owing to reduction of the rufescent element. In the other phase nearly black individuals resemble those in the corresponding phase of *C. lupus*.

The skulls of males, compared with those of females, are usually decidedly larger and more angular, as shown especially by the more prominent development of the sagittal crest and the heavier dentition. Individual variation, however, extends to cases in which there is little or no discernible sex difference. Irregular individual variations in the relative size of the large cheek teeth are not infrequent. Owing to individual deviations from the subspecific pattern, some specimens from unknown localities may be difficult to identify.

One or both of the small anterior premolars or posterior molars in either jaw may be absent, and in a few skulls supernumerary teeth were noted. In a skull of *C. n. rufus* from Kerr County, Tex. (No. 146744, U. S. National Museum), two small additional posterior upper molars are present. These have triangular crowns and are three-rooted. Similar additional posterior upper molars are in evidence in a skull of *C. n. gregoryi* from Solo, Pope County, Tex. (No. 243306, U. S. National Museum). These have nearly oval crowns, transverse in greatest diameter to the longitudinal axis of the skull. In another skull of *C. n. gregoryi* from Cooks Station, Mo. (No. 244426, U. S. National Museum), a supernumerary incisor placed slightly behind and between the second and third normal upper incisors on the right side projects slightly beyond the other teeth.

XIII

EXPLANATIONS

MEASUREMENTS

All measurements of specimens are in millimeters. The weights given are in pounds. Owing to the limited number of specimens of which external measurements and weights were available, more reliance is placed on conclusions based on the measurements of skulls. The external measurements, unless otherwise stated, were taken in the flesh by the collector, as follows: *Total length,* nose to end of terminal vertebra; *tail vertebrae,* upper base of tail to end of terminal vertebra; *hind foot,* back of heel to end of longest claw. Adult males usually exceed females in size, and the measurements are, therefore, presented according to sex. In some cases, so few nearly typical examples are available that the measurements given may not represent the normal range of individual variation, and too broad generalizations should not be based on them. The following cranial measurements of typical adults, unless otherwise stated, were taken with vernier calibers by the author. In measuring irregularly curved contours the vernier reading is apt to be altered with each slight change in the application of the points, or even the degree of pressure exerted. The calipers were, therefore, always held in as nearly the same position as possible; and whenever practicable, the vernier was read before the calipers were removed.

Greatest length.—Length from anterior tip of premaxillae to posterior point of inion in median line over foramen magnum.

Condylobasal length.—Length from anterior tip of premaxillae to posterior plane of occipital condyles.

Zygomatic breadth.—Greatest distance across zygomata.

Squamosal constriction.—Distance across squamosals at constriction behind zygomata.

Width of rostrum.—Width of rostrum at contriction behind canines.

Interorbital breadth.—Least distance between orbits.

Postorbital constriction.—Least width of frontals at constriction behind postorbital processes.

Length of mandible.—Distance from anterior end of mandible to plane of posterior ends of angles, the right and left sides measured together.

Height of coronoid process.—Vertical height from lower border of angle.

Maxillary tooth row, crown length. Greatest distance from curved front of canine to back of cingulum of posterior upper molar.

Upper carnassial, crown length (outer side), and crown width.—Antero-posterior diameter of crown on outer side, and transverse diameter at widest point anteriorly.

First upper molar, antero-posterior diameter, and transverse diameter.—Greatest antero-posterior diameter of crown on outer side, and greatest transverse diameter.

Lower carnassial (crown length).—Antero-posterior diameter at cingulum.

COLORS

Owing to the banding of the individual hairs, the pelage of wolves, like that of many other mammals, presents blended colors difficult to segregate and describe. The names employed of colors in quotation marks are from Ridgway's "Color Standards and Nomenclature, 1912." They represent approximations to color tones and are supplemented by generally understood modifying or comparative terms.

SPECIMENS EXAMINED

Specimens examined, unless otherwise indicated, are in the United States National Museum, including the Biological Surveys collection.

USE OF DISTRIBUTION MAPS

No attempt has been made to present keys to the subspecies of wolves. The construction of satisfactory keys to closely intergrading subspecies is not very practical, and it is suggested that recourse to the distribution maps will afford more reliable clues to the identification of specimens.

XIV

LIST OF NORTH AMERICAN SPECIES AND SUBSPECIES, WITH TYPE LOCALITIES

Subspecies of *Canis lupus*:

Canis lupus tundrarum Miller—Point Barrow, Alaska.

Canis lupus pambasileus Elliot—Susitna River, region of Mount McKinley, Alaska,

Canis lupus alces Goldman—Kachemak Bay, Kenai Peninsula, Alaska.

Canis lupus occidentalis Richardson—Fort Simpson, District of Mackenzie, Northwest Territories, Canada.

Canis lupus hudsonicus Goldman—Head of Schultz Lake, District of Keewatin, Canada.

Canis lupus arctos Pocock—Melville Island, District of Franklin, Northwest Territories, Canada.

Canis lupus orion Pocock—Cape York, northwestern Greenland.

Canis lupus labradorius Goldman—Fort Chimo, Quebec, Canada.

Canis lupus beothucus Allen and Barbour—Newfoundland, Canada.

Canis lupus lycaon Schreber—Quebec, Quebec, Canada.

Canis lupus nubilus Say—Engineer Cantonment, near Blair, Nebr.

Canis lupus irremotus Goldman—Red Lodge, Carbon County, Mont.

Canis lupus columbianus Goldman—Wistaria, north side of Ootsa Lake, Coast District, British Columbia.

Canis lupus ligoni Goldman—Head of Duncan Canal, Kuprean- of Island, Alexander Archipelago, Alaska.

Canis lupus fuscus Richardson—Banks of the Columbia River, below the Dalles, between Oregon and Washington.

Canis lupus crassodon Hall—Tahsis Canal, Nootka Sound, Vancouver Island, British Columbia, Canada.

Canis lupus youngi Goldman—Harts Draw, north slope of Blue Mountains, 20 miles northwest of Monticello, San Juan County, Utah.

Canis lupus mogollonensis Goldman—S. A. Creek, 10 miles northwest of Luna, Catron County, N. Mex.

Canis lupus monstrabilis Goldman—Ten miles south of Rankin, Upton County, Tex.

Canis lupus baileyi Nelson and Goldman—Colonia Garcia (about 60 miles southwest of Casas Grandes), Chihuahua, Mexico (altitude 6,700 feet).

Canis lupus bernardi Anderson—Cape Kellett, southwestern part of Banks Island, District of Franklin, Northwest Territories, Canada.

Canis lupus mackenzii Anderson—Imnanuit, west of Kater Point, Bathurst Inlet, District of Mackenzie, Northwest Territories, Canada.

Canis lupus manningi Anderson—Hantzsch River, east side of Foxe Basin, west side of Baffin Island, District of Franklin, Northwest Territories, Canada.

Subspecies of *Canis niger*:

Canis niger niger Bartram—Alachua Savanna (now Payne's Prairie), Alachua County, Fla.

Canis niger gregoryi Goldman—Mack's Bayou, 3 miles east of Tensas River, 18 miles southwest of Tallulah, La.

Canis niger rufus Audubon and Bachman—Fifteen miles west of Austin, Tex.

XV

CANIS LUPUS AND SUBSPECIES

CANIS LUPUS Linné
[Synonymy under American subspecies treated]

[*Canis*] *lupus* Linné, Syst. Nat. 1 (10th ed.): 39, 1758. Type from Sweden.

Distribution.—The original range of *C. lupus* was circumpolar in the Arctic land areas. From the Far North it extended south in the Old World, including Ireland and the British Isles in the West and Japan in the East, to southern Eurasia; in America it ranged from Cape Morris Jesup, Greenland, the most northern point of land in the world, 380 miles from the Pole, to the Valley of Mexico at the southern end of the high interior plateau of Mexico. Outlying islands included are Vancouver near the west coast and Newfoundland off the Atlantic coast. Throughout most of the vast general range of the species in America, wolves were formerly well distributed, but were absent in the extremely arid desert sections of the Far West and Southwest, particularly in central Washington, central Oregon, much of Nevada, the Great Salt Lake basin in Utah, southwestern Arizona, most of California, Baja California, and

Figure 14. Distribution of subspecies of *Canis lupus*

1. *Canis lupus tundrarum*
2. *C. l. pambasileus*
3. *C. l. alces*
4. *C. l. occidentalis*
5. *C. l. hudsonicus*
6. *C. l. arctos*
7. *C. l. orion*
8. *C. l. labradorius*
9. *C. l. beothucus*
10. *C. l. lycaon*
11. *C. l. nubilus*
12. *C. l. irremotus*
13. *C. l. columbianus*
14. *C. l. ligoni*
15. *C. l. fuscus*
16. *C. l. crassodon*
17. *C. l. youngi*
18. *C. l. mogollonensis*
19. *C. l. monstrabilis*
20. *C. l. baileyi*
21. *C. l. bernardi*
22. *C. l. mackenzii*
23. *C. l. manningi*

414

western Sonora. They were absent also west of the Sierra Nevada in California where conditions were apparently favorable, and did not enter the tropical parts of Mexico. The species has been extirpated from many regions formerly occupied, but is still present over vast areas, especially in the Far North.

General characters.—Size largest of the existing feral species of the genus; form robust; color variable, from mixtures of white with gray, brown, cinnamon, tawny, and black, to nearly uniform black in some color phases, and nearly pure white in Arctic races; skull heavy; first upper molar with cingulum on outer side indistinct.

Color.—*North American races in normal phase:* Upper parts in general widely varying mixtures of white with black and intermediate shades of gray, "cinnamon" or "cinnamon-buff," and brown; the back is usually more or less profusely overlaid with black; light post-humeral and nuchal bands are usually discernible where the black-tipped hairs thin out, but these bands are commonly interrupted along the median line; the muzzle, ears, and limbs, especially in the more southern forms, incline toward "cinnamon," "cinnamon-buff," or even tawny; under parts varying from whitish to "pinkish buff"; tail above similar to back, the black conspicuous over tail gland, paler below to tip which is black all around. *Black phase:* Upper parts brownish black to nearly pure black, with varying admixtures of white as a rule; under parts somewhat lighter in tone; a pure white median pectoral spot often present. *Young in first pelage:* Upper parts "drab-gray" to "drab," overlaid with brownish black; under parts usually somewhat paler, but chin blackish; ears blackish varying to buffy in some subspecies.

Skull.—Size large, and form massive. Comparison with *C. niger:* Size usually much larger, but small individuals may be exceeded by large ones of *niger;* form more massive; large molariform teeth with crowns less deeply cleft, the cusps more rounded and conical, less compressed laterally, the points and shearing edges less trenchant; upper carnassial with protocone, or antero-internal cusp more frequently absent, or if present usually less prominent; first upper molar with less prominent cingulum and with postero-external cusp less distinctly smaller as compared with antero-external cusp, also inner lobe bearing more reduced cusplets and enamel ridges; second upper molar variable but usually smaller.

Remarks.—The gray wolves are readily distinguished from any other North American canid, except possibly the red wolf, *C. niger,* in certain cases. In central Texas, gray wolves, *C. l. monstrabilis,* and red wolves, *C. n. rufus,* overlapped in geographic range. Specimens of the two from the same localities contrast strongly in size and present other differential characters that are unmistakable. Some specimens of *C. l. lycaon,* however, are of about the same size as *C. n. gregoryi* and *C. n. floridanus,* and while the pelage is longer, the color may not be very different. Similarity is also remarkably close in most other respects. Even the skulls are very much alike in form and in dental details. The most reliable distinguishing characters seem to be the reduction of the cingulum on the outer side in the first upper molar, the less deeply cleft crowns and more rounded, less laterally compressed cusps of the large molariform teeth. All discernible characters are subject to individual variation that may tend to obscure true relationship. It seems evident, however, that the cranial and dental similarities are superficial, with no direct bearing on specific distinction.

Gray wolves are often similar in external appearance to some of the large domestic dogs with which they readily cross, especially in the Far North. In cranial and dental details, however, wolves and dogs usually present marked contrasts. Among points of difference, the skulls of wolves tend to be flatter, with less elevated frontal region, and as a result the orbital angle, measured across orbits or at postorbital processes of frontals and jugals, rises less steeply. The orbits are more elliptical, less evenly rounded, owing to lesser concavity of the frontal border near the lachrymals, and are directed more obliquely outward. The auditory bullae are larger, more rounded and fully inflated, instead of flattened, with surface smoother, less rugose than in dogs. In dental sculpture the two animals are much alike, but in wolves the canines are longer, and the crowns of the upper carnassials, or large cheek teeth, exceed those of dogs in antero-posterior diameter.

CANIS LUPUS TUNDRARUM Miller
Alaska Tundra Wolf (Pls. 88-89)

Canis tundrarum Miller, Smiths. Misc. Coll. 59 (15): 1, June 8, 1912.

Type locality.—Point Barrow, Alaska.

Type specimen.—No. 16748, probably female, skull only, U. S. National Museum; collected by Lt. P. H. Ray.

Distribution.—Tundra region bordering Arctic coast of northwestern Alaska; south to Noatak River Valley. Intergrading on the south with *pambasileus,* and on the east along the Arctic coast with *mackenzii.*

General characters.—Size large; color light; pelage and claws very long; skull with heavy dentition. Closely allied to *pambasileus* of Mount McKinley region, but color paler and grayer, the white less mixed with brown or buff on head, and back more sparingly overlaid with black; skull with heavier dentition. Similar also to *occidentalis* and *mackenzii* of Mackenzie in size, but color darker, the general dorsal area more extensively mixed with black, and the tendency toward pure white less evident than in *occidentalis;* dentition heavier.

Color.—*Winter pelage:* Upper parts in general from nape to rump a mixture of white and black, the overlying black rather thinly distributed (compared with *pambasileus*); short pelage on top of head a grizzled mixture of white and black, faintly suffused in one specimen with "pale pinkish buff." Lip blackish in one specimen, white in another; entire under parts white; upper surface of muzzle pale buffy; ears pale buffy, mixed with black; outer surfaces of legs and feet faintly suffused with buff; soles and interdigital spaces "onion skin pink"; tail above similar to back, white below to tip which is blackish all around. No specimens in the black phase from the vicinity of the type locality have been examined, but two in this phase from the Noatak River appear to be referable to *tundrarum.*

Skull.—In close agreement with that of *pambasileus* in size and general structure, but dentition usually heavier, the difference most noticeable in the molariform teeth; crowns of second and third upper premolars, and of second, third, and fourth lower premolars usually distinctly longer. Not very unlike that of *occidentalis,* but dentition usually heavier.

Measurements.—*Body measurements approximated from tanned skins:* An adult male and female from Meade River, near Point

Barrow, respectively: Total length, 2020, 1940 mm.; tail vertebrae, 500, 475; hind foot, 295, 286. *Skull:* Type specimen (adult, probably female): Greatest length, 258.7; condylobasal length, 138.5; squamosal constriction, 76.1; width of rostrum, 43.2; interorbital breadth, 47.3; postorbital constriction, 41.9; length of mandible, 188.1; height of coronoid process, 74.7; maxillary toothrow, crown length, 110.6; upper carnassial, crown length (outer side), 25.9, crown width, 15; first upper molar, antero-posterior diameter, 17.7; transverse diameter, 24.7; lower carnassial, crown length, 30.5. An adult male and female from Meade River, near Point Barrow, respectively: Greatest length, 267.5, 270.5; condylobasal length, 248, 244.2; zygomatic breadth, 143.7, 140.5; squamosal constriction, 81.4, 77.2; width of rostrum, 47.1, 47; interorbital breadth, 46.9, 50.5; postorbital constriction, 43.7, 46.2; length of mandible, 199.4, 195.5; height of coronoid process, 84, 80; maxillary toothrow, crown length, 112.9, 112.6; upper carnassial, crown length (outer side), 27.2, 24.5, crown width, 16.3, 13.4; first upper molar, antero-posterior diameter, 18, 15.9; transverse diameter, 25.3, 21.1; lower carnassial, 30.9, 28.4.

Remarks.—Specimens examined indicate that *tundrarum* is a rather slightly differentiated, but recognizable subspecies. It appears to be most closely allied to *pambasileus*, but probably meets the range of *mackenzii* along the Arctic coast to the eastward. No specimens are available for study from the Arctic coast of Alaska east of the type locality of *tundrarum*. Wolves are known to occur, however, and in view of the close agreement of *tundrarum* with *mackenzii*, the intergradation of the two may safely be assumed. Six skins from points near the head of the Noatak River are variable in color: Two are similar to *pambasileus* in the gray phase, two resemble that subspecies in the black phase, and two are paler and more like typical specimens of *tundrarum*. The two skulls available from the Noatak area agree closely, especially in dental details, with *tundrarum*. These specimens are probably somewhat intermediate, but seem more properly referable to *tundrarum* than to *pambasileus*.

Specimens examined.—Total number, 13, all from Alaska, as follows: Meade River (near Point Barrow), 2[1]; Noatak River (near head), 6 (4 skins without skulls)[2]; Point Barrow (type locality), 5 (skulls only).

---

[1]Colo. Mus. Nat. Hist.
[2]One in Stanley P. Young coll.

CANIS LUPUS PAMBASILEUS Elliot
Interior Alaskan Wolf (Pls. 90-91)

Canis pambasileus Elliot, Proc. Biol. Soc. Washington 18: 79, February 21, 1905.

Canis lupus pambasileus Goldman, Jour. Mamm. 18 (1): 45, February 14, 1937.

Type locality.—Susitna River, region of Mount McKinley, Alaska.

Type specimen.—No. 13481, ♂ adult, skin and skull, Field Museum of Natural History; collected by C. F. Periolat.

Distribution.—Interior and most of western and southwestern Alaska, including the Seward Peninsula, the Yukon, Kuskokwim, and Susitna river valleys, and the Mount McKinley region; ranging east into southern Yukon. Intergrades with *occidentalis* on the east, with *tundrarum* toward the northwest, and probably with *alces* near the base of the Kenai Peninsula.

General characters.—Size among the largest of North American wolves; black color phase frequent; upper parts in gray phase mainly white moderately overlaid with black, with a buff suffusion in some specimens; pelage long; skull very large with elongated rostrum. Similar in size to *occidentalis* of Mackenzie, but color usually darker; upper parts in normal gray phase more profusely overlaid or mixed with black, and more or less suffused with pale buff, instead of the more uniform white or grayish shades exhibited by *occidentalis;* black color phase more prevalent; skull with longer palate. Similar in size to *tundrarum* of the Arctic coast of Alaska; color darker, the white more extensively mixed with brown or buff on head, and back more extensively overlaid with black; skull very similar in general form, but dentition lighter. Much larger and paler, in normal gray color phase, and *pelage* longer than in *ligoni* of the Alexander Archipelago. Size apparently smaller than *alces* of the Kenai Peninsula, and cranial details different.

Color.—*Winter pelage:* Upper parts from nape to rump a mixture of white and black, the black moderately extensive near the median line, thinning out along sides, more or less suffused in some specimens with "ivory yellow"; longer guard hairs near top of shoulders 130 to 140 mm. in length, tipped with black for about 25 mm., below which there is a white band, interrupted again by black giving way to white toward base; short pelage on top of head a grizzled mixture of white and black, varying in some specimens to white and "cinnamon-buff"; chin more or less distinctly brownish or blackish; under side of neck finely flecked with black, the rest of under parts white; upper surface of muzzle "cinnamon-buff" varying to blackish; ears "pinkish buff" or "cinnamon-buff" mixed with black; outer surfaces of legs and feet near "pale pinkish buff," a narrow blackish line present on forearm in some specimens, absent in others; tail above similar to back, below whitish near base, usually becoming suffused with "pinkish buff," and distinctly black all around at tip. *Summer pelage:* Shorter and much worn, but not materially different in color. In the black phase, while black or brownish black is predominant, especially over the back, specimens commonly present varying combinations of black or brown, thinly mixed with white in a grizzled pattern. The grizzled areas usually include the under parts, limbs, sides of head and lips, but intermingled white hairs may be present anywhere. According to Stanley P. Young, the recently-born pups are often of a light maltese slate color. Five very young pups from Toklat River are nearly uniform very dark brownish black everywhere, except for a small pure white pectoral spot on each.

Skull.—Closely approaches that of *occidentalis* in size and general form, but rostrum and palate slightly longer; maxillary tooth row longer. In close agreement with that of *tundrarum* in size and general structure, but molariform teeth usually smaller. Decidedly larger, more massive than in *ligoni*, with relatively heavier dentition. Differs from that of *alces* in apparently smaller size and less extreme elongation; rostrum and palate shorter; nasals narrower, less divergent anteriorly; supraoccipital shield narrower; molariform teeth relatively broader. Distinguished from *columbianus* by larger usual size; supraoccipital shield narrower; postorbital processes broader, less tapering, more bluntly pointed; carnassials relatively broader, less elongated (antero-posteriorly); second lower molars larger, less elongated.

Measurements.—An adult male from the Mount Hayes region, about 100 miles northeast of the type locality: Total length, 1753 mm. Two adult males from White River, Yukon, respectively: Total length, 1880, 1829; tail vertebrae, 532, 507. An adult female from same locality: Total length, 1765; tail vertebrae, 482. *Skull:*

An adult male from Gold Creek, a tributary of the Susitna River in the region of the type locality, and an adult male from Sushana River, north of Mount McKinley, respectively: Greatest length, 281.4, 286.9; condylobasal length, 261.4, 268.4; zygomatic breadth, 147.3, 151.6; squamosal constriction, 85.5, 82.8; width of rostrum, 48.6, 46.4; interorbital breadth, 47.3, 47.4; postorbital constriction, 45.8, 42.8; length of mandible, 203.7, 210.3; height of coronoid, 85.3, 89.1; maxillary tooth row, crown length, 120.4, 119; upper carnassial, crown length (outer side), 29.5, 27.1; upper carnassial, crown width, 14.7, 13.6; first upper molar, antero-posterior diameter, 19.7, 17.8; transverse diameter, 25.2, 24.1; lower carnassial, crown length, 33.8, 29.4. Two adult females, one from Tanana and the other from Fairbanks, Alaska, respectively: Greatest length, 269, 265.9; condylobasal length, 246.8, 245.5; zygomatic breadth, 129.4, 133; squamosal constriction, 79.8, 74.9; width of rostrum, 41.1, 44.6; interorbital breadth, 46.1, 44.3; postorbital constriction, 40.5, 40.7; length of mandible, 191.1, 191.3; height of coronoid process, 74.6, 71.6; maxillary tooth row, 111, 111.9; upper carnassial, crown length (outer side), 25.7, 25.4, crown width, 14.5, 14.8; first upper molar, antero-posterior diameter, 17, 17.1, transverse diameter, 23.2, 22.8; lower carnassial, 27.7, 28.7.

Remarks.—*C. l. pambasileus* agrees closely with *occidentalis* in size, and differs only slightly in cranial details, but is apparently distinguished by darker color in the normal color phase. It also differs in darker color from skins of *tundrarum* from the vicinity of the type locality, Point Barrow, Alaska. The type of the subspecies, *pambasileus*, is a black wolf. Individuals in the black phase are numerous.

Specimens examined.—Total number, 84, as follows: Alaska: Anchorage, 1 (skull only); Beaver, 2 (skulls only); Big Creek, Mount McKinley National Park, 1 (skull only); Big Delta, Tanana River, 2 (skulls only); Birch Creek (14 miles southwest of Circle), 1 (skull only); Chicken (Mesquite Forks, Forty-Mile River), 4 (skulls only); Cook Inlet (headwaters), 1 (skull only);[1] Cordova Bay (head), 1 (skull only)[2]; Dry Creek, north of McKinley National Park, 2 (skulls only); Eagle, 1 (skull only); East Fork, Mount McKinley National Park, 1 (skull only); Etchepuk River, Golovin Reindeer Range, Seward Peninsula, 1; Fairbanks, 2 (1 skull without skin); Fairbanks (100 miles north), 1; Farewell Mountain (south fork of Kuskokwim River), 1 (skull only); Fort Yukon, 1 (skull only); Fort Yukon (100 miles northwest), 1; Fort Yukon (head of Salmon Fork of Black River 120 miles northwest), 1 (skull only);[2] Gold Creek (near head; tributary of Susitna River above Curry), 1 (skull only); Jarvis Creek, 1 (skull only); Kenai Peninsula (probably near base), 1 (skull only);[2] Little Delta River, 2 (skulls only); Matanuska River (mouth), 1; Mount Hayes (headwaters Little Delta River), 2 (skulls only); Mount Hayes region, 9 (6 skulls without skins); Mount McKinley National Park, 5 (skulls only); O'Brien Creek (tributary of Forty-Mile River), 1 (skull only); Old Rampart House, 1 (skull only);[3] Savage River, 1 (skull only); Seventy Mile, 1 (skull only); Sushana River (north of Mount McKinley), 1 (skull only); Susitna River, 1 (skull only);[4] Tanana, 2 (skulls only); Tanana River (above Salcha River), 1 (skull only); Teklanika River (north of Mount McKinley National Park), 6 (skulls only); Toklat River, 6 (skins only); White River Glacier (near), Wrangell Mountains, 1; Yukon River (35 miles below Beaver), 3 (skulls only).

Yukon: Hoole Canyon, Pelly River, 1 (skull only); Hoole River, 1 (skull only); New Rampart House (6 miles north), 1 (skull only); Pelly River (mouth of Trummell River), 1 (skull only); White River, 8 (skulls only).[5]

CANIS LUPUS ALCES Goldman
Kenai Peninsula Wolf (Pls. 92-93)

Canis lupus alces Goldman, Proc. Biol. Soc. Washington 54: 109, September 30, 1941.

Type locality.—Kachemak Bay, Kenai Peninsula, Alaska.

Type specimen.—No. 147471, ♀ adult, skull only, U. S. National Museum (Biological Surveys collections); collected by C. A. Lambert, 1904. X-catalog number 5133.

---

[1]Kans. Univ. Mus. Nat. Hist.
[2]Mus. Vert. Zool.
[3]Stanley P. Young Coll.
[4]Field Mus. Nat. Hist.
[5]6 in Royal Ont. Mus. Zool.; 2 in Mus. Vert. Zool.

Distribution.—Known only from the type locality near the south-end end of the Kenai Peninsula.

General characters.—Size large, perhaps the largest of North American wolves; skull elongated with broad rostrum and narrowly spreading zygomata; canines large, but molariform teeth comparatively small. Similar in general to *pambasileus* of the Mount McKinley region, but apparently larger and differing in cranial details.

Color.—No skins available and color undetermined.

Skull.—Similar in general to that of *pambasileus*, but apparently larger, more elongated; rostrum and palate longer; nasals broader, more divergent anteriorly; supraoccipital shield broader; dentition similar, but molariform teeth relatively narrower.

Measurements.—No body measurements available. *Skull:* type, and an adult female topotype, respectively: Greatest length, 280.5, 272; condylobasal length, 263.5, 253.2; zygomatic breadth, 141.3, 141.4; squamosal constriction, 82.2, 81.8; width of rostrum, 47.4, 46.6; interorbital breadth, 49, 45.9; postorbital constriction, 44.3, 42.1; length of mandible, 201.3, 194.3; height of coronoid process, 79.1, 82; maxillary tooth row, crown length, 118.5, 112.3; upper carnassial, crown length (outer side), 25.5, 24.5, crown width, 12.8, 13; first upper molar, antero-posterior diameter, 17.1, 17.1, transverse diameter, 22.3, 22.3; lower carnassial, 30.3, 29.1. Two immature male topotypes (canines not fully in place), respectively: Greatest length, 263, 262.8; condylobasal length, 245, 250; zygomatic breadth, 133.8, 130.5; squamosal constriction, 80.7, 82.3; width of rostrum, 44.7, 45.7; interorbital breadth, 43.9, 42.5; postorbital constriction, 42.4, 40.9; length of mandible, 185, 190; height of coronoid process, 76.5, 74; maxillary tooth row, 108.6, 113.2; upper carnassial, crown length (outer side), 26, 27.5, crown width, 14.4, 15.4; first upper molar, antero-posterior diameter, 16.8, 17.3, transverse diameter, 23.3, 23.3; lower carnassial, 28.9, 31.1.

Remarks.—Five skulls without skins, from Kachemak Bay, Kenai Peninsula, not satisfactorily assignable to any of the races described, have accordingly been regarded as representatives of a new subspecies. This peninsular race reaches the maximum size attained by the species in North America. The skulls of two adult females are longer than those of any others examined, and present other peculiarities pointed out. Skulls of three immature males are not widely different from those of *pambasileus* of comparable age, but differ uniformly in the greater width of the supra-occipital shield. The new subspecies may range throughout the Kenai Peninsula, which at its base is narrowly connected with the mainland of Alaska. Specimens from north of Turnagain Arm of Cook Inlet are assignable to *pambasileus*. The principal natural prey of the Kenai wolf is doubtless the giant moose of the region. The large size of the wolf may be the result of adaptation enabling it to cope with so large an animal.

Specimens examined.—Total number, 5 (skulls only), all from Kachemak Bay, Kenai Peninsula, Alaska.

CANIS LUPUS OCCIDENTALIS Richardson
Mackenzie Valley Wolf (Pls. 94-95)

Canis lupus occidentalis Richardson, Fauna Boreali-Americana 1: 60, 1829.

Canis lupus-albus Sabine, Franklin's Narr. Jour. Polar Sea, p. 655, 1823. From Fort Enterprise, Mackenzie, Canada.

[*Canis lupus occidentalis*] var. C, *Lupus sticte* Richardson, l. c., p. 68. From banks of the Mackenzie River, Canada.

[*Canis lupus occidentalis*] var. E, *Lupus ater* Richardson, l. c., p. 70. From banks of the Mackenzie and Saskatchewan Rivers, Canada.

Type locality.—Name restricted by Miller (1912: 4) to subspecies occurring at Fort Simpson (now Simpson near mouth of Liard River), Mackenzie, Canada.

Type specimen.—Not designated.

Distribution.—Upper Mackenzie River Valley, north to Great Bear Lake, south over the vast lowlands interior of Mackenzie to central Alberta (Edmonton), Saskatchewan, and central Manitoba (Norway House); west in the Peace River Valley to eastern British Columbia. Intergrades on the west with *pambasileus*, and *columbianus*; on the north with *mackenzii*; on the east with *hudsonicus*; on the south with *nubilus*.

General characters.—Size among the largest of North American wolves; ratio of black to normally colored individuals apparently lower than in some of the other subspecies; upper parts in normal color phase varying from nearly pure white to white thinly overlaid or mixed with black or shaded with gray, usually lacking any buffy suffusion; skull very large and massive. Similar in size to *pambasileus* of Alaska, and somewhat larger than *columbianus* of British Columbia, but lighter, more predominantly white or plain grayish in normal color phase, without the buffy suffusion of upper parts seen in *pambasileus and columbianus*. Similar in size to *tundrarum* of the Arctic coast of Alaska, but color lighter, the tendency toward pure white more prevalent or the white less extensively mixed with black; dentition usually lighter. Apparently larger than *mackenzii* of northern Mackenzie and differs from *arctos*, the little-known race of Melville Island, Arctic America, in larger size and cranial details, including the broader brain case. Differs from *hudsonicus* of Keewatin in larger size and distinctive cranial features. Differs from *nubilus* of Nebraska most notably in larger size and more predominantly white pelage.

Color.—Very similar to *nubilus* in range of variation presented, but usually more extensively white; black patch on tail gland present, but black tip of tail usually inconspicuous. A skin from Fort Simpson, Mackenzie, in winter pelage is nearly uniform brownish black, the guard hairs with concealed white at base over dorsum.

Skull. About the size of that of *pambasileus*, but rostrum and palate slightly shorter; maxillary tooth row shorter. About like that of *tundrarum* in size and general structure, but molariform teeth usually smaller. Very similar to that of *columbianus*, but usually larger; postorbital processes stouter, less tapering, more bluntly pointed; dentition as a whole heavier, but second lower molars smaller. Apparently larger than that of *mackenzii*. Compared with *arctos:* Size larger, more massive; brain case broader; frontal region decidedly broader and flatter, less highly arched and convex in profile, more broadly and deeply V-shaped along median line; postorbital processes stouter, more bluntly pointed; auditory bullae smaller, less fully inflated; dentition similar. Compared with *hudsonicus:* Size decidedly larger; postorbital processes stouter, more bluntly pointed, the posterior borders turned less abruptly inward. Differs from that of *nubilus* most noticeably in larger size, supraoccipital shield usually broader, less projecting posteriorly, with a lesser tendency to develop a descending terminal hook.

Measurements.—A young adult male from Fort Simpson (type locality), Mackenzie: Total length, 1680 mm.; tail vetebrae, 480;

hind foot, 320. An adult male and an adult female from Wood Buffalo Park (10 miles from Slave River), Alberta, respectively: Total length, 1690, 1620; tail vertebrae, 430, 410; hind foot, 295, 290. *Skull:* Two adult males, one from Fort Simpson, Mackenzie, and the other from Wood Buffalo Park (10 miles from Slave River), Alberta, respectively: Greatest length, 292.8, 278.2; condylobasal length, 266, 262.5; zygomatic breadth, 156.5, 145.5; squamosal constriction, 85.4, 90.5; width of rostrum, 50.1, 47.2; interorbital breadth, 53.2, 46.2; postorbital constriction, 44.9, 44.6; length of mandible, 204.8, 197.6; height of coronoid process, 85.3, 80.8; maxillary tooth row, crown length, 116, 114.1; upper carnassial, crown length (outer side), 30.6, 27.2, crown width, 17.1, 14.4; first upper molar, antero-posterior diameter, 18.8, 17.6, transverse diameter, 24.8, 24.2; lower carnassial, crown length, 33.8, 30.8. Two adult females from Great Bear Lake, Mackenzie, and Wood Buffalo Park (10 miles from Slave River), Alberta, respectively: Greatest length, 249.5, 257.3; condylobasal length, 233, 237.5; zygomatic breadth, 130, 143; squamosal constriction, 75.5, 83.1; width of rostrum, 42.7, 44.6; interorbital breadth, 42.3, 42.3; postorbital constriction, 36, 45; length of mandible, 176.7, 185.5; height of coronoid process, 70.1, 76.4; maxillary tooth row, crown length, 106.6, 104.8; upper carnassial, crown length (outer side), 26.5, 25.8, crown width, 14.2, 14.2; first upper molar, antero-posterior diameter, 18, 17, transverse diameter, 24.1, 23.4; lower carnassial, crown length, 29, 29.7.

Remarks.—The wolves of the vast area here assigned to *occidentalis* are still very imperfectly known. Study of more ample material, when available, may result in a revision of range boundaries. The few body measurements at hand may suggest that *occidentalis* is smaller than *pambasileus,* but the skull dimensions of a larger number indicate that the two are very similar in size. The most obvious cranial difference appears to be the somewhat shorter rostrum and palate usually shown in *occidentalis* by the shorter maxillary tooth row. The prevailing color in the present race, like that of the other far northern subspecies ranging east of the continental divide, is white mixed to a very limited but widely varying extent with black or gray. In pallid general coloration, *occidentalis* closely resembles the paler specimens of *nubilus,* and contrasts rather strongly with *pambasileus, columbianus,* and other subspecies ranging mainly west of the continental divide. *Canis lupus-albus* Sabine, from Fort Enterprise, Mackenzie, as has been shown by Miller (1912, p. 1), is preoccupied by *C*[*anis*] *lupus albus* Kerr, 1792 (*Animal Kingdom,* p. 137), applied to the wolf of the Yenisei Region, Russia. *Lupus sticte* and *Lupus ater* are names applied by Richardson to color phases and are assignable to the synonymy of *occidentalis*.

Specimens examined.—Total number, 42, as follows:

Alberta: Edmonton, 1 (skull only); Smith landing (50 miles southwest), 1; Wood Buffalo Park (10 miles from Slave River), 7 (skulls only).[1]

British Columbia: Cache Creek, Peace River District, 2 (skulls only);[2] Cameron River, Peace River District, 1 (skull only);[2] Carbon River (35 miles west of Hudson Hope), Cariboo District, 2 (skulls only); Fort McLeod, Cariboo District, 1 (skull only);[1] Henry River (above Tuchade Lake), 1 (skull only).

Mackenzie: Artillery Lake, 1; Aylmer Lake, 1 (skull only);[1] Caribou Point, Great Slave Lake, 1 (skull only);[1] Fort Rae, Great Slave Lake, 1 (skull only); Fort Resolution, 1 (skull only); Fort Simpson, 5 (4 skulls without skins); Fort Smith, 1 (skull only); Great Slave Lake, 1 (skull only).[1]

Manitoba: Norway House (near north end of Lake Winnipeg), 1 (skull only).

Yukon: Crow Base (35-40 miles southeast), 3 (skulls only); Macmillan River (north fork), 2 (skulls only); Pelly Lakes, 7 (skulls only); Riddell River, 1 (skull only).

CANIS LUPUS HUDSONICUS Goldman
Hudson Bay Wolf (Pls. 96-97)

Canis lupus hudsonicus Goldman, Proc. Biol. Soc. Washington 54: 112, Sept. 30, 1941.

Type locality.—Head of Schultz Lake, Keewatin, Canada.

---

[1]Amer. Mus. Nat. Hist.
[2]Brit. Col. Prov. Mus.

THE WOLVES OF NORTH AMERICA

Type specimen.—No. 180281, made adult, skin and skull, U. S. National Museum (Biological Surveys collection); collected by H. V. Radford, January 4, 1912. Original number 92.

Distribution.—Northern Keewatin, including the northwestern coast of Hudson Bay (Cape Fullerton), and west to northeastern Mackenzie (Back's River, 20 miles below Lake Beechey).

General characters.—A light-colored subspecies of medium size; winter pelage nearly white, but hairs becoming grayish or brownish toward base over dorsum; skull with rather broad postorbital region and narrow, acutely pointed postorbital processes. Similar in general to *Canis lupus occidentalis* of the upper Mackenzie River Valley, but smaller, and cranial features distinctive. Apparently larger than in *mackenzii* of the lower Mackenzie River Valley. Size and color about as in *Canis lupus arctos* of Melville Island, but cranium flatter, less highly arched, the frontal outline much less strongly convex in lateral view, and differing in other details. Differs from *Canis lupus lycaon* of Quebec in larger size and whiter coloration.

Color.—*Type (winter pelage):* Upper parts in general yellowish white, or "cream color"; top of head and middle of face with dark brown under color faintly showing through; guard hairs over dorsum with a brownish band near middle below which they are whitish to base, the shorter under fur on the same area brownish at base, becoming pale yellowish toward tips; under parts overlaid with yellowish white, the under tone whitish to base of hairs; limbs about like under parts; feet "onion-skin pink" between the toes, as usual in the group; tail "cream color," except on the median line near upper base, where black-tipped hairs form a conspicuous, elongated patch on glandular area. A skin from Cape Fullerton, Hudson Bay, is whiter, the yellowish tone being absent, and the tail lacks the dusky spot on gland. Three April skins from Back's River, 20 miles below Lake Beechey, Mackenzie, are essentially white, with thinly distributed dark hairs on ears and over back, black tail gland, and scantily black-tipped tail.

Skull.—Similar in general to that of *occidentalis*, but differs in decidedly smaller size; postorbital processes more slender and more acutely pointed, the posterior borders turned more abruptly inward. Apparently larger than that of *mackenzii*. Similar in size to that of *arctos* but flatter, the frontal region less highly arched and convex in lateral view, more deeply V-shaped along median line in posterior view; zygomata tending to spread more widely; auditory bullae slightly larger, more fully inflated; postorbital processes narrow and acute as in *arctos;* dentition similar, but antero-internal cusps of upper carnassials less prominent.   Compared with that of *lycaon,* the skull is much larger, with relatively broader rostrum.

Measurements.—Type: Total length, 1720 mm.; tail vertebrae, 519; hind foot, 323; height at shoulder, 848; weight, 101 pounds. An adult female topotype: Total length, 1570; tail vertebrae, 420; hind foot, 290.   Three apparently adult males (skins only) from Back's River (20 miles below Lake Beechey, Mackenzie), respectively: Total length, 1593, 1650, 1605; tail veterbrae, 413, 431, 368; hind foot, 298, 307, 282. *Skull* (type and an adult female topotype, respectively): Greatest length, 258.3, 251; condylobasal length, 241, 228.8; zygomatic breadth, 146.4, 134.8; squamosal constriction, 83.9, 77.4; width of rostrum, 46, 42.4; interorbital breadth, 47.2, 44.4; postorbital constriction, 41.8, 43.2; maxillary tooth row, 110.1, 104.1; upper carnassial, crown length (outer side), 26.8, 24.5 crown width, 14.2, 13.8, first upper molar, antero posterior diameter, 17.4, 17.4, transverse diameter, 24.2, 22.6; lower carnassial, crown length, 32.6, 27.6.

*Remarks.—*The wolves of northern Keewatin and Back's River drainage in Mackenzie, and the northwest coast of Hudson Bay, are closely allied to *occidentalis,* the geographic neighbor on the west, but the differential characters pointed out seem to warrant the recognition of a regional race.   Comparison with a skull from Ellesmere Island, assumed to represent *arctos,* indicates more distant relationship.

*Specimens examined.—*Total number, 9, as follows:

Keewatin: Cape Fullerton, 1[1]; Hudson Bay (without definite locality), 1;[1] Schultz Lake, 3 (2 skulls without skins); Wager River, 1 (skull only).[1]

Mackenzie: Back's River (20 miles below Lake Beechey), 3 (skins only).

---

[1]Amer. Mus. Nat. Hist.

CANIS LUPUS ARCTOS Pocock
Melville Island Wolf (Pl. 98)

Canis lupus arctos Pocock, Zool. Soc. London Proc., part 3, p. 682, September 1935.

Type locality.—Melville Island, Arctic America.

Type specimen.—No. 55.11.26.4, adult, probably male, skull only, British Museum; collected on Sir E. Belcher's expedition, 1853-54.

Distribution. — Melville Island and probably neighboring islands; north and east to Ellesmere Island.

General characters.—A nearly white subspecies of medium size. Differs from *occidentalis* of Mackenzie in smaller size, more predominantly white coloration, and narrower braincase. Closely resembles *orion* of Greenland in coloration, but may be larger; skull with more elevated frontal region.

Color. — A female from Ellesmere Island (*winter pelage, April*): General coloration white, with blackish-tipped hairs thinly and inconspicuously distributed along median line of dorsum and across upper side of tail near base; sides of muzzle and small areas near angles of mouth mixed with dusky; throat yellowish; underfur over dorsum "light mouse gray"; soles of feet and interdigital areas near "buff-pink" on fore feet and "shell pink" on hind feet.

Skull.—Compared with *occidentalis:* Size smaller, less massive; braincase narrower, more highly arched; frontal region decidedly narrower, more convex in profile, less broadly and deeply V-shaped along median line; postorbital processes slenderer, more acutely pointed; auditory bullae larger, more fully inflated; dentition similar, but rather light; protocone of upper carnassial prominent. Compared with *orion:* Very similar in general form, but frontal region less elevated and less convex in outline.

Measurements. — Tanned skin of a female from Ellesmere Island: Total length, 1515; tail vertebrae, 360; hind foot, 225. *Skull:* From original description of type specimen: "Total length, 255; condylobasal length, 232; zygomatic width, 142; postorbital width, 43; interorbital width, 47; maxillary width above fourth upper premolar, 76; maxillary width at canines, 48; palate length, 114;

width of upper incisors, 39; upper cheek teeth, 108; mandibular length, 185; fourth upper premolar, 27 x 15.5; first upper molar, 18 x 21; first lower molar, 31." An adult male from Ellesmere Island: Greatest length, 264.7; condylobasal length, 236.9; zygomatic breadth, 138.7; squamosal constriction, 79.4; width of rostrum, 46; interorbital breadth, 45.6; postorbital constriction, 40.4; length of mandible, 186.8; height of coronoid process, 76.1; maxillary tooth row, crown length, 108.6; upper carnassial, crown length (outer side), 26.4; upper carnassial, crown width, 15.3; first upper molar, antero-posterior diameter of crown, 17.6, transverse diameter of crown, 23; lower carnassial, crown length, 30.1.

Remarks.—In describing *arctos*, Pocock referred to it a skull from Discovery Bay, Ellesmere Island. A somewhat larger skull from Ellesmere Island in the collection of the American Museum of Natural History also seems to agree with the original description, especially in the elevation of the frontal region, and is assumed to be representative. Characters differentiating *arctos* from *occidentalis* appear to be well marked, but relationship to *orion* is not so clear, owing to the lack of adequate material for comparison.

Specimens examined.—Two (one skin without skull, one skull without skin),[1] from Ellesmere Island.

CANIS LUPUS ORION Pocock
Greenland Wolf (Pl. 99)

Canis lupus orion Pocock, Zool. Soc. London Proc., part 3, p. 683, September 1935.

Type locality.—Cape York, on Baffin Bay, northwestern Greenland.

Type specimen.—No. 97.3.5.1, skin and skull, apparently male adult, British Museum.

Distribution.—Northern Greenland, Arctic America; limits of range unknown. Donald B. MacMillan writes me that wolves were found by his party at Cape Morris Jesup, the most northern point of land in the world, 380 miles distant from the Pole. He points out

---

[1]Amer. Mus. Nat. Hist.

their apparent absence at present in southern Greenland, but also evidence of their former occurrence, as the Norsemen arriving in 986 reported finding wolf traps, such as are built by Eskimos today.

General characters.—Described as a "whitish gray" subspecies, perhaps smaller than *arctos;* skull with less elevated frontal region.

Color.—From original description: "The coat is everywhere long and densely thickened with underwool about 60 mm. in length, the length of the contour hairs (in mm.) being approximately as follows: Back 70, flank 65, shoulder-mat 134, nape 105. There are also long hairs, from 60 to 70 mm., on the backs of the legs above the paws, the latter being long-haired round the margins and between the pads, which are completely overlapped and concealed. The general colour is a uniform whitish grey, except for the tolerably extensive marbling and streaking of the black-tipped contour hairs of the upper side, but the ears are pale buff, turning to drab towards the point; the top of the head, as far as the angle of the eye, and of the muzzle, apart from its white tip, is very pale brownish grey; there is some buff about the lower jaw and some black hair-tips on the hind throat; the rest of the underside and the legs are white; the tail has a black tip, but the rest of its upper side is not so conspicuously black and white as the back. Judging from the condition of the coat, and especially the hairiness of the backs of the legs and the soles of the feet, this skin is in winter coat." Two skins in the American Museum of Natural History were taken on the Crockerland Expedition from "Greenland." One of these is marked female, March 26, 1914, and both are almost entirely white. In one a few inconspicuous dark-tipped hairs appear on the lower part of the rump, and the upper side of the tail near the base. In the other, dark-tipped hairs are restricted to a few over the tail gland. In both of these skins the concealed woolly under-fur is pale gray, near "pallid mouse gray." Tufts of hairs between the median toes on the fore feet are about 55 millimeters in length, tinted basally with "shell pink."

Skull.—Type skull of doubtful sex, described as smaller than that of *arctos,* with less elevated and convex frontal profile. The skull of a female from "Greenland" is very similar to that of a male believed to represent *arctos* from Ellesmere Island in general form. The frontal region is less elevated, and thus in accord with the description of the type, but the range of individual variation is unknown.

Measurements.—No external measurements of specimens from very near the region of the type locality are available. Measurements of two wolves (sex and age not stated) shot by the Denmark Expedition on the east coast of Greenland in latitude between 75° and 83° 10′ N., furnished by Donald B. MacMillan, are respectively as follows: Total length, 1,500, 1,530 mm.; length of tail, 420, 440; height at shoulder, 760, 730; circumference of chest, 750, 670; weight, 63.8, 45.1 pounds. *Skull* (type specimen from original description): "Total length, 235; condylobasal length, 220; zygomatic width, 130; postorbital width, 40; interorbital width, 43; maxillary width above fourth upper premolars, 68; maxillary width at canines, 42; palate length, 110; palate between second upper premolars, 32; width of upper incisors, 34; upper cheek-teeth, 101; mandibular length, 171; fourth upper premolar, 23 x 14; first upper molar, 16 x 19; first lower molar, 27." An adult female from "Greenland": Greatest length, 242.4; condylobasal length, 227.5; zygomatic breadth, 132.8; squamosal constriction, 74.7; width of rostrum, 39.6; interorbital breadth, 42.1; postorbital constriction, 35.8; length of mandible, 173.4; height of coronoid process, 71; maxillary tooth row, crown length, 102.6; upper carnassial, crown length (outer side), 24.5, crown width, 13.8; first upper molar, anteroposterior diameter, 16.2, transverse diameter, 2.2; lower carnassial, crown length, 28.

Remarks.—The Greenland wolf was not fully characterized by its describer, and owing to lack of adequate material for comparison, its relationship to *arctos* remains somewhat uncertain. General conditions, however, point to the probable occurrence of more than one geographic race on the great island of Greenland. Degerbol (1927, p. 23) refers in comparative remarks to the wolves of the northwestern coast and the Scoresby Sound region on the east side of Greenland.

Specimens examined. — Two (one skin without skull) from Greenland (without definite locality).[1]

---

[1]Amer. Mus. Nat. Hist.

CANIS LUPUS LABRADORIUS Goldman
Labrador Wolf (Pls. 100-101)

Canis lupus labradorius Goldman, Mamm. Jour. 18 (1): 38, Feb. 14, 1937.

Type locality.—Vicinity of Fort Chimo (now Chimo), Quebec, Canada.

Type specimen.—No. 23136, probably ♀, adult skull only, U. S. National Museum; collected by Lucien M. Turner in 1882 or 1883. Original number 2190.

Distribution.—Northern Quebec and Labrador, Canada.

General characters.—Size medium; color light; frontals remarkably broad behind postorbital processes (usually broader than between orbits). Most closely allied to *lycaon* of southern Quebec, but larger; color lighter; cranial details, especially the greater postorbital width of the frontals, distinctive.

Color.—Varying from "dark somewhat grizzly gray to almost white" (Turner manuscript).

Skull.—Compared with that of *lycaon*, the skull is larger, more massive; rostrum heavier; postorbital region relatively broader (broader than interorbital region in most skulls examined); dentition heavier.

Measurements.—No body measurements available. *Skull.*—An adult, probably male, from Hopedale, Labrador, and the type, an adult, probably female, from Fort Chimo, Quebec, respectively: Greatest length, 262.2, 247.1; condylobasal length, 243.5, 222.7; zygomatic breadth, 141.5, 132.7; squamosal constriction, 78.8, 73; width of rostrum, 49.5, 41.7; interorbital breadth, 46.6, 43.5; postorbital constriction, 46.9, 46.9; length of mandible, 189.6, 175.5; height of coronoid process, 81.8, 73.8; maxillary tooth row, crown length, 110.1, 98.4; upper carnassial, crown length (outer side), 25.7, 25; upper carnassial, crown width, 13.7, 12.4; first upper molar, antero-posterior diameter, 17.1, 15.3, transverse diameter, 23.3, 21.3; lower carnassial, crown length, 29.4, 28.1.

Remarks.—The Labrador wolf appears to be an inhabitant of the barren grounds, requiring close comparison only with *lycaon* of the forested region of eastern Canada and the northeastern United States. A skull, probably of a female, from Hopedale, Labrador, agrees closely in general size and proportions with some examples of *lycaon* from southern Quebec, but the frontals are broader and the dentition is decidedly heavier. The skull, conforming so closely in many of the more essential details, suggests the probability of intergradation.

Specimens examined.—Total number, 11, as follows:

Labrador: Adlavik, 1 (skull only);[1] Hopedale, 3 (skulls only);[1] Kippokak, 1 (skull only);[1] Porcupine (near Cartwright), 1 (skull only).

Quebec: Fort Chimo, 5 (skulls only).

CANIS LUPUS BEOTHUCUS Allen and Barbour
Newfoundland Wolf (Pl. 102)

Canis lupus beothucus Allen and Barbour, Mamm. Jour. 18 (2): 230, May 14, 1937.

Type locality.—Newfoundland.

Type specimen.—No. 351, adult, probably ♂, skull only, Museum of Comparative Zoology; collected by J. M. Nelson, about 1865.

Distribution.—Confined to Newfoundland; now extinct.

General characters.—A white subspecies of medium size, with rather robust skull. Compared with *labradorius* of northern Labrador: Size and perhaps color similar; cranial details distinctive. Compared with *lycaon* of Quebec: Size larger; color whiter; skull heavier, the rostrum decidedly broader.

Color.—From original description of a skin from north of Grand Lake, Newfoundland, collected many years ago by Dr. Elwood Worcester: "Entirely pure white with a slight tinge of ivory yellow on the head and limbs. The under fur is dense and woolly, about 45 mm. deep on the shoulders, while the overlying guard hairs in the same region are about 160 mm. long. The short ears are densely hairy. According to Dr. Worcester, black individuals may occur."

Skull.—Similar to that of *labradorius* in size and general form including the broad rostrum, but differs in structural detail; frontal region more deeply groved, or V-shaped, along median line; postorbital processes less tapering, more obtusely pointed; supraoccipital

---

[1]Mus. Comp. Zool.

shield narrower; ascending branches of premaxillae shorter and broader; nasals less deeply excised to the median line anteriorly, leaving the narial borders more broadly U-shaped, instead of V-shaped; dentition similar. Exhibits a departure from that of *lycaon* in decidedly heavier rostrum and larger carnassials, and differs otherwise in about the same details as from *labradorius*.

Measurements.—From original description of a nearly complete skin collected many years ago north of Grand Lake, Newfoundland: "The ears measure about 80 mm. in length and hardly exceed the surrounding long guard hairs. This skin measures in head and body length, in its present condition, about 1390 mm." *Skull.*—From original description of type, regarded as a male, and a Newfoundland skull believed to be of a female, respectively: "Greatest length, 265, 245; basal length, 238, 227; palatal length, 125, 120; zygomatic width, 140, 130; mastoid width, 79.2, 71.8; width outside pm^4, 82, 75; upper cheek teeth, $c-m^2$, 107, 103; lower cheek teeth, $c-m_3$, 118, 126; length of upper pm^4, 24.2, 23; length of alveoli, pm^4, 21.8, 20.6; length of lower molar m_1, 28, 27.9." A larger skull, doubtless of an adult male from Newfoundland (also from original description): "Greatest length, 276; zygomatic width, 143. Skull of an adult, probably male (measured by author), from Newfoundland: Greatest length, 254; condylobasal length, 230; zygomatic breadth, 138.7; squamosal constriction, 78.2; width of rostrum, 44.1; interorbital breadth, 46.7; postorbital constriction, 45.4; length of mandible, 182.7; height of coronoid process, 78.6; maxillary tooth row, crown length, 104; upper carnassial, crown length (outer side), 26.2, crown width, 14.7; first upper molar, antero-posterior diameter, 17.5, transverse diameter, 23; lower carnassial, crown length, 29."

Remarks.—The Newfoundland wolf appears to have been more closely allied to *labradorius* than to *lycaon*. Its natural prey was the native caribou. With the settlement of the island, however, much injury to young cattle was reported, and a price put by the legislature on its head. This wolf probably became extinct during recent years.

Specimens examined.—Four skulls and one skin are known to exist. All of these were in the Museum of Comparative Zoology, but one skull of this lot has recently passed to the U. S. National Museum (Biological Surveys collection) in exchange. The exchanged skull is the only one examined by the author.

CANIS LUPUS LYCAON Schreber
Eastern Wolf (Pls. 103-104)

Canis lycaon Schreber, Die Saugthiere, theil 2, heft 13, pl. 89, 1775; name *Canis lycaon* also appears in Nachtrag zum 26 heft, theil 3, p. 585, 1778.

Canis lupus canadensis Blainville, Ostiogr. Mamm. Recents et Foss., vol. 2, facs. 13 (Atlas), Genre Canis, p. 45, pl. 7, 1843. Presumably from Canada.

Canis lupus canadensis Allen and Barbour, Jour. Mamm. 18 (2): 230, May 14, 1937.

Canis lupus lycaon Goldman, Jour. Mamm. 18 (1): 45, Feb. 14, 1937.

Canis tundrarum ungavensis Comeau, Ann. 1, Acfas, Montreal, 6: 121, 1940.

Type locality.—Vicinity of Quebec, Quebec, Canada. Type locality fixed by Goldman (Jour. Mamm. 18 (1): 38, Feb. 14, 1937).

Type.—Name used by Schreber in plate illustration (l.c.) derived from Buffon's description and figure (1761, pp. 362-370, pl. 11) of a "loup noir," a female, captured in Canada when very young, kept chained, and taken alive to Paris by a French naval officer.

Distribution.—Formerly southern Quebec, Ontario, north probably to Hudson Bay, eastern Minnesota, Michigan, Ohio, northeastern and middle Atlantic states; southern limit of range indefinitely determined but believed to extend to Florida. Still present in southern Quebec, Ontario, and parts of northern Minnesota, Wisconsin, and northern Michigan. Doubtless intergrading with *labradorius* and *hudsonicus* on the north, east and west of Hudson Bay, respectively, and formerly with *nubilus* west of the Great Lakes.

General characters.—A small, dark-colored subspecies; skull with remarkably slender rostrum. Size smaller than *labradorius* of northern Quebec, *hudsonicus* of Keewatin, or *nubilus* of Nebraska, and color darker than in any of them. Superficially similar to some specimens of large subspecies of *Canis niger*.

Color.—*Winter pelage:* Upper parts in general grayish, usually heavily overlaid with black from upper side of neck over back; head more or less suffused with "cinnamon"; under parts, including throat and thoracic area, varying from white to "pale pinkish buff," with scattered dark hairs intermingled, becoming clearer white on inguinal region; chin and space between lower jaws varying from white to blackish; ears "cinnamon" to near "tawny"; outer surfaces of limbs ranging from "cinnamon-buff" to rich "cinnamon," the forearms with a narrow black line, prominent in some specimens and obsolescent in others; feet near pinkish buff; tail grayish above, the guard hairs tipped with black, the black tending to mass over tail gland as usual in the group; under side of tail more or less distinctly suffused with buff to tip, which is black. *Summer pelage:* Similar to winter pelage, but somewhat paler, the black less in evidence.

The skin of a wolf taken on the grounds of the Tourelli Club, 50 miles north of Quebec, about November 1, 1916, and presented by Theodore Roosevelt, is mainly dark brown or brownish black, or more or less distinctly "fuscous," and may be not very unlike the animal figured as the type. In this specimen the upper parts from nape to rump are brownish black along the median line, but the guard hairs bear a nearly concealed subterminal buffy band about 10 millimeters wide, below which is a brownish section giving way to white at base. The under fur is brown. The sides of body are grayish brown. The muzzle and ears are clear brown or "fuscous," passing into a grizzled mixture of white and brown on the face. The throat and thoracic areas, except a pure white pectoral spot, are dark brown, becoming lighter, more grayish brown on abdominal region. The limbs are mainly brownish black. The tail is blackish above, grayish brown below.

Skull.—Similar in general to that of *nubilus*, but smaller, with much slenderer rostrum; supraoccipital shield less projecting posteriorly over foramen magnum; nasals usually more deeply emarginate anteriorly; upper carnassials smaller, the protocones prominent in some specimens, absent in others; posterior upper molars usually actually as well as relatively larger. Differs from that of *hudsonicus* in much smaller size and relatively slenderer rostrum. Compared with that of *labradorius*, the skull is much smaller and slenderer; frontal region narrower; nasals more deeply emarginate anteriorly; dentition in general lighter, but posterior upper molars relatively larger. Similarity in size and cranial details to large subspecies of *niger* is rather close; but in *lycaon* the skull is usually broader, with higher brain case and more massive in general form; zygomata more widely spreading; postorbital processes with posterior margins turned less abruptly inward; large molariform teeth with crowns less deeply cleft, the cusps more rounded, less compressed laterally, and the cingulum on the outer side in the first upper molar is less prominent.

Measurements.—An adult male from Montebello, Quebec, and one from Algonquin National Park, Ontario, respectively: Total length, 1575, 1626; tail vertebrae, 393, 419; hind foot, 323, 267. Average of three adult females from Montebello, Quebec: Total length, 1473 (1423-1524); tail vertebrae, 360 (356-368); hind foot, 269 (260-286). An adult female from Lucerne, Ontario: Total length, 1601; tail vertebrae, 482; hind foot, 253. *Skull:* Two adult males from Montebello, Quebec, respectively: Greatest length, 253, 250.5; condylobasal length, 233, 236; zygomatic breadth, 140.3, 136; squamosal constriction, 76.2, 78.8; width of rostrum, 41.4, 41.5; interorbital breadth, 45.3, 43.9; postorbital constriction, 38.1, 37.6; length of mandible, 181.7, 178.5; height of coronoid process, 75, 71; maxillary tooth row, crown length, 104.8, 106.6; upper carnassial, crown length, outer side, 23.7, 23.4, crown width, 13.7, 12.5; anterior upper molar, antero-posterior diameter, 16.3, 17.7, transverse diameter, 21.3, 21.9; lower carnassial, 27.9, 28.2. Two adult females from Montebello, Quebec, respectively: Greatest length, 213.6, 224.7; condylobasal length, 203.3, 211.4; zygomatic breadth, 118.2, 117.9; squamosal constriction, 69.6, 70.2; width of rostrum, 34.4, 35.3; interorbital breadth, 35.8, 37.2; post-orbital constriction, 30.4, 33.8; length of mandible, 155, 157.7; height of coronoid process, 62.5, 65.8; maxillary tooth row, crown length, 91, 94.5; upper carnassial, crown length (outer side), 22.5, 21.8, crown width, 12, 12.4; first upper molar, antero-posterior diameter, 16, 15.8; transverse diameter, 19.5, 21; lower carnassial, crown length, 25.8, 25.9.

Remarks.—*Canis lupus lycaon* is characterized by small general size, and particularly the relative slenderness of the rostrum. Specimens from the Great Lakes region present a wide range of individual variation in size and cranial details, and grade toward the more robust plains wolf, *nubilus*. The color is grayer, but in size and even in many details of cranial structure, some examples of *lycaon* bear a rather close resemblance to certain of the larger specimens of *Canis niger*. The subspecies *lycaon* differs, however, from the subspecies of *Canis niger* in combination of cranial details, as pointed out, and the resemblances are evidently superficial. A skull (No. 11179, Mus. Comp. Zool.) labeled Florida, without definite locality, is quite unlike that of the type of *floridanus*, now regarded as representing typical *niger*, the red wolf of the region.   In the height and massiveness of the cranium, obliquely directed temporal ridges and absence of well developed cingula on the outer borders of the first upper molar, this skull shows closer alliance with the true wolves. It is tentatively referred to *lycaon*, but is rather massive, with heavier but more narrowly spreading zygomata, shorter nasals, and heavier canines than usual in that form.   More material might indicate that it represents an unrecognized extinct southeastern race of *C. lupus*. *Canis tundrarum ungavensis* was not compared by the describer with *lycaon*, the type locality of which had been fixed as Quebec, which is within 200 miles. The two names are undoubtedly synonymous.

The name *Canis lycaon* was first used by Schreber (l.c.) under the figure on plate 89 in 1775. The animal was regarded as a black fox, and in synonymy reference is made to the "loup noir" of Buffon in theil 3, p. 353 of his great work, published in 1776.   The name *Canis lycaon* again appears, with further reference to the "loup noir" of Buffon, in Nachtrag zum 26 Heft, theil 3, p. 585, published in 1778.   The name *Canis lupus canadensis* Blainville appears to be assignable to the synonymy of *lycaon*, as shown by Allen and Barbour (1937, p. 230).

Specimens examined.—Total number, 77, as follows:

Florida: Without definite locality, 1 (skull only).[4]

Michigan: Calderwood, 2 (1 skull without skin); Cusino, 1; Dickinson County, 1 (skull only); Duluth, 7 (skulls only);[5] Eckerman (9 miles north), 1; Escanaba River (west branch), Dickinson County, 2 (skulls only); Grand Isle, 1 (skin only); Hulbert, 1 (skull only); Kenton, 1 (skull only); L'Anse, 2 (skulls only); Mackinac County, 1; Marquette (30 miles northwest), 3; Marquette County, 1 (skull only);[6] Newberry (22 miles northeast), 1 (skin only); Pine Lake, Marquette County, 2 (skulls only); Randville, 1; Saul Sainte Marie, 1 (skull only); Taquamenaw River (east branch, 5 miles from mouth), 1 (skull only); Taquamenaw River (2 miles above falls), 1; Walsh, Schoolcraft County, 1 (skull only).[7]

Minnesota: Elk River, 2 (skulls only); Gunflint Lake (east of), Superior National Forest, 8 (skulls only).[8]

New York: Adirondack Mountains, 1 (skull only).
Ohio: Without definite locality, 1 (skull only).[9]
Ontario: Brent, Algonquin National Park, 1 (skull only);[1] Dacre, Renfrew, 1 (skull only);[1] Gaudette Twp., Algoma, 1 (skull only);[1] Hurkett, Thunder Bay, 1 (skull only);[1] Little Island Lake, Algonquin National Park, 1 (skin only);[1] Mattawa, Nipissing (40 miles northeast), 2 (skulls only); McCoy's Lake, Algonquin National Park, 1 (skull only); Norway Creek, Algonquin National Park, 1 (skin only);[1] Port Sydney, Muskoka, 1 (skull only);[1] Searchmont, Algoma, 1 (skull only);[1] Silver Islet, Thunder Bay, 1 (skull only);[1] Sundridge, Parry Sound, 1 (skull only);[1] Whitney, Nipissing, 1 (skull only).[2]
Pennsylvania: Without definite locality, 2 (skulls only).[9]
Quebec: Lucerne, Hull, 3 (skulls only);[3] Montebello, Papineau, 6 (skulls only);[1] Quebec (Tourelli Club, 50 miles north), Quebec, 1 (black skin).
Tennessee: Hamilton County, 1 (ramus of mandible only).
Wisconsin: Antigo, Langlade County, 1 (skull only);[6] Eagle River, 1 (skull only); Perkinstown, Taylor County, 1 (skull only); Vilas County, near Michigan line, 2 (skulls only).[6]

CANIS LUPUS NUBILUS Say
Great Plains Wolf; Buffalo Wolf; Loafer (Pls. 105-106)

Canis nubilus Say, Long's Expedition Rocky Mountains 1: 169, 1823.
Canis variabilis Wied, Reise in das innere Nord Amerika 2: 95, 1841. From Fort Clark, near Stanton, Mercer County, N. Dak.
Canis lupus var. *nubilus* Richardson, Fauna Boreali-Americana, p. 69, 1829.

---

[1]Royal Ontario Mus. Zool.
[2]Mus. Vert. Zool.
[3]2 in Mus. Vert. Zool.; 1 in Royal Ontario Mus. Zool.
[4]Mus. Comp. Zool.
[5]Amer. Mus. Nat. Hist.
[6]Field Mus. Nat. Hist.
[7]Stanley P. Young collection.
[8]Minn. Mus. Nat. Hist.
[9]Acad. Nat. Sci. Phila.

Type.—No type specimen designated.

Type locality.—Engineer Cantonment, near present town of Blair, Washington County, Nebr.

Distribution.—Formerly Great Plains region from southern Saskatchewan and Manitoba south to northeastern New Mexico and southern Oklahoma, and from near the eastern base of the Rocky Mountains east to western Minnesota, western Iowa, and Missouri; now probably extinct. Intergraded on the north with *occidentalis,* on the west with *irremotus* and *youngi,* on the east with *lycaon,* and on the south with *monstrabilis.*

General characters.—Size medium; color rather light; skull short, broad, and massive, with supraoccipital region narrow, the inion strongly projecting backward and tending to develop a descending hook. Averaging smaller than *youngi* of the southern Rocky Mountain region, with upper parts less suffused with buff; skull with supraoccipital region projecting farther posteriorly. Resembling *irremotus* of the northern Rocky Mountain region, but usually grayer, less inclining toward white; frontals narrower. Differs from *occidentalis* of Mackenzie in smaller size and shorter, less extensively white pelage. Similar in size to *monstrabilis* of Texas, but usually paler, pelage longer and denser; skull flatter. Differs from *lycaon* of southern Quebec in paler color and much more robust skull.

Color.—*Winter pelage:* Upper parts in general a mixture of white and varying shades of light buff, moderately overlaid with black, tending to produce a grayish tone; more distinctly grizzled black and white on face and top of head where the pelage is short; under parts varying from white to near "pale pinkish buff"; outer sides of limbs to feet "pale pinkish buff," becoming lighter, more whitish along inner sides; ears "pale pinkish buff" to near "cinnamon-buff," usually edged with black; tail above whitish to "pale pinkish buff," overlaid with black most profusely over gland near base, becoming pure white or buff below, and black all around with a few white hairs usually interspersed at tip. Many color variations are presented. Individuals may be nearly white at any season, except for a sprinkling of black hairs over the back, a small, narrow, but conspicuous black patch over the tail gland, and a more or less distinctly black tip. Black individuals may occur in the same litter with those normally colored. A male in winter pelage from Mizpah Creek, 65 miles southeast of Miles City, Montana, is light "tawny" in prevailing color of upper parts. *Young:* In first pelage, sooty brown or near "wood brown" in general tone, varying to blackish on lower part of rump and upper surface of tail; facial area and top of head suffused with "cinnamon-buff"; cars "ochraceous tawny" edged with black. This pelage, short and velvety at first, grows rapidly, and thinly outstanding guard hairs appear. In about six to eight weeks it gives way to a new and shorter coat of a somewhat lighter shade, due to the removal of dusky guard hairs. In young specimens taken 20 miles south of Higbee, Colorado, on April 26, 1910, this first molt had advanced to the base of the tail, leaving this appendage in the earlier stage. In the new pelage the color markings of the adult, especially the post-humeral whitish areas and tendency to exhibit a whitish collar, become more clearly apparent. The black patch over the tail gland is more or less distinctly in evidence from early puppyhood.

Skull.—Relatively short and massive in general form, with heavy rostrum and narrow supraoccipital shield and inion prominently projected posteriorly. Similar in general form to that of *youngi,* but averaging smaller; rostrum shorter and supraoccipital shield narrower, rising less steeply, the inion projecting farther posteriorly over foramen magnum, and tending to develop a descending terminal hook. Compared with *irremotus:* Frontal region narrower, and differing otherwise in about the same characters as from *youngi.* Compared with *lycaon:* Larger, more massive; rostrum broader; supraoccipital shield and inion more projecting posteriorly; nasals less deeply emarginate anteriorly; dentition as a whole heavier, but posterior upper molars usually actually as well as relatively smaller. Differs from that of *occidentalis* most noticeably in smaller size. Compared with *monstrabilis:* Size similar, but more flattened; frontals less highly arched and less convex in profile; rostrum less depressed across middle, sloping more gradually upward to frontals; nasals with inner margins usually turned less strongly downward to form a V-shaped median trough.

Measurements.—An adult male from Douglas, Wyo.: Total length, 1,982; height at shoulder, 940. *Skull:* Two adult males from Kearney, Nebr., respectively: Greatest length, 258.4, 253.5; condylobasal length, 228.9, 232.3; zygomatic breadth, 137.7, 135.2; squamosal constriction, 80.4, 75.7; width of rostrum, 44.3, 42.2; interorbital breadth, 46.6, 48.1; postorbital constriction, 35.7, 40.3;

length of mandible, 180.3, 183.5; height of coronoid process, 81, 81.2; maxillary tooth row, 102.8, 106.3; upper carnassial, crown length (outer side), 26.1, 25.2, crown width, 13.1, 12.4; first upper molar, antero-posterior diameter, 15.9, 17.2, transverse diameter, 22.6, 22.7; lower carnassial, 29.2, 28.9. Two adult females, one from Kearney and the other from Platte River, Nebr., respectively: Greatest length, 228.7, 231; condylobasal length, 210.7, 212.5; zygomatic breadth, 119.4, 130.5; squamosal constriction, 70.6, 71.4; width of rostrum, 38.7, 40.9; interorbital breadth, 38.9, 40.3; post-orbital constriction, 34.8, 38; length of mandible, 161.7, 165.5 height of coronoid process, 66.5, 71.4; maxillary tooth row, crown length (outer side), 24.1, 24.2, crown width, 12.8, 14.1; first upper molar, antero-posterior diameter, 16.9, 15.5, transverse diameter, 23.2, 20.2; lower carnassial, crown length, 27.8, 28.

Remarks.—The Great Plains wolf was a well-marked race, mid-continental in geographic position. Its range included that of the greatest game herds of North America, which afforded an ample food supply. The individual cranial variation that may be expected in wolves is well shown by 88 skulls of this subspecies taken many years ago in the vicinity of Fort Union, Mont. Evidence of inter-gradation with neighboring races is shown by specimens from various localities along the borders of the general range. Specimens from eastern Minnesota and Michigan seem more properly refera-ble to *lycaon,* but relationship to *nubilus* is shown in somewhat inter-mediate characters.

Specimens examined.—Total number, 191, as follows:

Colorado: Bent County, 15 (7 skulls only); Fort Massachusetts (now Fort Garland), San Luis Valley, near head of Rio Grande, 1 (skull only); Higbee, Otero County (20 miles south), 3; Re-publican Fork of Kansas River, 1 (skull only); Thatcher (11 miles north), 1 (skull only.)[1]

Kansas: Fort Harker, 1; Gove County, 1 (skull only).

Manitoba: Duck Mountain, 2 (skulls only).

Minnesota: Crookston, 1 (skull only).

Missouri: Without definite locality, 1 (skull only).[2]

Montana: Ekalaka, 1 (skull only); Fort Union, 88 (skulls only); Glendive, 1 (skull only); Kinsey, 1; Meredith, 5 (skin and skull); Miles City, 7 (1 skull only); Mizpah, 1; Mizpah Creek (65 miles southeast of Miles City), 1; Stone Shack, Custer

County, 3 (1 skull only); Upper Missouri River, 1 (skull only).
Nebraska: Fort Kearney, 14 (skulls only); Platte River, 5 (skulls only).
New Mexico: Carthage, 5; Gallo Canyon (40 miles southeast of Corona), 1 (skull only); Mountainair, Torrance County, 2 (skin and skull); Santa Rosa (18 miles north), 2 (skulls only).
North Dakota: Medora (20 miles south), 6 (skulls only).
Oklahoma: Afton, 1 (skull only); Beaver Creek, 1 (skull only);[3] Wichita Mountains, 4 (skulls only).
South Dakota: Dewey, Custer County, 1; Faith, Meade County, 1; Folsom, Custer County, 1; Fort Randall, 2 (1 skull only); Harding County, 1 (skull only); Imlay, Pennington County, 1.
Wyoming: Douglas, 5 (1 skull only); Natrona County, 2 (skulls only).

CANIS LUPUS IRREMOTUS Goldman
Northern Rocky Mountain Wolf (Pls. 107-108)

Canis lupus irremotus Goldman, Mamm. Jour. 18 (1): 41, Feb. 14, 1937.

Type locality. — Red Lodge, Carbon County, southwestern Montana.

Type specimen.—No. 214869, ♂ adult, skin and skull, U. S. National Museum (Biological Surveys collection); collected by M. E. Martin, April 19, 1916. X-catalog number 16243.

Distribution.—Formerly the northern Rocky Mountain region and high adjoining plains, from southern Alberta (Calgary) south through Idaho, and western Montana to western Wyoming; east to the Black Hills (Belle Fourche) of South Dakota.

General characters.—A light-colored subspecies of medium to rather large size, with narrow but flattened frontal region. Similar in size to *youngi* of the more southern Rocky Mountain region, but whiter, the upper parts less heavily overlaid with black; skull differs in detail, especially in the narrowness of the frontal region. Size larger and color whiter than in *nubilus* of Nebraska, or in *fuscus* of Oregon, and differs from both in cranial features, including the rela-

---

[1]Coll. Stanley P. Young.
[2]Coll. Acad. Nat. Sci. Phila.
[3]Coll. Amer. Mus. Nat. Hist.

tive narrowness of the frontal region. Differs from *occidentalis* of Mackenzie in decidedly smaller size. Differs from *columbianus* of central British Columbia in smaller average size, paler, less "cinnamon-buff" coloration, and narrower postorbital region of skull.

Color.—*Winter pelage:* Upper parts from nape to rump usually near "light buff" or varying shades of gray, sparingly overlaid with black, becoming nearly white on sides and limbs; short pelage on top of head light buffy white, the hairs tipped with black; ears and upper surface of muzzle light buffy; under parts in general more or less soiled white; tail above light buffy, thinly and inconspicuously overlaid with black, light buffy below to tip, which is a mixture of buff and black all around. Individuals in the black phase appear to be rare. In a skin from the vicinity of Kelly, Wyoming, the prevailing color is brownish black, extending down over the legs to the feet. A skin from near Elk, Wyoming, is unusual in "pale drab-gray" general tone, becoming whitish on legs and feet; ears brownish black in marked contrast with surrounding pelage; tail grayish, tipped with white.

Skull.—Very similar in size and spread of zygomata to that of *youngi,* but frontals usually narrower between orbits and behind postorbital processes; supraorbital shield tending to project farther posteriorly over foramen magnum. Usually larger than that of *nubilus,* but frontals narrower; supraoccipital shield broader and rising more steeply, less projecting posteriorly, over foramen magnum. Compared with *fuscus:* Size similar; frontal region flatter, less convex in profile, and distinctly narrower, less inflated behind postorbital processes; rostrum and nasals longer, the nasals usually ending well behind posterior plane of maxillae. Compared with *columbianus:* Size smaller; frontal region narrower, more constricted behind postorbital processes; supraoccipital shield narrower, more tapering toward apex; dentition similar.

Measurements.—Type (approximated from tanned skin): Total length, 1870 mm.; tail vertebrae, 410; hind foot, 240. An unusually large adult male from 15 miles south of Three Forks, Gallatin County, Montana (measured in flesh by collector): Total length, 1834; height at shoulder, 839; weight, 106 pounds. A male, not quite full grown, from Soda Springs, Idaho: Total length, 1904; tail vertebrae, 412; hind foot, 263. Two adult females from the same locality, respectively: Total length, 1929, 2046; tail vertebrae, 480, 440; hind foot, 236, 254. Two females, not quite full-grown, from Montpelier, Idaho, respectively: Total length, 1803, 1854; tail vertebrae, 440, 470; hind foot, 232, 242. *Skull:* Type and an adult male topotype, respectively: Greatest length, 259.2, 262; condylobasal length, 237, 241; zygomatic breadth, 144.9, 142.7; squamosal constriction, 81.1; 81; width of rostrum, 47.7, 49.5; interorbital breadth, 44.6, 43.1; postorbital constriction, 34.7, 35.5; length of mandible, 186, 193.5; height of rostrum, 74.4, 82.6; maxillary tooth row, 105.7, 106.2; upper carnassial, crown length (outer side), 25.7, 26.1, crown width, 13.9, 15.3; first upper molar, antero-posterior diameter, 17.6, 18.4; transverse diameter, 20.2, 24.1; lower carnassial, crown length, 28.8, 29.5. Two adult females from Dillon, Montana, respectively: Greatest length, 254.5, 244.5; condylobasal length, 237.7, 225.5; zygomatic breadth, 127, 123.3; squamosal constriction, 76.8, 69.1; width of rostrum, 42.8, 40.8; interorbital breadth, 45.7, 41.7; postorbital constriction, 39.7, 36.9; length of mandible, 179.4, 173; height of coronoid process, 73.5, 70.6; maxillary tooth row, 109.2, 102.3; upper carnassial, crown length (outer side), 26, 25.2, crown width, 13.4, 14.8; first upper molar, antero-posterior diameter, 16.8, 16.4, transverse diameter, 22.9, 23.7; lower carnassial, crown length, 30.3, 28.

Remarks.—*C. l. irremotus* occupied a section along the backbone of the continent extending northward from the United States into Canada. An individual was killed 15 miles south of Three Forks, Gallatin County, Mont., April 30, 1941, by Al Johnson of the Fish and Wildlife Service. This remarkable animal from a region in which the wolves were believed to have been extirpated was found to have the longest skull (285.3) of any measured from the entire United States. It equals some of the larger, more northern wolves (*pambasileus* and *occidentalis*) in general dimensions, but differs notably in lighter dentition. A few wolves may still persist in the mountainous region between southwestern Alberta and southeastern British Columbia. Specimens from northwestern Wyoming are somewhat intermediate between *irremotus* and *youngi*, which ranged to the southward. One of the largest wolf skulls from the United States is that of an old male referred to *irremotus* from 15 miles northwest of Manville, Wyo. Skulls from the Snake River Desert and other localities in central-southern and southwestern Idaho are rather small and variable. They do not appear to be typical, but agree more closely with *irremotus* than any other race. Specimens from the Black Hills region of Wyoming and South Dakota are variable and grade toward *nubilus,* the area forming an eastern salient loop in the range of the subspecies. In southern British Columbia, *irremotus* probably intergrades with *columbianus.*

Specimens examined.—Total number, 149, as follows:

Alberta: Calgary, 7;[1] Gleichen, 4 (skulls only);[1] Lethbridge, 3;[1] Lethbridge (25 miles southeast), 1.

Idaho: Aldridge, 5; Argora, Clark County, 1; Bear Park (35 miles northeast of Minidoka), 4 (skulls only); Boise National Forest, 1 (skull only); Castleford, Twin Falls County, 1 (skull only); Dry Valley (20 miles northeast of Soda Springs), 1; Hammett, Owyhee County, 3 (skins only); Leodore, 1; Leodore (10 miles south), 1 (skull only); Montpelier, 3; Priest River, 1 (skull only); Pocatello (head of Port Neuf River), 3 (skins only); Pocatello (10 miles east), 1; Soda Springs, 11 (4 skulls only); South Fork of Boise River, Elmore County, 1 (skull only); Spark's Well (23 miles northeast of Minidoka), 3 (skulls only); Tyhee Basin, Bannock County, 2 (1 skull only).

Montana: Beaverhead Mountains (12 and 25 miles southeast of Leadore, Idaho, respectively), 2; Belt, 5; Continental Divide (Montana side, 20 miles east of Leadore, Idaho), 1; Delphia 1 (skin only); Dillon, 2; Fort Conrad, 1 (skull only); Ingomar, 2 (1 skin without skull); Kruger, 1 (skull only); Lame Deer, Rosebud County, 1 (skull only); Little Belt Mountains, 4 (skulls only); Lodge Grass, Big Horn County, 1; Musselshell River, 1 (skull only);[1] Powderville, 4; Red Lodge (type locality), 3; Red Rock, Beaverhead County, 1; Riceville, 1 (skull only); Ridge, 1 (skull only); Spring Creek, Madison County, 1 (skin only); Sun River Valley, 1 (skull only); Three Forks (15 miles south), Gallatin County, 1 (skull and scalp); Warm Springs, deer Lodge County, 2; White Sulphur Springs (20 miles northwest), 1.

South Dakota: Belle Fourche, 1 (skull only).

Wyoming: Arvada, Sheridan County, 2 (1 skull only); Barber, 2 (skulls only); Big Piney, Sublette County, 4; Cokeville, Lincoln County, 1 (skull only); Converse County, 4 (skulls only); Cora, Sublette County, 6; Elk and vicinity, Teton County, 5; Fort Washakie, 1; Gillette, 1 (skull only); Glenrock, Converse

County, 1; Hell Roaring Creek, 7; Howard, 1; Kelly (Bacon Creek Ridge), Teton County, 1; Lenore, Fremont County, 3; Lost Springs (10 miles north), Converse County, 3 (1 skull without skin); Manville (15 miles northwest), 1; Otto, 1 (skull only);[1] Pinedale, 1 (skull only); Sand Creek Canyon, Black Hills, 1 (skull only); Shell, 1 (skin only); Split Rock, 2; Yellowstone National Park, 3 (skulls only).

CANIS LUPUS COLUMBIANUS Goldman
British Columbia Wolf (Pls. 109-110)

Canis lupus columbianus Goldman, Proc. Biol. Soc. Wash. 54: 110, September 30, 1941.

Type locality.—Wistaria, north side of Ootsa Lake, Coast District, British Columbia.

Type specimen.—No. 3559, ♂ adult, skull only, British Columbia Provincial Museum; collected by J. C. Shelford, November 1938.

Distribution.—Greater part of British Columbia, west of the Rocky Mountains and the Stikine Mountains, passing into *fuscus* near the southwestern coast and into *ligoni* along the coast bordering the Alexander Archipelago of southwestern Alaska; grades into *occidentalis* in the Peace River region, and farther south into *irremotus*.

General characters.—Size large; upper parts rather dark; ears light "cinnamon buff"; skull with broad supraoccipital shield and narrow carnassials. Approaches *pambasileus* of Alaska and *occidentalis* of Mackenzie in size, but reaches less extreme maximum cranial dimensions; color similar to *pambasileus*, less uniformly grayish or whitish than in *occidentalis*. Differs from *irremotus* of Montana in larger usual size, more buffy coloration, and broader postorbital region of skull. Differs from *fuscus* of Oregon in larger size, paler color, and cranial features, especially the longer nasals. Differs from *crassodon* of Vancouver Island in paler color and lighter dentition. Differs from *ligoni* of the Alexander Archipelago, Alaska, mainly in greater average size.

Color.—Variable but similar to *pambasileus*. A somewhat worn skin from Chezacut, north shore of Chilcotin Lake: Upper parts in

[1] Amer. Mus. Nat. Hist.

general mixed white and black with a pale buffy or yellowish suffusion, the back moderately overlaid with black; short pelage on middle of face a grizzled mixture of white and black, becoming suffused
pith "pinkish buff" at top of head; upper surface of muzzle "pinkish
buff"; under parts across middle of abdomen thinly overlaid with
pale buff, the under color near "avellaneous" showing through;
middle and sides of chest white; the hairs white to roots; ears "cinnamon-buff" mixed with black near tips; outer sides of limbs "pinkish buff," the usual narrow black line on anterior surface of forearm
narrow and indistinct; tail above similar to back, a black line over
glandular area, below "pale pinkish buff."

In another, a female in fresh pelage from Chezacut, the buffy
element is darker and richer in tone and the color in detail as follows: Upper parts in general suffused wtih light "cinnamon-buff,"
purest and most intense on sides of shoulders, flanks, and thighs; top
of head "cinnamon-buff" mixed with black, becoming abruptly grizzled grayish on forehead and face; muzzle and chin brownish; under
side of neck "pale pinkish buff" slightly darkened by black tips of
longer hairs; chest and thorax "pinkish buff"; inguinal region white;
ears "cinnamon" mixed with black; lower part of legs "pinkish buff,"
a narrow blackish line along anterior surface of forearm; upper side
of tail near base suffused with "pale pinkish buff," the glandular
area heavily overlaid with black, passing distally into "cinnamon-
buff" more moderately darkened by black-tipped hairs, becoming
black at end as usual in the species; under side of tail "pale pinkish
buff" on proximal two-thirds, passing into a "pinkish-buff" suffusion overlaid with black toward tip.   Three from Chezacut and
others from the vicinity of Takla and Bear Lakes in the black phase
are similar to those of *pambasileus* and *ligoni* in the same color phase.
In these the hairs are more or less distinctly buff-banded along the
median line of the back, and brown rather than black is predominant.
A skin from near the south end of Bear Lake presents an unusual
coarsely grizzled mixture of black and white or gray, the blend producing an "iron-gray" general tone, with no trace of a buffy element,
and resembling a similar color phase seen in *ligoni* and other subspecies. A female taken in August on the Little Tahltan River, Cassiar District, is intensively suffused with "cinnamon-buff," and the
ears are near light "cinnamon-rufous."

Skull. — Closely resembles that of *pambasileus,* but usually smaller; subpraoccipital shield broader; postorbital processes slenderer, more tapering and acutely pointed; carnassials relatively narrower, more elongated (antero-posteriorly); second lower molars larger, more elongated. Very similar to that of *occidentalis,* but usually smaller; postorbital processes slenderer, more tapering; dentition as a whole lighter, but second lower molars larger; canines slenderer; carnassials relatively narrower. Compared with *irremotus:* Size larger; frontal region broader, less constricted behind postorbital processes; supraoccipital shield usually broader, more rounded near apex; dentition similar. Compared with *fuscus:* Size larger; nasals relatively longer, extending farther posteriorly beyond ends of maxillae; second lower molar relatively larger. Differs from that of *crassodon* in lighter dentition, especially the narrower carnassials. Differs from that of *ligoni* most obviously in greater average size.

Measurements.—Approximated from tanned skin of a female from Chezacut: Total length, 1600 mm.; tail vertebrae, 370. *Skull: Type* (male) and an adult male topotype, respectively: 272.9, 263.9; condylobasal length, 260, 244.4; zygomatic breadth, 148.4, 147.7; squamosal constriction, 82.5, 80.8; width of rostrum, 46, 45; interorbital breadth, 48.8, 43.1; postorbital constriction, 45.7, 38.3; length of mandible, 196.2, 193; height of coronoid process, 75, 80.9; maxillary tooth row, 112.1, 107.3; upper carnassial, crown length (outer side), 27.1, 26.8, crown width, 13.8, 14; first upper molar, antero-posterior diameter, 17.3, 16.4, transverse diameter, 24.1, 22.9; lower carnassial, crown length, 31.1, 29.5. Two adult female topotypes, respectively: Greatest length, 262.2, 266.5; condylobasal length, 235.8, 246.4; zygomatic breadth, 140, 133.8; squamosal constriction, 79.3, 79.5; width of rostrum, 45.4, 43.1; interorbital breadth, 46.8, 42.7; postorbital constriction, 44.6, 37; length of mandible, 185.3, 188.7; height of coronoid process, 73.6, 73, maxillary tooth row, 105.8, 108.4; upper carnassial, crown length (outer side), 25.6, 24.7, crown width, 12.9, 13.4; first upper molar, antero-posterior diameter, 16.7, 17.1, transverse diameter, 22, 21.8; lower carnassial, 29, 28.2.

Remarks.—The British Columbia wolf, *columbianus,* approaches its larger northern neighbors in size but differs in its combination of color and cranial details. Two skulls from Iskut summit, 60 miles south of Telegraph Creek, are large for *columbianus*, but present somewhat mixed characters in detail. They probably represent intergradation with *pambasileus* or *occidentalis*. Although from a locality not far distant from the range of *ligoni*, which is mainly confined to the Alexander Archipelago, these specimens exhibit a marked departure from those of that race in size and detailed characters. The British Columbia subspecies is believed to be increasing in numbers in some of the more remote sections of the country.

Specimens examined.—Total number, 25, as follows:

British Columbia: Bear Lake (5 miles north and 4 miles east of south end, respectively), 2 (skins only);[1] Bear Lake (12 miles northeast and 6 miles northwest, respectively), 2 (skins only);[1] Bowron Lake, Cariboo District, 1 (skull only)[2]; Chezacut, north shore of Chilcotin Lake, 5 (2 skins without skulls);[2] Iskut Summit (60 miles south of Telegraph Creek), 2 (skulls only)[3]; Kettle River, 2 (skulls only);[4] Little Prairie, Horsefly River, Cariboo District, 1 (skull only);[2] Little Tahltan River, Cassiar District, 1 (skin only);[5] Pemberton, Lillooet District, 1 (skull only);[2] Roche River (tributary of Similkameen River), Yale District, 1 (skull only); Tacla Lake (18 miles northwest of north end), 1 (skin only);[1] Telegraph Creek, 1 (skull only);[2] Vernon, Yale District, 1 (skull only);[2] Wistaria, north side of Ootsa Lake, Coast District, 4 (skulls only).[2]

CANIS LUPUS LIGONI Goldman
Alexander Archipelago Wolf (Pls. 111-112)

Canis lupus ligoni Goldman, Mamm. Jour. 18 (1): 39, Feb. 14, 1937.

Type locality.—Head of Duncan Canal, Kupreanof Island, Alexander Archipelago, Alaska.

Type specimen.—No. 243323, ♂ adult, skin and skull, U. S. National Museum (Biological Surveys collection); collected by J. Stokley Ligon, November 7, 1922. X-catalog number 23022.

---

[1]John F. Stanwell-Fletcher Coll.
[2]Provincial Museum of British Columbia.
[3]Mus. Vert. Zool.
[4]Kansas Univ. Mus. Nat. Hist.
[5]Amer. Mus. Nat. Hist.

Distribution.—Alexander Archipelago, and adjacent mainland of southeastern Alaska; northward along the coast to Yakutat Bay.

General characters.—A dark-colored subspecies of medium size; pelage short. Differs from *columbianus,* of central British Columbia, in smaller usual size and paler buff suffusion of upper parts. Similar in general to *fuscus,* of the lower Columbia River Valley, but somewhat larger; ratio of blackish to normally colored individuals higher; upper parts in normally colored examples similarly overlaid with black, but usually less suffused with buff; skull more elongated and differing in detail. Much smaller and darker in normal gray color phase and pelage shorter than in *pambasileus* of the Mount McKinley region, Alaska. Similar to *crassodon* of Vancouver Island, British Columbia, in size and color, but differs in cranial details, notably the smaller auditory bullae.

Color.—*Type (winter pelage, November):* Short pelage on top of head a mixture of black and white, producing a grizzled effect; upper parts from nape to rump pale buff heavily overlaid with black, the black giving way to purer buff along sides; outer surfaces of legs cinnamon buff, paling gradually to near pinkish buff on feet; upper surface of muzzle cinnamon buffy; ears rich tawny, mixed with black; under parts in general buffy white; tail above about like back, becoming buffy below and deep black all around at tip.

Specimens from Zarembo, Kuiu, and Prince of Wales Islands present two distinct color phases—one which may be regarded as normal, and the other predominantly black. Four of the five skins available from Zarembo Island are in the blackish phase. In the latter the muzzle and feet usually are nearly pure black, but in one a mixture of black and white or gray includes the entire body in a combination suggesting the peculiar color of the glacier bear, which also inhabits the coast region of southern Alaska.

Skull. — Rather closely resembling that of *columbianus,* but smaller; auditory bullae usually larger, more fully inflated. Decidedly smaller, less massive than *pambasileus,* with relatively lighter dentition. Similar in size and general form to *crassodon,* but auditory bullae smaller, less inflated; upper carnassials distinctly smaller and narrower, the anterior borders more transverse to longitudinal axis of skull, instead of oblique and directed inward and backward as in *crassodon.*

Measurements.—Type: Total length, 1733 mm.; tail vertebrae, 477; hind foot, 300; weight (stomach empty), 91 pounds. An adult female topotype: 1556; 457; 285. Two adult males from Wrangell, Alaska, respectively: Total length, 1650, 1683; tail vertebrae, 453, 492; hind foot, 298, 292. Two adult females from Wrangell, Alaska, respectively: 1585, 1496; 435, 406; 279, 270. An adult female from Baker Island, Alaska: 1499; 393; 279. *Skull:* Type and an adult male from Wrangell, respectively: Greatest length, 262.1, 262; condylobasal length, 251, 239.4; zygomatic breadth, 145.3, 146.4; squamosal constriction, 80, 84.4; width of rostrum, 43.4, 47.9; interorbital breadth, 49.1, 47; postorbital constriction, 43.4, 41.5; length of mandible, 197, 184.5; height of coronoid process, 72.9, 73.3; maxillary tooth row, crown length, 112.8, 110.3; upper carnassial, crown length (outer side), 25.2, 25; upper carnassial, 13.9, 14.2; anterior upper molar, antero-posterior diameter, 17.7, 16.3; anterior upper molar, 24.5, 23.3; lower carnassial, crown length, 30.4, 28.3. An adult female topotype and an adult female from Wrangell, respectively: Greatest length, 250, 244; condylobasal length, 232.8, 229; zygomatic breadth, 135.5, 132.2; squamosal constriction, 76.1, 77.4; width of rostrum, 42.4, 43.4; interorbital breadth, 41.2, 43.9; postorbital constriction, 36.4, 41.6; length of mandible, 185.3, 178.5; height of coronoid process, 73.4, 66.7; maxillary tooth row, crown length, 106.1, 104.6; upper carnassial, crown length (outer side), 23.9, 22.8; upper carnassial, crown width, 12.9, 12.8; anterior upper molar, antero-posterior diameter, 16.4, 16.3; anterior upper molar, transverse diameter, 22.9, 21.6; Lower carnassial, crown length, 28.7, 27.5.

Remarks.—The wolf of the Alexander Archipelago and closely adjoining mainland of southeastern Alaska is a well-marked subspecies, differing from the wolves of the interior in smaller size, shorter pelage, and darker normal coloration. In the normal, or gray, color phase, the back is more profusely overlaid with black than in *pambasileus.* In the varying mixtures presented in the black phase, however, the two are much alike. Its principal natural prey is probably the black-tailed deer (*Odocoileus columbianus sitkensis*) of the region.

Specimens examined.—Total number 37, all from Alaska, as follows: Baker Island, 2; Conclusion Island, 1 (skull only); Dry

Bay, Alsek River, 1 (skull only);[1] Eleanor Cove, Yakutat Bay, 1 (skull only);[1] Juneau, 1 (skull only);[2] Ketchikan, 2; Kuiu Island, 7 (5 skulls without skins); Kupreanof Island (type locality), 5; Prince of Wales Island, 8 (6 skulls without skins; 2 skins without skulls); Revillagigedo Island, 1 (skull only); Wrangell, 3 (1 skin without skull); Zarembo Island, 5.

CANIS LUPUS FUSCUS Richardson
Cascade Mountains Wolf (Pls. 113-114)

Canis lupus var. *fusca* Richardson, Zool. Capt. Beechey's Voyage of the Blossom, 1839, p. 5. Reference is made to his earlier description under *Canis lupus occidentalis* (1829, p. 61).

Lupus gigas (Townsend), Acad. Nat. Sci. Phila., Ser. 2, vol. 2, Art. 8, p. 75, Nov. 1850. From near Vancouver, Clark County, Washington.

Canis gigas Miller, Smiths. Misc. Coll. 59 (15): 4, June 8, 1912.

Type.—Not designated.

Type locality.—Banks of the Columbia River, below the Dalles, between Oregon and Washington.

Distribution.—Formerly the forested region from the Cascade Range in Oregon and Washington west in places to the Pacific coast; south to undetermined limits along the Sierra Nevada in northeastern California, and probably northwestern Nevada, north along the coast of British Columbia to undetermined limits; on the east intergradation with *columbianus* and *irremotus* can safely be assumed. Probably still extant in some of the wilder sections near the coast of south western British Columbia and the Siskiyou Mountains of southern Oregon.

General characters.—A dark cinnamon or cinnamon-buffy subspecies, with dorsum profusely overlaid with black; size medium; skull rather short; rostrum and nasals short, the nasals usually ending near posterior plane of maxillae. Similar in size to *youngi* of Utah and *irremotus* of Montana, but color darker, more suffused with "cinnamon-buff" than either, the back more heavily overlaid with black; cranial details, especially the shorter nasals, distinctive.

---

[1]Roy. Ont. Mus. Zool.
[2]Field Mus. Nat. Hist.

Similar in size to *crassodon* of Vancouver Island, but ground color less grayish, more cinnamon-buffy; cranial and dental details different. Differs from *columbianus* of British Columbia in smaller size, darker color, and cranial features, especially the shorter nasals.

Color.—*Winter pelage:* Upper parts in general usually suffused with "cinnamon" or "cinnamon-buff," the top of head and entire back profusely overlaid with black; under parts varying from "cinnamon-buff" to "pinkish cinnamon," becoming white in some specimens on inguinal region; chin blackish; outer surfaces of fore and hind legs ranging from "cinnamon-buff" to rich "cinnamon," becoming somewhat paler on feet; ears externally suffused with "cinnamon," the hairs tipped with black; inner surfaces of ears more thinly clothed with "cinnamon-buff" hairs; tail above "cinnamon" or "cinnamon-buff," overlaid with black; tail below whitish or "pinkish buff" near base, passing gradually to "cinnamon-buff" overlaid with black toward tip which is black all around, as usual in the group. A skin from Sycan, Oregon, is nearly pure white, except for a sprinkling of dark hairs over rump and a black patch on tail gland. In one skin a few hairs white to roots are intermingled with the black on the tip of the tail.

Skull.—Similar in size to that of *youngi*, but frontal region more inflated behind postorbital processes; nasals shorter, less extended posteriorly, more nearly conterminous with maxillae. Compared with *irremotus*: Size similar; frontals broader between orbits and broader, more inflated behind postorbital processes; rostrum and nasals shorter, the nasals usually ending nearer the posterior plane of maxillae. Compared with *crassodon*: Size and general form similar; nasals usually shorter, more nearly conterminous with maxillae posteriorly; auditory bullae smaller, less inflated; dentition, especially the larger molariform teeth, lighter; upper carnassial narrower anteriorly, with border of crown more nearly transverse to longitudinal axis of skull (anterior border of crown directed more obliquely inward and backward in *crassodon*). Compared with *columbianus*: Size smaller, nasals relatively shorter, less extended posteriorly; second lower molars relatively smaller.

Measurements.—Two adult males from Cascadia, Oregon (approximated from tanned skins), respectively: Total length, 1670, 1800 mm.; tail vertebrae, 390, 470; hind foot, 230, 260. Two adult females from the same locality (tanned skins), respectively:

Total length, 1610, 1562; tail vertebrae, 390, 377; hind foot, 220, 240. An adult male from Elwha River, 22 miles south of Port Angeles, Washington: Weight, 86 pounds. *Skull:* Two adult males from Cascadia, Oregon, respectively: Greatest length, 256.5, 256; condylobasal length, 235.5, 238.3; zygomatic breadth, 137, 141.1; squamosal constriction, 78.8, 75.6; width of rostrum, 45, 44.3; interorbital breadth, 47.8, 50.3; postorbital constriction, 44.3, 44; length of mandible, 187, 187.2; height of coronoid process, 85, 83.3; maxillary tooth row, crown length, 109.1, 107.6; upper carnassial, crown length (outer side), 25.6, 25.5, crown width, 14.2, 12.3; first upper molar, antero-posterior diameter, 16.8, 16.9; transverse diameter, 22, 23.1; lower carnassial, crown length, 30.1, 28.4. Two adult females from Cascadia, Oregon, respectively: Greatest length, 239.8, 237.5; condylobasal length, 218.5, 222.8; zygomatic breadth, 128.3, 131.8; squamosal constriction, 75.4, 72; width of rostrum, 44, 40.6; interorbital breadth, 45, 46.8; postorbital constriction, 41.7, 43; length of mandible, 170.5, 172.4; height of coronoid process, 72.8, 71.8; maxillary tooth row, crown length, 98.6, 101.4; upper carnassial, crown length (outer side), 21.9, 22.8, crown width, 12.9, 12.5; first upper molar, antero-posterior diameter, 15.1, 15, transverse diameter, 21.3, 20.8; lower carnassial, crown length, 26.3, 26.4.

Remarks.—The Cascade wolf is distinguished by peculiar dark coloration in combination with cranial details in marked contrast with those presented by its geographic neighbors. Owing, no doubt, to the dark "cinnamon" or "cinnamon-buff" general ground color, the animal was referred to as the "brown wolf." This wolf undoubtedly passed gradually into *irremotus* in the region east of the Cascade Range, in northeastern Washington, and may still intergrade with that subspecies in southeastern British Columbia.

The name *Canis lupus fusca* Richardson (1839, p. 5) for the "large brown wolf" of Lewis and Clark, said to inhabit "California and the banks of the Columbia" River, seems to have been overlooked until brought to attention by Allen and Barbour (1937, p. 230). This name, proposed by Richardson, clearly takes precedence over *gigas* described by Townsend from the same general region in 1850. Lewis and Clark (Thwaites ed., 1905, p. 94) state that "The large brown wolf is like that of the Atlantic States, and are found only in the woody country on the Pacific Ocean embracing the

Mountains which pass the Columbia between the Great Falls an[d] Rapids of the same." The type region may, therefore, be restricted to the banks of the Columbia River below the Dalles, between Oregon and Washington.

The first naturalist to obtain a specimen of the Cascade Mountains wolf seems to have been David Douglas. According to his journal published in 1914 (p. 59), he procured in the summer of 1825, along with other mammals, a "new species of *Canis*" on the banks of the Santiam River, a branch of the Willamette River in Oregon. In this connection, there is a bare manuscript reference, no page being given, to Richardson's Fauna Boreali-Americana. It seems probable from the context that the *"Canis"* was the wolf. Mammals collected by Douglas, including a hunter's skin of *Arctomys? (Spermophilus?) douglasi* (equals *Citellus beecheyi douglasii*), were listed by Richardson; but he says (l. c., p. 61), "I have seen none of these brown wolves," and there seems to be no evidence that any wolf material taken by Douglas reached Richardson.

Specimens examined.—Total number, 28, as follows:

British Columbia: Burrard Inlet, 1 (skull only);[5] Calvert Island, 1 (skull only);[5] Swindle Island, 1 (skull only).[5]

California: Litchfield, Lassen County, 1 (skull only).[1]

Oregon: Cascadia, 3; Clackamas River (28 miles above Cazadero), 1;[2] Crane Prairie (25 miles northeast of Ashland), 1 (skull only); Estacada, 1; Foster, Linn County, 1 (skull only);[3] Foster (6 miles northeast), 1 (skin only);[2] Glide, 2 (one 40 miles east; one 15 miles northeast); Glide (north fork of east fork of north fork of Rock Creek, 20 miles northeast of Glide), 1;[2] Glide, 3;[4] Molalla River (at source), Clackamas County, 1;[2] Rogue River (Peavine Mountain, 40 miles northeast), 2; Tiller (15 miles southeast on Elk Creek), 2; Sycan (30 miles south of Silver Lake), 1.

Washington: Bitter Cottonwood, 1 (skull only); Elwha River (22 miles south of Port Angeles), 1 (skull only); Hoh River (base of Olympic Mountains), 1; Twin Peaks, Chelan County, 1.

---

[1]Mus. Vert. Zool.
[2]Oregon Agr. College Coll.
[3]Stanley P. Young Coll.
[4]One in Oregon Agr. College Coll.
[5]Provincial Mus. of British Columbia.

CANIS LUPUS CRASSODON Hall
Vancouver Island Wolf (Pls. 115-116)

Canis occidentalis crassodon Hall, Univ. Calif. Pub. Zool. 38 (12) 420, November 8, 1932.

Type locality.—Tahsis Canal, Nootka Sound, Vancouver Island, British Columbia.

Type.—No. 12456, ♂ adult, skull only, Museum of Vertebrate Zoology; collected during winter of 1909-10 by Carl Leiner, from whom procured on July 26, 1910, by Harry S. Swarth. Original number 8419, H. S. S.

Distribution.—Vancouver Island, British Columbia.

General characters.—An insular subspecies; size medium; upper parts gray, heavily overlaid with black; skull with postorbital region broad; dentition heavy; upper carnassial with outer side longest, the anterior border of crown directed obliquely inward and backward to protocone. Most closely allied to *fuscus* of adjacent mainland, but color grayer, apparently lacking the "cinnamon" or "cinnamon-buff" suffusion of the latter; cranial details distinctive. Differs from *columbianus* of British Columbia in darker upper parts and heavier dentition.

Color.—A skin from Nootka Sound, in winter pelage: Upper parts in general a drab grayish mixture, the top of head and dorsal area heavily overlaid with black; under parts in general dull white; throat grayish; chin blackish; outer surfaces of fore and hind legs "pinkish buff"; ears brownish; tail grayish overlaid with black above, the black most extensive near base, below dull white, becoming black all around at tip about 120 millimeters in length.

Skull.—Similar in size and general proportions to that of *fuscus*; nasals usually longer, extending farther beyond posterior plane of maxillae; auditory bullae larger, more inflated; dentition, especially the larger molariform teeth, heavier; upper carnassial distinctly broader anteriorly, with border of crown directed more obliquely inward and backward (anterior border of crown more nearly transverse to cranial axis in *fuscus*). Differs from that of *columbianus* in about the same details as from *fuscus*.

Measurements.—A tanned skin from Nootka Sound: Total length, 1885; tail vertebrae, 470; hind foot, 310. *Skull:* Type (from original description): "Condylobasal length, 240.1; length of tooth-rows, 126.6; postpalatal length, 98.1; greatest width across upper toothrows, 89.2; mastoid breadth, 88; depth of mandible through coronoid process, 70.5." An adult male from Tahsis Canal, Nootka Sound, and an adult female from Quatsino Sound, Vancouver Island, respectively: Greatest length, 256.2, 241.9; condylobasal length, 239.6, 222.1; zygomatic breadth, 143.4, 132; squamosal constriction, 80.1, 79; width of rostrum, 44.8, 40.8; interorbital breadth, 50.1, 43.3; postorbital constriction, 45.6, 43; length of mandible, 183.5, 170.8; height of coronoid process, 72.1, 70.1; maxillary tooth row, crown length, 107.5, 101.8; upper carnassial, crown length (outer side), 26.2, 24.9, crown width, 15.9, 14.6; first upper molar, antero-posterior diameter, 17.6, 17.2, transverse diameter, 24.6, 21.7; lower carnassial, 30.4, 28.8.

Remarks.—The Vancouver Island wolf is most closely allied to *fuscus* of the adjacent mainland, as might be expected. Color differences appear to be well marked, however, as are the cranial and dental features, especially the size and form of the upper carnassial.

Specimens examined.—Total number, 12, all from Vancouver Island, as follows: Alberni, 1 (skull only);[1] Cowichan Lake, 1 (skull only);[1] Englishman's River, 1 (skull only);[2] Nootka Sound, 1 (skin only);[2] Quatsino, 2 (skulls only); Quatsino Sound, 4 (skulls only); Tahsis Canal, Nootka Sound, 2 (skulls only).[2]

CANIS LUPUS YOUNGI Goldman
Southern Rocky Mountain Wolf (pls. 117-118)

Canis lupus youngi Goldman, Mamm. Jour. 18 (1): 40, February 14, 1937.

Type locality.—Harts Draw, north slope of Blue Mountains, 20 miles northwest of Monticello, San Juan County, Utah.

Type specimen.—No. 224001, ♂ adult, skin and skull, U. S. National Museum (Biological Surveys collection); collected by Bert Brown Turner, December 11, 1916. X-catalog number 17413.

Distribution.—Formerly numerous in Rocky Mountain region from northern Utah and southern Wyoming south through Utah and western Colorado to northern Arizona and northern New Mexico;

---

[1]Brit. Col. Prov. Mus.
[2]Mus. Vert. Zool.

west irregularly to central Nevada (Gold Creek, Elko County), and sporadically at least to southeastern California (Providence Mountains). Now extremely rare and restricted mainly to the rugged territory bordering the upper Colorado River in southeastern Utah and southwestern Colorado. Intergraded on the north with *irremotus*, on the east with *nubilus*, and on the south with *mogollonensis*.

General characters.—A light-colored subspecies of medium to rather large size. Averaging larger than *nubilus* of the prairie region of Nebraska, with upper parts usually more suffused with buff; skull with supraoccipital region much less prominently projecting posteriorly. Similar in size to *irremotus* of the more northern Rocky Mountain region, but upper parts more suffused with buff; skull differs in detail, especially the greater breadth of the frontal region. Larger than *mogollonensis* of the Mogollon Mountain and plateau region of New Mexico and Arizona, with upper parts usually paler, less extensively overlaid with black and more suffused with buff.

Color.—Similar to that of *nubilus*, some specimens being indistinguishable, but upper parts usually more suffused with buff. An unusually light colored skin from Salt Creek (about 22 miles north of Fruita, Colorado), is buffy white over nearly entire body, except a narrow thin line of black-tipped hairs along median line of back, a black patch on tail gland, and a few dark hairs on tip of tail.

Skull.—Averaging larger than that of *nubilus;* rostrum and palate longer; supraoccipital shield broader, rising more steeply, less projecting posteriorly over foramen magnum, usually without the descending terminal hook so frequently present in *nubilus*. Similar in most dimensions to that of *irremotus*, but frontals usually broader between orbits and behind postorbital processes; supraoccipital shield tending to rise more steeply with lesser posterior projection of apex. Larger, more massive than that of *mogollonensis;* zygomata relatively less widely spreading; fronto-nasal profile usually straighter, the rostrum and nasals less depressed across middle; nasals flatter, the inner margins less decurved to form a V-shaped median groove; dentition relatively as well as actually heavier.

Measurements.—*Type* (approximated from tanned skin): Total length, 1800 mm.; tail vertebrae, 470; hind foot, 255. An adult male from Castle Peak (Burns Hole, 15 miles northeast of Eagle),

Colorado: Total length, 1777; height at shoulder, 806; weight, 125 pounds. An adult female from Salt Creek (22 miles north of Fruita), Colorado: Total length, 1701; height at shoulder, 724; weight, 110 pounds. An adult male from Laramie, Wyoming: Total length, 1600; tail vertebrae, 420; hind foot, 270. *Skull:* Type and an adult male from Salt Creek (about 22 miles north of Fruita), Colorado, respectively: Greatest length, 258.5, 265; condylobasal length, 243.5, 248.5; zygomatic breadth, 136.7, 148; squamosal constriction, 82.8, 82.5; width of rostrum, 47.7, 48.2; interorbital breadth, 44.3, 51.5; postorbital constriction, 40.6, 45.4; length of mandible, 187.7, 193.4; height of coronoid process, 77.1, 82.1; maxillary tooth row, 107.8, 110.3; upper carnassial, crown length (outer side), 26.5, 25.2, crown width, 14.1, 13.4; first upper molar, antero-posterior diameter, 17.3, 17.1, transverse diameter, 23.7, 24.8; lower carnassial, 30, 29.1. Two adult females from Piceance, Rio Blanco County, Colorado, respectively: Greatest length, 244.5, 242.8; condylobasal length, 228.7, 226.5; zygomatic breadth, 130.9, 128.8; squamosal constriction, 73.2, 72.5; width of rostrum, 42.7, 40; interorbital breadth, 43.2, 44.1; postorbital constriction, 39, 39.9; length of mandible, 175.8, 172.2; height of coronoid process, 70.6, 70.4; maxillary tooth row, crown length, 106.7, 104; upper carnassial, crown length (outer side), 24.6, 24.5; crown width, 12.7, 13.4; first upper molar, antero-posterior diameter, 16.1, 15.3, transverse diameter, 22, 22.1; lower carnassial, 28, 27.8.

Remarks.—C. l. youngi was evidently the wolf of the southern part of the Rocky Mountains and high adjacent plains, displacing *nubilus* west of the prairie region of Nebraska and Kansas. It appears to have been most typical in the Colorado River drainage along the western side of the continental divide. Its range marked the western limit of wolves in the arid Southwest. Small numbers extended into Nevada. One only, perhaps a wanderer from southern Nevada, was trapped in the Providence Mountains, southeastern California, in 1922.

Specimens examined.—Total number, 111, as follows:
California: Providence Mountains (Old Barnett Mine, 12 miles west of Lanfair), 1 (skull only).[1]
Colorado: Castle Peak (Burns Hole, 15 miles northeast of Eagle), 1 (skin only);[2] Chico Creek (near Dove Creek), Dolores Coun-

ty, 1; Glade Park (Black Ridge), Mesa County, 3; Piceance, Rio Blanco County, 3 (1 skull without skin); Pueblo (20 miles northeast), 2 (skulls only); Redvale (25 miles northwest), 1 (skull only);[2] Salt Creek (about 22 miles north of Fruita), 2;[3] Sulphur, Rio Blanco County, 1 (skull only); Turman's Creek, Rio Blanco County, 1; West Creek, Garfield County, 2.

Nevada: Gold Creek, Elko County, 1 (skull only).[1]

New Mexico: Abiquiu, 3;[4] Canjilon, 4; Cuba, 3; Dulce (35 to 45 miles southwest), 14; El Rito, 2; El Vado (20 miles south), Rio Arriba County, 6; Haynes, 6; Jemez, 1; Jemez Mountains, 1; Lamy, 2 (1 skull without skin); La Plata, San Juan County, 1; San Mateo, 5; San Mateo Mountains, 1; Senorito, 12;[5] Tusas, 1.

Utah: Duchesne, 3; Greasewood Valley (10 miles southeast of LaSal, San Juan County), 1; Grouse Creek, Boxelder County, 1 (skull only); Harts Draw (type locality—north slope of Blue Mountains, 20 miles northwest of Monticello), San Juan County, 2; South Eden, Weber County, 1.

Wyoming: Dry Lake (15 miles north of Rawlins), 1 (skull only);[2] Federal, 7 (2 skulls without skins); Jelm, Albany County, 5 (2 skins without skulls); Laramie, 2 (1 skull without skin); Rock Springs, 5 (4 skulls without skins); Wagon Creek (Southwestern Wyoming), 2.

CANIS LUPUS MOGOLLONENSIS Goldman
Mogollon Mountain Wolf (Pls. 119-120)

Canis lupus mogollonensis Goldman, Mamm. Jour. 18 (1): 43, Feb. 14, 1937.

Type locality.—S. A. Creek, 10 miles northwest of Luna, Catron County, N. Mex.

Type specimen.—No. 224548, ♂ adult, skin and skull, U. S. National Museum (Biological Surveys collection); collected by Bart Burnam, July 1, 1916. X-catalog 18119.

---

[1]Mus. Vert. Zool.
[2]Stanley P. Young Collection.
[3]One in Stanley P. Young Collection.
[4]One skull without skin in Field Mus. Nat. Hist.
[5]Four skulls without skins in Field Mus. Nat. Hist.

Distribution.—Formerly the Mogollon Plateau region, extending nearly across central Arizona, and east through the Mogollon Mountains of central western New Mexico; now rare, if not extinct. On the north *mogollonensis* gave way to *youngi*, and east of the Rio Grande to *nubilus* and *monstrabilis*. On the south it passed rather abruptly into *baileyi*, which still inhabits the Sierra Madre of Mexico.

General characters.—A rather small, usually dark-colored, but varying to nearly white, subspecies. Similar in general to *youngi* of the Rocky Mountain region to the northward, but smaller and usually darker in color. Decidedly larger and usually lighter in color than *baileyi* of the Sierra Madre of Mexico. Closely resembles *monstrabilis* of Texas, but differs in cranial characters, especially the more elevated frontal region. Differs from *nubilus* of Nebraska mainly in darker color and cranial details.

Color.—*Winter pelage:* Upper parts from nape to rump varying from dull white to "cinnamon-buff," rather heavily overlaid with black; short pelage on middle of face a mixture of "light buff" and black, tending to become "cinnamon-buff" on top of head; under parts and inner sides of legs mainly dull white, the under side of neck thinly mixed with black in some specimens; outer sides of legs varying from "pale pinkish buff" to "cinnamon-buff," usually becoming somewhat paler on feet; anterior surface of forearm with a narrow dusky line present in some specimens, absent in others; upper surface of muzzle near "cinnamon-buff"; ears "cinnamon-buff" to "ochraceous tawny," tinged with black; tail above similar to back, the black patch on tail gland conspicuous; tail dull white below on basal two-thirds, becoming more or less suffused with buff toward tip, which is black all around with a few white hairs often intermixed. In an unusually colored skin from 50 miles west of Chloride, New Mexico, the upper parts from muzzle to base of tail are overlaid with clear "pinkish cinnamon" instead of black; a few scattered black hairs appear on the upper surface and tip of the tail.

Skull.—Resembles that of *baileyi*, but is larger, more massive; rostrum distinctly broader. Smaller, less massive than that of *youngi*; zygomata relatively more widely spreading; inner margins of nasals tending to decurve more strongly to form a deeper V-shaped median groove; sagittal and lambdoid crests forming supraoccipital shield usually projecting farther posteriorly over foramen magnum; dentition lighter. Very similar in size to that of *nubilus*, but usually less flattened; rostrum more depressed near middle, sloping upward more steeply to frontals; inner margins of nasals usually more decurved. Differs from that of *monstrabilis* mainly in less elevated frontal region.

Measurements.—Two adult males, one from Fairview and the other from Reserve (25 miles northwest), N. Mex., respectively: Total length, 1,600, 1,470; tail vertebrae, 406, 420; hind foot, 254, 255. Two adult females from Chloride (24 miles northwest), respectively: Total length, 1,455, 1,480; tail vertebrae, 400, _____; hind foot, 245, 235; weight, 58, 49 pounds. An adult female from Escudilla Mountains, Ariz., 1,416; 394; 241. *Skull: Type* (male) and an adult male from Escudilla Mountains, Ariz., respectively: Greatest length, 253.5, 257; condylobasal length, 236.3, 238.7; zygomatic breadth, 142.1, 137.5; squamosal constriction, 80.8, 78.1; width of rostrum, 43.7, 44; interorbital breadth, 46.1, 45.2; postorbital constriction, 36.8, 41.6; length of mandible, 184.7, 184.5; maxillary tooth row, 107, 105.6; upper carnassial, crown length (outer side), 25.1, 24.4, crown width, 13.9, 14.2; first upper molar, antero-posterior diameter, 16.7, 15.9, transverse diameter, 22.8, 22.9; lower carnassial, crown length, 30, 27.9. Two adult females, a topotype and one from Escudilla Mountains, Ariz., respectively: Greatest length, 240.2, 238.3; condylobasal length, 222.4, 219; zygomatic breadth, 133.5, 129.7; squamosal constriction, 75.2, 73.5; width of rostrum, 44.1, 42.1; interorbital breadth, 46, 41.1; postorbital constriction, 42.3, 39.8; length of mandible, 174, 168.7; maxillary tooth row, 101.3, 96.1; upper carnassial, crown length (outer side), 24.7, 23.9, crown width, 14.3, 13.5; first upper molar, antero-posterior diameter, 16.7, 15.9, transverse diameter, 22.9, lower carnassial, crown length, 27.8, 27.4.

Remarks.—The Mogollon Mountain wolf is somewhat intermediate in characters, as well as in geographic position, between *youngi* and the smaller race *baileyi* which ranged north from the Sierra Madre and the high plateau region of Mexico into southeastern Arizona and southwestern New Mexico. It stands somewhat apart in combination of features, however, as a fairly well-marked regional race. Evidence of intergradation is clear, but the geographic transition from *mogollonensis* to the neighboring races, especially to *youngi* in northern New Mexico, and from *mogollonen-*

sis to *baileyi* in the southwestern part of the State, was remarkably abrupt.

Specimens examined.—Total number, 111, as follows:

Arizona: Aguila, Maricopa County, 1 (skull only);[1] Cibecue, 1; Clifton, 3; Cooney Tank (south of Springerville), 3; Escudilla Mountains, 5 (skulls only); Galiuro Mountains, 1 (skull only); Heber, 1; Kendrick Peak, 1 (skull only); Peloncillo Mountains, 1 (skull only).[1]

New Mexico: Alma (25 miles southwest), 1; Black Range, Socorro County, 7 (2 skulls only); Chloride (24-50 miles west), 14 (2 skins without skulls; 2 skulls without skins); Capitan Mountains, 2 (skulls only); Datil, 1; Datil Mountains, 1 (skull only); Datil National Forest, 2 (skulls only); Fairview, 5; Gila National Forest, 39 (skulls only); Head of Mimbres River, 2 (1 skull without skin); Hurley, 1; Luna, 2; Magdalena, 4; Monticello, 1; Reserve, 3 (2 skulls without skins); Reserve (20 miles northwest), 2 (skulls only); S. A. Creek (type locality—10 miles northwest of Luna), 1; Silver City, 6.

CANIS LUPUS MONSTRABILIS Goldman
Texas Gray Wolf (Pls. 121-122)

Canis lupus monstrabilis Goldman, Mamm. Jour. 18 (1): 42, Feb. 14, 1937.

Type locality.—Ten miles south of Rankin, Upton County, Texas.

Type specimen.—No. 209497, ♂ adult, skin and skull, U. S. National Museum (Biological Surveys collection); collected by W. F. DeLong, September 3, 1915. X-catalog number 12646.

Distribution.—Formerly southern and most of western Texas (apparently replaced by *baileyi* in extreme western part), southeastern New Mexico, and south into northeastern Mexico (Matamoros); now probably extinct. Intergraded on the north with *nubilus*, and on the west with *mogollonensis* and *baileyi*.

---

[1]Stanley P. Young Collection.

General characters.—Size medium; color usually dark, but varying to nearly white; skull with highly arched frontal region.   Resembles *baileyi* of the Sierra Madre of Chihuahua but is larger and
grayer, less strongly inclined toward buffy or tawny along flanks and
on outer surfaces of limbs.   Similar in size to *nubilus* of Nebraska,
and *mogollonensis* of New Mexico, but usually darker than the former; pelage thinner and coarser; cranial characters, especially the
more highly arched frontal region, differing from either.

Color.—About as in *mogollonensis*.   An unusually colored skin
from Mayhill, New Mexico, taken in April, is entirely pale yellowish, except a few black hairs on tail gland and along upper terminal
two-thirds of tail.

Skull.—Most closely resembles that of *baileyi* in general form,
but is decidedly larger and heavier; frontal region usually more
highly arched; nasals strongly depressed along inner sides, tending
to form a deep median groove as in *baileyi*.   Similar in size to that
of *nubilus*, but less flattened; frontal region more highly arched and
fully inflated; nasals more depressed along median line.   Differs
from that of *mogollonensis* in higher, more inflated frontal region.

Measurements.—*Type* (adult male, approximated from tanned
skin): Total length, 1,620 mm.; tail vertebrae, 423, hind foot, 230.
Two adult females from 15 miles north of Elk, New Mexico, respectively: Total length, 1,372, 1,499; tail vertebrae, 419, 406; hind
foot, 241, 254.   An adult female from Mescalero, New Mexico:
1,422; 368; 222. *Skull: Type* (male) and an adult male topotype,
respectively: Greatest length, 260, 255.5; condylobasal length,
236.8, 237.8; zygomatic breadth, 137.5, 131.5; squamosal constriction, 80.4, 74.7; width of rostrum, 43.7, 46.2; interorbital breadth,
45.4, 46.9; postorbital constriction, 39.5, 40.7; length of mandible,
184.4, 178.2; height of coronoid process, 83.9, 79.1; maxillary
tooth row, crown length, 103.8, 106.3; upper carnassial, crown
length (outer side), 24.7, 25.8, crown width, 14.3, 14.8; first upper
molar, antero-posterior diameter, 15.1, 17.1, transverse diameter,
22.5, 24.2; lower carnassial, 28, 30.   Two adult female topotypes,
respectively: Greatest length, 250.4, 251.7; condylobasal length,
231.3, 228.1, zygomatic breadth, 138.5, 126; squamosal constriction,
78.1, 74.3; width of rostrum, 45.3, 39.3; interorbital breadth, 45.2,
45.1; postorbital constriction, 40.3, 40.3; length of mandible, 178.8,

171.3; height of coronoid process, 73.5, 69.2; maxillary tooth row, crown length, 103.3, 104.2; upper carnassial, crown length (outer side), 24.8, 24.2, crown width, 13.8, 13.8; first upper molar, antero-posterior diameter, 17.1, 17, transverse diameter, 22.1, 22.5; lower carnassial, crown length, 28, 27.7.

Remarks.—The distribution of the Texas gray wolf, extending to northeastern Mexico, marks the southern limit of the range of the species south over the great plains. Gray wolves were formerly plentiful in Texas, but apparently were never very numerous in northeastern Mexico. In central Texas, the range of the gray wolf meets that of the Texas red wolf (*Canis niger rufus*), but these forms are specifically distinct. The gray wolf is distinguished externally from the red wolf by decidedly larger size and more robust form. It is usually grayer, less rufescent as the common name implies, but owing to wide variation in both species, color is not always diagnostic. The skull of the Texas gray wolf, compared with that of the Texas red wolf, is much more massive and more highly arched. The dentition is very similar, but somewhat simpler. The larger molariform teeth above and below tend to be less deeply cleft, with less prominent cusp development. In the upper carnassial the antero-internal cusp when present is usually smaller, and is less frequently obsolete or absent. In the first upper molar, the large external cusps forming the high part of the crown are less unequal in size, the posterior one being less distinctly the smaller of the two. A small postero-median cusp in the first upper molar, absent or very small in the gray wolf, is more prominently developed in the red wolf. The posterior upper molars are relatively smaller than in *rufus* as a rule.

Specimens examined.—Total number, 41, as follows:

New Mexico: Capitan Mountains, (skulls only); Elk, 2; Mayhill, 1; Mescalero, 2; Sacramento Mountains, 7.

Tamaulipas: Matamoros, 1 (skull only).

Texas: Big Lake, Reagan County, 1; Fort Richardson, 1 (skull only); Guadalupe Mountains, 1 (skull only); Kimble County, 1 (skull only); Llano, 1 (skull only); Monahans, 1 (skull only); Nueces River, Edward County, 1 (skull only); Ozona N. H. Ranch, 25 miles west), 10; Rankin, 9 (10 miles south, 3; Harris Ranch, 18 miles southeast, 6).

CANIS LUPUS BAILEYI Nèlson and Goldman
Mexican Wolf (Pls. 123-124)

Canis nubilus baileyi Nelson and Goldman, Mamm. Jour. 10 (2): 165, May 9, 1929.
Canis lupus baileyi Goldman, Mamm. Jour. 18 (1): 45, Feb. 14, 1937.

Type locality.—Colonia Garcia (about 60 miles southwest of Casas Grandes), Chihuahua, Mexico (altitude 6,700 feet).

Type specimen.—No. 98312, ♂ adult, skin and skull, U. S. National Museum (Biological Surveys collection); collected by E. W. Nelson and E. A. Goldman, July 10, 1899. Original number 13895.

Distribution.—Sierra Madre and adjoining tableland region of western Mexico, formerly extending north to southeastern Arizona (Fort Bowie), southwestern New Mexico (Hatch), and western Texas (Fort Davis), south to the Valley of Mexico; still living in the northern part of the Sierra Madre, the exact southern and eastern limits undetermined.

General characters.—Size smallest of the American subspecies of *Canis lupus;* color dark; skull small, with slender rostrum and widely spreading zygomata. Size smaller and color usually darker than *mogollonensis* of New Mexico. Compared with *monstrabilis* of Texas: Smaller and less grayish, more strongly inclining toward buffy or tawny along flanks and on outer surfaces of limbs.

Color.—Winter pelage: Upper parts varying from "pinkish buff" to "pale pinkish buff" rather heavily overlaid with black; short pelage on head and face, a grizzled mixture of varying shades of buff and black; upper surface of muzzle and ears "cinnamon-buff" to tawny, more or less mixed with black; under parts, inner sides of legs, and lower surface of tail mainly "light buff" to "pinkish buff"; outer sides of legs ranging from rich "tawny" to "pinkish buff," becoming paler on feet; tail above about like back, with the usual black patch on gland, the tip black all around. In the usual pattern of coloration, as shown by topotypes, the muzzle, top of head, ears, and outer sides of limbs incline toward tawny, but these parts vary in occasional pallid examples to near "pale pinkish buff." A skin from Helvetia, Arizona, is unusually rich rufescent. The upper surface of the muzzle and the ears are deep "tawny," the upper parts in general are suffused with "cinnamon," and the under parts are "cinnamon-buff." One from 18 miles east of Parker Canyon, Huachuca Mountains, Arizona, presents an unusual mixture of black and gray, with the black predominating above and below.

Skull.—Closely resembling that of *monstrabilis* in general form, but decidedly smaller and more slender in proportions; zygomata widely spreading, frontal region rather high and nasals depressed along inner sides, much as in *monstrabilis;* dentition rather light. Similar to that of *mogollonensis,* but distinctly smaller, less massive; rostrum relatively slenderer.

Measurements.—Type specimen (adult male): Total length, 1,570 mm.; tail vertebrae, 410; hind foot, 260. An adult male from Canelo Hills, 4 miles south of Canille, Arizona: Total length, 1,520; tail vertebrae, 400; hind foot, 270, weight, 98 lbs. An adult female from same vicinity; weight, 65 lbs. An adult male from Walnut Canyon, 35 miles southeast of Animas, New Mexico: Total length, 1,486; weight, 51 lbs. *Skull:* Two adult males, type specimen, and a topotype: Greatest length, 232.1, 246.5; condylobasal length, 221.4, 231.5; zygomatic breadth, 129.7, 144.7; squamosal constriction, 74.8, 82.8; width of rostrum, 39.5, 43.4; interorbital breadth, 44.5, 46.2; postorbital constriction, 38.9, 44.8; length of mandible, 171, 183; height of coronoid process, 70.4, 77.8; maxillary tooth row, crown length, 100.2, 104.2; upper carnassial, crown length (outer side), 24.7, 25.1, crown width, 12, 14.6; first upper molar, antero-posterior diameter, 15.8, 15.9, transverse diameter, 21.5, 22.2; lower carnassial, crown length, 27.2, 27. Two adult females from type locality: Greatest length, 224.4, 234.2; condylobasal length, 209.5, 215.9; zygomatic breadth, 126.1, 130.9; squamosal constriction, 74.1, 74.6; width of rostrum, 37.9, 38.1; interorbital breadth, 43.1, 40; postorbital constriction, 42.8, 40.3; length of nasals, 165, 168; height of coronoid process, 69, 69; maxillary tooth row, 95.4, 99.3; upper carnassial, crown length (outer side), 24.5, 23.4, crown width, 12.2, 12.1; first upper molar, antero-posterior diameter, 15.1, 15.5, transverse diameter, 20.4, 19.5; lower carnassial, 26.3, 24.9.

Remarks.—The range of *baileyi* marks the southern limits of the gray wolf group in geographic distribution. Wolves formerly occupied the plateau or tableland region to its southern extremity near the Valley of Mexico. Owing to their inroads on domestic stock, strychnine was used, and elaborate pit traps were constructed. As a result, the wolves were believed for many years to have been extingunished on the southern part of the plateau, but remained fairly numerous in the Sierra Madre as far south as Durango. Some recent reports have, however, indicated their reappearance in the mountains not far north of the Valley of Mexico. The Mexican wolf is similar in small size to geographically remote *lycaon*, and both are notable for the slenderness of the rostral portion of the skull; but they differ in other respects. In *baileyi* the zygomata are decidedly heavier than in *lycaon*. In southeastern Arizona and southwestern New Mexico, *baileyi* intergraded with *mogollonensis*. Although wolves are known to wander over considerable distances, the transition from *baileyi* to *mogollonensis* is remarkably abrupt. An adult female was recently killed 16 miles northwest of Fort Davis, Tex., in a section from which wolves were believed to have been extirpated. The animal is clearly referable to *baileyi*, which was previously unknown from Texas, and was taken under conditions suggesting that it may have been a wanderer from northern Chihuahua.

Specimens examined.—Total number, 61, as follows:

Arizona: Arivaca, 3;[1] Canelo Hills (4 to 6 miles south of Canille), 2; Chiricahua, 1; Fort Bowie, 1; Helvetia, 2; Parker Canyon (18 miles east, southwest side Huachuca Mountains), 1; Parker Ranch (Santa Rita Mountains), 2; Patagonia (15 miles west), 1; Santa Rita Mountains, 1 (skull only); Seep Springs (35 miles east of Douglas), 1.

Chihuahua: Casas Grandes, 2 (skulls only);[2] Colonia Garcia, 13 (5 skulls without skins); Colonia Juarez, 1; Gallego, 1; Rio Alamos, 1;[3] Sierra Madre (near Guadalupe y Calvo), 1 (skull only).

Durango: El Salto, 1.

New Mexico: Animas, 4; Animas Valley, 1; Animas Mountains, 1; Cloverdale, 7 (2 skulls without skins); Hachita, 8; Hatch, 1; San Luis Mountains, 2.

Sonora: Santa Cruz, 1 (skull only).

Texas: Fort Davis (16 miles northwest), 1.

---

[1]Stanley P. Young Collection.
[2]Field Mus. Nat. Hist.
[3]Amer. Mus. Nat. Hist.

CANIS LUPUS BERNARDI Anderson
Banks Island Tundra Wolf

Canis lupus bernardi Anderson, Journ. Mamm. 24 (3): 389, August 17, 1943.

[*Canis lupus*] *banksianus* Anderson, Journ. Mamm. 24 (3): 390, August 17, 1943.

Type locality.—Cape Kellett, southwestern part of Banks Island, District of Franklin, Northwest Territories, lat. about 72° N., long. 125° W., Canada.

Type specimen.—No. 2796, ♂ adult, skin and skull, National Museum of Canada; collected by Peter Bernard, February 27, 1916.

Distribution.—Known only from Banks Island, but probably occurs also on Victoria Island, at least on the northwestern part, as suggested by Anderson.

General characters.—From original description: "Color mostly whitish, with less buffy than shown by average specimens of *mackenzii* and *manningi*; all specimens examined showing a greater or lesser number of blackish-tipped hairs forming a more or less distinct median dorsal line. A rather large rangy wolf, with long narrow skull, slender rostrum and exceedingly large upper and lower carnassials."

Color.—From original description: "In the type specimen the general color is white with no yellowish tinge, except on back of ears. Top of head from nose to nape with hairs dusky gray at base and with short white tips, giving the hair a clean grayish appearance; a darker gray streak under each eye; cheeks and side of nose dull whitish, more grayish under chin. Mane very long, with hairs whitish at base, distal to this a broad black band, sometimes with white tip, but many of the hairs have a second black band at tip, making a hair with four distinct bands; blackish-tipped dorsal area overlapping on shoulders and hips, narrower medially and fading out on shoulders and thighs; tail thickly intermixed on dorsal surface with black-tipped hairs; white below and with tip black and the usual black spot on top of tail; feet white; claws blackish. No. 3505, adult female (allotype), Dec. 15, 1915, is almost completely white; ears light buffy at base, duller at tips; a faint trace of black-tipped hairs along median dorsal line from nape to tail; tail white, with the usual black spot on top, but with no black at tip of tail; claws horn color. One additional male and one adult female and a subadult male and female are between the above extremes. One young wolf of the year, taken September 9, 1914, at Cape Kellett, is remarkable in having no buffy coloring; whitish, with a fairly well-defined median dorsal area produced by sparse black-tipped hairs on dull whitish background; tail white with a few black-tipped hairs, black spot on top and black tip; in almost all respects a miniature of the adult male type."

Skull.—From original description: "Distinguished by great comparative length, narrow zygomatic breadth, long, slender rostrum, and exceedingly large carnassials. Nasals narrower than in *tundrarum* and extending much farther behind posterior extensions of maxillaries and with shorter distance across postorbital processes. From its nearest neighbor on the north, *Canis lupus arctos* (of Melville Island, Sverdrup Islands, and Ellesmere Island) with which it might be expected to have the closest relationship, *bernardi* differs the most widely, with skull of only slightly less length, but much less massive, with narrower rostrum, lesser zygomatic breadth, lighter lower mandible, of less depth and more nearly straight. The tooth-row is about the same length as in *arctos,* but the molars and premolars are all longer, broader, and heavier; canines and incisors project forward at a noticeably greater angle. Coronoid process slender, sloping backward more than in *mackenzii* and *tundrarum;* ramus of mandible lower than in *mackenzii* and nearly straight as in *tundrarum,* but slightly less in depth and heavier horizontally; coronoid processes usually more truncated at tip than in these other races."

Measurements.—From original description: "Tanned skins of type, and no. 3506, adult female, allotype, measure, respectively: Total length, 1,870, 1,562 mm.; tail, 366, 362; hind foot, 261, 235. Field measurements of one male and one female which did not reach the museum are: Total length, 1,625, 1,422; tail, 432, 406; hind foot, 305, 254; height at shoulders, 813, 660; depth of chest, 406, 305; girth, 736, 660." *Skull* (type, from table accompanying original description): Greatest length, 252; condylobasal length, 233; zygomatic breadth, 136; maxillary tooth row, 107; upper carnassial, crown length, 28, crown width, 16; first upper molar, anteroposterior diameter, 18, transverse diameter, 25; lower carnassial, crown length, 31. Average of 3 adult males and 2 adult females (same table), respectively, from type locality: Greatest length,

245.3, 238.8; condylobasal length, 232, 219; zygomatic breadth, 129.3, 120; maxillary tooth row, 106, 101.4; upper carnassial, crown length, 27.4, 26, crown width, 16.6, 15.4; first upper molar, antero-posterior diameter, 17.6, 17.4, transverse diameter, 24.2, 27; lower carnassial, crown length, 29.7, 29.6.

Remarks.—No specimens of this race have been examined by me. It was based by the describer on 6 skins and 8 skulls from the type locality.

In the table of cranial measurements given by Anderson (*op. cit.*) the name *banksianus* appears for specimens from Banks Island. The name was evidently used inadvertently for *bernardi,* of which it is, therefore, a synonym.

CANIS LUPUS MACKENZII Anderson
Mackenzie Tundra Wolf

Canis lupus mackenzii Anderson, Journ. Mamm. 24 (3): 388, August 17, 1943.

Type locality.—Imnanuit, west of Kater Point, Bathurst Inlet, District of Mackenzie, Northwest Territories, lat. 67° 44′ 20″ N., long. 109° 04′ 03″ W., Canada.

Type specimen.—No. 2792, ♂ adult, skin and skull, National Museum of Canada; collected by R. M. Anderson, May 14, 1916. Original number 658.

Distribution.—Arctic coast and tundra region from west side of Mackenzie River delta, east to undetermined limits beyond Bathurst Inlet, south to the northern side of Great Bear Lake.

General characters.—From original description: "Color variable, adults more frequently white, but adult specimens are often buffy with dorsal band of black-tipped hairs; some specimens are almost black. Considerably smaller than *occidentalis,* slightly smaller than *hudsonicus, tundrarum* and *bernardi,* and considerably larger than *manningi.*"

Color.—From original description: "The type specimen is entirely yellowish white with exception of brownish black spot on dorsal side of tail; claws pale horn color. . . . An adult male, N. M. C. No. 2791, taken at Port Epworth, Coronation Gulf, July 20, 1915, is yellowish white, with top of head tawny brown, mixed with black-tipped hairs; neck sparsely black-tipped, and dorsal region with most of hairs black-tipped; legs buffy brown anteriorly, white posteriorly. An adult female, N. M. C. No. 4868, taken on Kogaryuak River, Coronation Gulf, June 10, 1917, by Jos. F. Bernard, is mostly slaty gray, with hairs on back having paler brownish tips; legs and under parts mostly plumbeous or dusky."

Skull.—From original description: "Much larger than in *manningi* of Baffin Island, smaller than in *hudsonicus* from west of Hudson Bay, and *tundrarum* from northern Alaska, with teeth about the same size as in the last two forms but larger than in *manningi*. Compared with *bernardi* from Banks Islands, the teeth of *mackenzii* are much smaller, particularly the upper and lower carnassials. Ramus of mandible short and heavy, with lower edge of ramus much more convex than in *tundrarum;* coronoid processes lower than in *tundrarum* and with tips slightly recurved posteriorly."

Measurements. — From original description: "Approximated from tanned skin of male: Total length, 1,676 mm.; tail vertebrae, 361; hind foot, 247. Specimens of this race measured in the flesh by the writer are as follows: No. 2789, Rae River, west of Coronation Gulf: Total length, 1,570; tail vertebrae, 385; hind foot, 281; weight, 78 pounds. No. 2551, ♀ adult and one other ♀ taken the same month on lower Coppermine River measured, respectively: Total length, 1,565, 1,460; tail vertebrae, 425, 470; hind foot, 285, 295." *Skull* (type, from original description): Greatest length, 248; condylobasal length, 226; zygomatic breadth, 131.8; maxillary tooth row, 102; upper carnassial, crown length, 26.2, crown width, 14; first upper molar, antero-posterior diameter, 17, transverse diameter, 22; lower carnassial, crown length, 30. Average of 3 adult males and 2 adult females (original description), respectively, from Bathurst Inlet, Coronation Gulf: Greatest length, 251, 241; condylobasal length, 228.8, 223.5; zygomatic breadth, 132.8, 129.8; maxillary tooth row, 102.6, 101.5; upper carnassial, crown length, 26.7, 25.4, crown width, 13.9, 13.5; first upper molar, antero-posterior diameter, 17.3, 17, transverse diameter, 22.3, 21.8; lower carnassial, crown length, 29, 28.

Remarks.—The description of *mackenzii*, recently published, was received too late for detailed consideration of the status of the race in relation to neighboring forms. The new race appears to be smaller than the other continental forms with which it must intergrade. The specimens examined are in part the same as those listed by Anderson.

Specimens examined. — Total number, 8, all from Mackenzie District as follows: Coronation Gulf (south side), 1; Dease River, 1 (skull only);[1] Fort Anderson, 1 (skull only); Fort Good Hope, 1; Great Bear Lake, 1 (skull only);[1] Langton Bay, 1 (skull only);[1] Peel River, 1 (skull only), Reliance, Great Slave Lake, 1 (skull only).[1]

CANIS LUPUS MANNINGI Anderson
Baffin Island Tundra Wolf

Canis lupus manningi Anderson, Jour. Mamm. 24 (3): 392, August 17, 1943.

Type locality. — Hantzsch River, east side of Foxe Basin, west side of Baffin Island, District of Franklin, Northwest Territories, lat. about 67° N., long. 24° W., Canada.

Type specimen. — No. 17236, ♀ young adult, skin and skull, National Museum of Canada; collected by Tom H. Manning, December 7, 1938. Original number 70.

Distribution. — Baffin Island, and probably smaller neighboring islands.

General characters. — From original description: "Considerably smaller than any of the other Arctic wolves, but with somewhat larger skull and teeth than in *Canis lupus labradorius,* from south of Hudson Strait. Color somewhat variable, but adults are generally white, and juveniles and subadults have more or less buffy, often with black-tipped hairs along median dorsal line."

Color. — From original description: "The type specimen has hair mostly pure white, with very faint tint of buffy on nose; ears pale buffy at tips; dorsal region with faint buffy tint; feet and tail white; tail with black spot on top but with no black at tip. Two subadult females (nos. 65 and 69, Manning collection) caught at the same place and supposed to belong to the same family group as the type specimen, have top of head faintly tinged with reddish buff, ears similar; a narrow black edging around lower lip and posterior portion of upper lip; back with longitudinal wash of yellowish buff in-

---

[1]Amer. Mus. Nat. Hist.

clined to reddish, with a few dorsal hairs blackish at tip; black spot on top of tail and tip of tail blackish. No. 68, also a young female, has more grayish on head, with a narrow dorsal band intermixed with blackish-tipped hairs; sides buffy; under parts and tail pure white."

Skull.—From original description: "Much smaller and less massive than in *arctos* in all respects, with rostrum more slender and zygomata proportionately much smaller; bullae much smaller; carnassials much shorter and less massive; tooth-row shorter and all teeth smaller. Compared with *mackenzii*, *manningi* has much smaller skull and teeth, palate more narrow and with posterior end of nasals projecting less far behind maxillaries; bullae smaller, more elongated and subtriangular. Compared with *tundrarum*, from which it is still farther separated geographically, *manningi* shows even greater difference in size; coronoid process much lower than in *tundrarum* and sloping backward, rounded at tip."

Measurements. — From original description: "Type: Total length, 1,003 mm.; tail vertebrae, 389; hind foot, 262. Adult male, no. 94, N.M.C., Ashe Inlet (from tanned skin) and one female adult from Foxe Basin (from tanned skin), respectively: Total length, 1,588, 1,524; tail, 387, 368; hind foot, 191, 191." *Skull* (type, from original description): Greatest length, 231; condylobasal length, 214; zygomatic breadth, 121; maxillary tooth row, 94; upper carnassial, crown length, 22, crown width, 11.8; first upper molar, antero-posterior diameter, 16.6, transverse diameter, 19.8; lower carnassial, crown length, 27.6. Average of 2 adult males and 3 adult females (original description), respectively, from Baffin Island: Greatest length, 253.5, 247.8; condylobasal length, 227.5, 224.3; zygomatic breadth, 137.5, 129.5; maxillary tooth row, 103.4, 101.7; upper carnassial, crown length, 24.3, 24.3, crown width, 13.9, 13.5; first upper molar, antero-posterior diameter, 16, 16.1, transverse diameter, 20.3, 21.6; lower carnassial, crown length, 27.9, 27.3.

Remarks.—No specimens of *manningi* have been examined by me. The subspecies was based on 13 specimens from various localities on Baffin Island. Owing to isolation of habitat and other geographic considerations, the name may be expected to represent a well-marked race.

XVI

CANIS NIGER AND SUBSPECIES

CANIS NIGER Bartram
[Synonymy under subspecies]

Distribution.—Formerly Mississippi River Valley and affluents, north at least to Warsaw, Ill., and Wabash, Ind., south through southern Missouri, eastern Oklahoma, Arkansas, and doubtless western Kentucky and western Tennessee to the Gulf Coast in Louisiana and Mississippi; west from the coastal region to the Pecos River Valley in Texas, and east through Alabama to the Atlantic Coast in Georgia and Florida; exact limits undetermined. Now restricted mainly to the Ozark Mountain region in Missouri, Arkansas, and southeastern Oklahoma and a few outlying sections in Louisiana and Texas.

General characters.—Size rather small; form slender; color inclining toward tawny, especially on muzzle, ears, and outer surfaces of limbs; skull slender; first upper molar with a distinct cingulum on outer side. In typical form, *niger*, resembling *Canis latrans* externally, but larger, more robust; pelage usually somewhat coarser; rhinarium and feet larger; tawny element in coloration more predominant; cranial characters very similar in general but differing in detail. Differs from *Canis lupus* in smaller size and much slenderer

Figure 15. Distribution of subspecies of *Canis niger*
1. *Canis niger niger*
2. *C. n. gregoryi*
3. *C. n. rufus*

proportions, as a rule (*C. n. niger* and *C. n. gregoryi*, large subspecies of *niger*, are similar in size to *C. l. lycaon* and *C. l. baileyi*, small subspecies of *lupus*); rhinarium and foot pads smaller; general coloration more tawny; cranial features usually quite distinctive.

Color.—*Normal phase:* Upper parts in general a varying mixture of "cinnamon-buff," "cinnamon," or "tawny" with gray and black; dorsal area more or less heavily overlaid with black, and black is conspicuously massed over the tail gland; muzzle, ears, and outer surfaces of limbs usually distinctly tawny; light post-humeral and nuchal bands varying in distinctness about as in the true wolves and coyotes; forearm with a narrow, more or less conspicuous, black line on anterior surface (present also in true wolf and coyote); under parts varying from whitish to "pinkish buff"; tail tipped with black. *Black phase:* Upper parts, limbs, and tail above black or brownish black, thinly and inconspicuously mixed with all white or white-banded hairs; light post-humeral and nuchal bands faintly indicated; under side of neck and pectoral region similar to back, except for a small, nearly pure white median pectoral spot sometimes present; inguinal area, inner sides of thighs, and under side of tail near base more extensively mixed with white. *Young (in first pelage):* Near "wood brown" above and below, somewhat lighter on inguinal region, darkened over back by brownish black-tipped hairs; ears and forearms tinged with "cinnamon."

Skull.—Size comparatively small and form slender. Closely approaches that of *C. latrans* in form, but is usually larger and differs in combination of details; cranium higher; rostrum deeper; zygomata more widely spreading; supraoccipital shield tending to project farther posteriorly; jugal heavier, more deeply inserted in maxilla, the orbital border more distinctly thickened and tending to bow outward; occipital condyles usually extending farther transversely; auditory bullae usually larger; dentition very similar, but first upper molar with postero-external cusp more nearly equaling antero-external cusp. Comparison with *C. lupus:* Size usually much smaller, but large individuals may exceed small ones of *lupus;* form more slender; large molariform teeth with crowns more deeply cleft, the cusps more compressed laterally, and points and shearing edges more trenchant; upper carnassial with protocone, or antero-internal cusp, usually more prominent, but in some specimens absent; first upper molar with a more prominent cingulum and with postero-external cusp more distinctly smaller as compared with antero-external cusp, also inner lobe bearing more prominent cusplets and enamel ridges; second upper molar variable, but usually larger.

Remarks.—The species is subdivisible into three subspecies: *niger, gregoryi,* and *rufus.* Of these, the larger subspecies, *gregoryi* and *niger,* exhibit a remarkable approach in size and general proportions to the small eastern gray wolf, *C. l. lycaon.* They differ externally, however, in shorter pelage and more rufescent instead of predominantly grayish coloration, and internally in combination of cranial details as already pointed out. Perhaps the most reliable distinguishing characters are the more prominent cingulum on the outer side of the first upper molar, and the more deeply cleft crowns and laterally compressed cusps of the large molariform teeth. Subspecies *rufus* in central Texas and Oklahoma, on the other hand, is so small and in general characters agrees so closely with *C. latrans,* which it overlaps in geographic range, that some specimens are difficult to determine. Representatives of the two species occur at the same localities but typical specimens are easily recognized by the contrast in size and the differing combinations of cranial details. Owing to wide range of individual variation, however, some of the smaller specimens of subspecies *rufus* may be confused with large examples of *latrans.* Specimens collected in the vicinity of Llano, Tex., include typical examples of both species and individuals not sharply distinctive of either. Close approach in essential details and the apparent absence of any invariable unit character suggests the possibility of hybridism in some localities in Texas.

CANIS NIGER NIGER Bartram
Florida Red Wolf (Pl. 129)

Lupus niger Bartram, Travels, p. 199, 1791.

Canis floridanus Miller, Proc. Biol. Soc. Wash. 25: 95, May 4, 1912.
From Horse Landing, St. Johns River, about 12 miles south of Palatka, Putnam County, Fla.

Canis rufus floridanus Goldman, Jour. Mamm. 18 (1): 45, Feb. 14, 1937.

Canis niger niger Harper, Jour. Mamm. 23 (3): 339, Aug. 14, 1942.

Type locality.—Alachua Savanna (now Payne's Prairie), Alachua County, Fla.

Type specimen.—Not designated.

Distribution.—Formerly Florida, Georgia, and Alabama; limits of range undetermined, but probably included South Carolina; believed to be extinct.

General characters.—Size largest of the subspecies of *rufus*. Similar in color to *gregoryi*, but size apparently somewhat larger; proportions more robust as indicated by skulls examined.

Color.—Type of *floridanus* (= *niger*): Upper parts in general (worn pelage) a coarsely grizzled light buff and gray mixture; muzzle "cinnamon" above, becoming dull white on sides; outer surfaces of limbs near "tawny" or "ochraceous tawny," becoming paler and near "cinnamon-buff" on feet; forearms with a narrow blackish line anteriorly as usual in the group; chin and throat dull white; under side of neck and chest pale buff, tinged with black; abdominal and inguinal areas and inner sides of limbs pinkish buff; ears "cinnamon" mixed with black to near base where the black is thinned out, leaving the cinnamon brighter in tone; tail (much worn) light buffy with a blackish patch over gland. The name, *niger*, was evidently based by Bartram on a specimen in the black phase. No specimens of the Florida wolf in this phase have been examined by me. A skin in winter pelage (March) from 12 miles south of Cherokee, Ala., referred to *niger* is similar to the type and lighter in general color than average specimens of *gregoryi*. The lighter tone is noticeable on the limbs and on the back where the overlying black, as seen in *gregoryi*, is somewhat reduced.

Skull.—Similar in general to that of *gregoryi*, but somewhat larger, more massive; frontal region and rostrum broader; zygomata heavier; dentition heavier. Size and general form much as in *C. l. lycaon*, but frontal region less highly arched; nasals with a more evenly U-shaped, instead of deeply V-shaped, space between the anterior ends; molariform teeth with crowns more deeply cleft, the cusps more compressed laterally and points and shearing edges more tranchant; first upper molar with more prominent cingulum along outer side, and postero-external cusp more distinctly smaller as compared with antero-external cusp, also inner lobe bearing more prominent cusplets and enamel ridges.

Measurements.—An adult male from 12 miles south of Cherokee, Alabama: Total length, 1650; tail vertebrae, 410. *Skull:* Type (♀) from Florida: Zygomatic breadth, 122.2; squamosal constriction, 67.2; width of rostrum, 36.1; interorbital breadth, 43.2; postorbital constriction, 38.9; length of mandible, 158.9; height of coronoid process, 65.5; upper carnassial, crown length (outer side), 23.2, crown width, 12.8; first upper molar, antero-posterior diameter, 15.8, transverse diameter, 21.7; lower carnassial, crown length, 25.6. An adult male from 12 miles south of Cherokee, Alabama: Greatest length, 236; condylobasal length, 219; zygomatic breadth, 125.9; squamosal constriction, 72.3; width of rostrum, 39.7; interorbital breadth, 39.7; postorbital constriction, 37.6; length of mandible, 170; height of coronoid process, 70.7; maxillary tooth row, 98.5; upper carnassial, crown length (outer side), 24.1, crown width, 14.1; first upper molar, antero-posterior diameter, 22; transverse diameter, 21; lower carnassial, crown length, 27.3.

Remarks.—A specimen from 12 miles south of Cherokee, Ala., may be grading toward *gregoryi*, but owing to heavy cranial proportions and large teeth, seems referable to the present subspecies. In rather light coloration also this specimen is not very unlike the type of *floridanus* (= *niger*). The subspecies *niger* rather closely approaches *lycaon* in size and general appearance, but the resemblance is probably superficial, and the two are regarded as specifically distinct.

Specimens examined.—Total number, 2, as follows:
Alabama: Cherokee (12 miles south), 1.
Florida: Horse Landing, 12 miles south of Palatka, 1.

CANIS NIGER GREGORYI Goldman
Mississippi Valley Red Wolf (Pls. 127-128)

Canis rufus gregoryi Goldman, Jour. Mamm. 18 (1): 44, Feb. 14, 1937.

Canis niger gregoryi Harper, Jour. Mamm. 23 (3): 339, Aug. 14, 1942.

Type locality.—Mack's Bayou, 3 miles east of Tensas River, 18 miles southwest of Tallulah, Madison Parish, La.

Type specimen.—No. 136731, ♂ adult, skin and skull, U. S. National Museum (Biological Surveys collection); collected by B. V. Lilly, April 25, 1905. X-catalog number 5338.

Distribution.—Formerly the Mississippi River Valley, north at least to Warsaw, Ill., and Wabash, northern Indiana; probably western Kentucky and western Tennessee; west throughout the Ozark Mountain region in southern Missouri, Arkansas, except northwestern part, to southeastern Oklahoma, and from the lowlands of Louisiana west to eastern Texas; east to southeastern Mississippi. Intergradation with *rufus* on the west and with *niger* on the east is evident.

General characters.—Similar to *rufus* of Texas but much larger, and color averaging less vividly rufescent. Size somewhat smaller, but color similar to *niger* of Florida.

Color.—About as given for the species, but averaging less tawny than *rufus*.

Skull.—Closely resembling that of *rufus*, but decidedly larger and of heavier proportions, with notably broader rostrum. Usually smaller, less massive than that of *niger*; frontal region narrower; dentition lighter.

Measurements.—Two adult males from Barren, Missouri, respectively: Total length, 1650, 1473; tail vertebrae, 393, 362; hind foot, 254, 235. Weight of an adult male from same locality: 67 lbs. Two adult females from Barren, Missouri, respectively: Total length, 1448, 1422; tail vertebrae, 355, 343; hind foot, 216, 222. Weight of an adult female from same locality: 50 lbs. *Skull:* Type (♂) and an adult male from 15 miles northwest of Tallulah, Louisiana, respectively: Greatest length, 250, 249.5; condylobasal length, 228, 230.7; zygomatic breadth, 126, 124.7; squamosal constriction, 73.2, 75.4; width of rostrum, 34.7, 35.9; interorbital breadth, 40.6, 42.6; postorbital constriction, 32.4, 36.7; length of mandible, 173, 176; height of coronoid process, 68.6, 67.8; maxillary tooth row, crown length, 103.8, 104; upper carnassial, crown length (outer side), 23.5, 24.9; crown width, 12, 12; first upper molar, antero-posterior diameter, 15.9, 16.1, transverse diameter, 20.6, 22.6;

lower carnassial, crown length, 26.5, 26.8. An adult female from type locality and one from Sikes, Louisiana, respectively: Greatest length, 222.7, 218.5; condylobasal length, 202.5, 207.7; zygomatic breadth, 114.2, 114.5; squamosal constriction, 67.9, 68.7; width of rostrum, 38, 32.6; interorbital breadth, 35.6, 40.2; postorbital constriction, 31, 37.5; length of mandible, 156.7, 157.7; height of coronoid process, 68.6, 66.8; maxillary tooth row, crown length, 91.2, 93.1; upper carnassial, crown length (outer side), 22.6, 20.1, crown width, 11.7, 11; first upper molar, 15.1, 14.8, transverse diameter, 20, 19; lower carnassial, 24.7, 23.4.

Remarks.—*C. n. gregoryi* is somewhat intermediate in characters, as well as geographic position, between *rufus* and *niger*. The combination of characters presented over a wide range appear, however, to warrant the recognition of the Mississippi River Valley animal as a separate race. Red wolves remained until recently fairly numerous west of the Mississippi River, but of the occurrence of *gregoryi* in the more densely settled country to the eastward, little is known. An interesting early record is that of a specimen from the Maximilian collection in the American Museum of Natural History, Museum Number 112. Translation of the German script on the tag is as follows: "Skull of the bitch wolf in the exhibition gallery from Wabash [Indiana] 1832. Weight of bitch wolf 60 pounds." This skull exhibits the light cranial structure and narrow, compressed dental cusps characterizing the red wolves. The skin and skull of a young male in the same museum, received from C. K. Worthen, is labeled Warsaw, Ill., February 7, 1893. A more recent record of a specimen, also in the American Museum of Natural History, is Biloxi, Miss., collected in November 1931 by Frank Parker.

Specimens examined.—Total number, 247, as follows:

Arkansas: Almond, 1; Aly (8 miles northwest), 1; Aplin, 1; Ava, 3; Bergman, 2; Blue Ball (3 miles south), 4; Cardiff, 1; Carthage (5 miles west), 1; Cedar, 2; Crystal Springs, 1; Delaplaine (3 miles east), 1; Egger (radius of 12 miles), 7; Fallsville, 9; Ferndale, 8; Fifty-Six, 4; Forrest City, 1; Gladstone, 1; Graysonia (5 miles southeast), 1; Hartley, 1; Hollis, 1 (skull only); Hot Springs (9 miles east), 1; Isaac, 6; Lead Hill, 1; Lonsdale (6 miles west), 4; Lurton, 2; Maumelle Creek, Pulaski County, 1; Mena, 1; Mill Creek, 3; Mull, 4; Onyx,

11; Parkdale (12 miles east), 1; Parks (4 miles east), 1; Pinnacle, 6; Potter, 1; Rush, 2; Shady, 3; Signal Hill, Stone County, 1; Simpson, 6; Solo, 1; Stillwater, 8; Thornburg, 1; Wye (8 miles west), 2.

Illinois: Warsaw, Hancock County, 1.[1]

Indiana: Wabash, Wabash County, 1 (skull only).[1]

Louisiana: Avery Island (12 miles north), 1 (skull only); Floyd (10 miles southwest), 1; Indian Lake (23 miles southwest of Tallulah), 1; Jackson Parish, 1(skull only); Little River, La Salle Parish, 1 (skull only)[2]; Mack's Bayou (3 miles east of Tensas River, 18 miles southwest of Tallulah), 1; Madison Parish, 1 (skull only); Mer Rouge, 1; Sabine River, Beauregard Parish, 2 (skulls only); Sikes, 2; Tallulah, 4 (3 skulls only); Vidalia (20 miles southwest), 1 (skull only); Winn Parish, 2.

Missouri, Arcadia, 2; Barren, 7; Cooks Station, 7; Gatewood, 3; Reeds Spring, 2; Sabula (4 miles south), 1 (skull only); Stone County, 3; Tyrone, 2; Upalika, 1; Westover, 5: West Plains, 2.

Oklahoma: Bethel, 5; Big Cedar, 1; Broken Bow (15 miles north), 20; Cedar Creek, Pushmataha County, 2; Fewell, 2; Nashoba (Garland Creek), 1; Octavia (10 miles northeast), 3; Page, 9; Sherwood, 4; Smithville, 12; Talahina, 1 (skull only); Zafra, 1 (skull only).

Texas: Hardin County, 1; Kountze, 2 (1 skull without skin); Mont Belvieu, Chambers County, 1 (skull only); Newton County, 1 (skull only); Polk County, 2 (skulls only); Rock Creek, Newton County, 1 (skull only); Segno, 1; Wakefield, 2 (skulls only).

CANIS NIGER RUFUS Audubon and Bachman
Texas Red Wolf (Pls. 125-126)

Canis lupus var. *rufus* Audubon and Bachman, Quadr. North Amer. 2: 240, 1851.

Canis rufus Bailey, North Amer. Fauna 25: 174, Oct. 24, 1905.

Canis rufus rufus Goldman, Jour. Mamm. 18 (1): 45, Feb. 14, 1937.

---

[1]Amer. Mus. Nat. Hist.
[2]La. State Univ.

Canis niger rufus Harper, Jour. Mamm. 23 (3): Aug. 14, 1942.

Type locality.—Name restricted by Goldman (1937, p. 38) to subspecies occurring 15 miles west of Austin, Tex.

Type specimen.—Not designated.

Distribution.—Formerly northwestern Arkansas, eastern Oklahoma, except Ozark Mountains in southeastern corner, and south through central Texas to the Gulf Coast near Aransas Bay; west to the Pecos River Valley. Now believed to be restricted to parts of central and southern Texas, intergrading with *gregoryi* in the eastern part of the State.

General characters.—Very similar to *gregoryi* of the Mississippi Valley, but smaller, and color averaging more vividly rufescent.

Color.—About as given for the species, but tawny element usually more predominant than in the other subspecies.

Skull.—Closely resembling that of *gregoryi*, but decidedly smaller and of lighter proportions, with notably slenderer rostrum.

Measurements.—Two adult males from Redfork, Oklahoma, respectively: Total length, 1403, 1454; tail vertebrae, 381, 420; hind foot, 210, 221. An adult male from Noble, Cleveland County, Oklahoma: Weight, 55 lbs. *Skull:* Two adult males from vicinity of Llano, Texas, respectively: Greatest length, 225, 226.9; condylobasal length, 207.8, 209; zygomatic breadth, 117.5, 112.3; squamosal constriction, 68.7, 66; width of rostrum, 34.6, 33.3; interorbital breadth, 39.7, 35; postorbital constriction, 36, 34.8; length of mandible, 161, 160.7; height of coronoid process, 61.1, 62.8; maxillary tooth row, 98.2, 94.6; upper carnassial, crown length (outer side), 22.4, 21.3; upper carnassial, crown width, 11.6, 11.6; first upper molar, antero-posterior diameter, 14.3, 14.2, transverse diameter, 19.8, 18.7; lower carnassial, crown length, 24.6, 23.1. Two adult females from vicinity of Llano, Texas, respectively: Greatest length, 200.9, 207.3; condylobasal length, 194, 191.6; zygomatic breadth, 106, 110.2; squamosal constriction, 64.3, 63.1; width of rostrum, 29.8, 31.7; interorbital breadth, 39.7, 33.9; postorbital constriction, 40, 39.1; length of mandible, 149, 151.2; height of coronoid process, 61.1, 60.6; maxillary tooth row, 87.7, 89; upper carnassial, crown length (outer side), 19.4, 21.6, crown width, 9.8, 10.6; first upper molar, antero-posterior diameter, 12.7, 14.7, transverse diameter, 17.3, 18.7; lower carnassial, crown length, 20, 23.2.

Remarks.—The description of *rufus* by Audubon and Bachman clearly refers to the red wolf of Texas. No local habitat was formally designated. However, reference was made (1.c. 242) to the occurrence of the animal 15 miles west of Austin, and that place has been selected as the type locality.

The small size of *rufus* is the principal character distinguishing it from the decidedly larger subspecies inhabiting territory to the eastward. The intergradation of *rufus* with *gregoryi* is clearly shown by specimens from eastern Texas, southeastern Oklahoma, and northwestern Arkansas. In these regions the transition from one subspecies to the other is rather abrupt. As already pointed out in remarks on the species, there appear to be no very tranchant or entirely dependable characters distinguishing in all cases small specimens of *rufus* from large ones of the coyote, *Canis latrans;* and the status of typical *rufus* in relation to the latter is, therefore, not entirely clear. However, as most specimens of the two species are readily recognizable, even where they occur at the same locality, possible hybridism, rather than regular intergradation, is indicated.

Specimens examined.—Total number, 94, as follows:

Arkansas: Boxley, Newton County, 2; Frederick, 1; Hector, 1; Raspberry, 3 (1 skull without skin); Redstar, 1; Summers (5-12 miles north), 7 (3 skulls without skins).

Oklahoma: Atoka, 2; Ridden, 1 (skull only); Red Fork, 2; Tahlequah, 1 (skull only); Wedington, 3 (skins only); Wichita Mountains Refuge, 1.

Texas: Angleon, 4 (2 skulls without skins); Aransas Migratory Waterfowl Refuge, near Austwell, 1 (skull only); Bloomington (5 miles south), Calhoun County, 3; Brady, 3 (1 skull without skin); Bryan (15 miles south), Brazos County, 1; Burnet, 1; Burnet County, 2 (skulls only); Cantey Ranch, near Mineral Wells, Palo Pinto County, 1; Cisco, Hill Brothers Ranch, 12 miles northeast, 1; Cleveland, Liberty County, 1;[1] Click, Llano County, 1; Columbus, 1; Dayton, (6 miles north), 2 (skulls only); Doole (5 miles southeast), 1; Droyet Ranch (6 miles south of Marble Falls), 1; Fairland (5 miles east), 1 (skull only); Frelsburg, 1 (skull only); Kerrville, 2 (1 skull without skin); Kerr County, 1 (skull only); Llano (radius of 22 miles), 14 (1 skin without skull); Loving (Ferguson Ranch, 6 miles northeast), 1; Llano County, 1 (skull only); Magnolia, Montgomery County, 1; Marble Falls, Burnet County, 2; Menard (35 miles west), 3; Murray (Graham Ranch, 6 miles northeast), 1; New Chaney, Montgomery County, 1; New Waverly, Montgomery County, 1 (skull only); Nueces River, Edwards County, 1 (skull only); Parker County, 2 (skeletons with skulls); Port Lavaca (7 miles southwest), 2 (skulls only); Port O'Connor, 4 (skulls onyy); Porters, Montgomery County, 2 (1 skull without skin); Security, Montgomery County, 3;[2] Sheffield (22 miles north), Pecos County, 1; Valley Spring (5 miles north), Llano County, 1 (skull only).

---

[1]Stanley P. Young Collection.
[2]One in Stanley P. Young Collection.

TABLE 4.—CRANIAL MEASUREMENTS OF ADULT MALES IN U. S. NATIONAL MUSEUM, UNLESS OTHERWISE INDICATED, OF *Canis lupus* GROUP

Species and locality	Number	Greatest length	Condylobasal length	Zygomatic breadth	Squamosal constriction	Width of rostrum	Interorbital breadth	Postorbital constriction	Length of mandible	Height of coronoid process	Maxillary tooth row, crown length	Upper carnassial, crown length (outer side)	Upper carnassial, crown width	First upper molar, antero-posterior diameter	First upper molar, transverse diameter	Lower carnassial, crown length
C. l. tundrarum:																
Alaska—																
Noatak River[1]	264415	282.0	256.3	143.4	82.4	46.8	55.0	47.8	195.5	79.4	115.1	28.8	15.8	20.1	25.4	33.2
Point Barrow[2]	4053	267.5	248.0	143.7	81.4	47.1	46.9	43.7	199.4	84.0	112.9	27.2	16.3	18.0	25.3	30.9
Average		274.8	252.2	143.6	81.9	47.0	51.0	45.8	197.5	81.7	114.0	28.0	16.1	19.1	25.4	32.1
C. l. pambasileus:																
Alaska—																
Big Delta	265100	280.0	261.2	151.8	84.2	52.6	59.8	47.6	205.5	88.2	118.5	....	....	....	....	....
Big Delta	265576	286.4	263.5	150.0	86.8	50.0	55.8	47.2	206.7	87.5	118.5	....	....	....	....	33.0
Chicken	203895	286.8	258.5	141.6	82.2	47.3	54.7	45.2	205.9	88.8	114.7	29.6	16.3	18.6	25.6	33.1
Dry Creek (N. of McKinley Park)	266409	275.2	253.7	149.4	81.7	44.9	48.1	43.6	198.5	86.1	114.7	26.4	14.6	17.4	23.8	31.6
Farewell Mountain	242704	288.2	266.0	148.4	87.1	51.2	47.3	48.5	208.7	86.4	121.5	26.2	14.9	17.5	24.0	30.0
Gold Creek	264226	281.4	261.4	147.3	83.5	48.6	50.3	45.8	203.7	85.3	120.4	29.5	15.6	18.6	25.2	33.8
Savage River	264227	277.3	251.5	153.0	84.4	46.4	45.9	45.9	199.3	89.5	119.5	29.6	14.7	19.2	24.2	31.5
Seventy Mile	265982	285.0	265.3	153.0	86.6	49.5	55.6	43.6	208.5	88.3	119.6	29.6	15.6	18.5	26.1	33.4
Sushana River	266406	286.9	268.4	151.6	86.8	46.4	47.4	43.9	210.3	89.1	119.0	27.1	13.6	17.8	24.1	29.4
Tanana	218341	287.2	258.7	145.7	87.2	54.3	54.4	46.5	202.5	84.0	114.4	25.2	14.1	16.7	22.6	28.7
Tanana River	255577	271.3	250.7	151.4	78.7	48.2	51.6	44.7	196.5	84.4	112.2	27.5	14.8	18.0	23.8	31.0
Teklanika River	266407	277.2	257.5	152.5	84.8	46.8	47.1	40.6	201.3	88.5	114.1	26.8	13.5	18.0	24.0	29.9
Yukon—																
White River[3]	33-9-20-5	293.7	269.3	151.5	87.0	49.4	50.3	43.0	208.0	92.9	118.1	26.6	13.7	17.3	24.3	29.8
White River[3]	31-2-16-2	292.8	263.9	149.0	84.2	47.0	49.6	43.5	207.0	84.2	118.5	27.6	13.6	17.7	24.6	30.2
White River[3]	33-9-20-8	282.0	252.7	144.0	83.1	45.5	49.3	49.2	202.4	80.6	114.3	25.4	13.1	17.1	22.7	29.3
Average		283.1	260.2	149.4	84.5	48.5	51.6	45.1	204.3	86.9	116.7	27.3	14.6	17.9	24.2	31.0
C. l. alces:																
Alaska—																
Kachemak Bay[4]	147470	263.0	245.0	133.8	80.7	44.7	43.9	42.4	185.0	76.5	108.6	26.0	14.4	16.8	23.3	28.9
Kachemak Bay[4]	136743	262.8	250.0	130.5	82.3	45.7	42.5	40.9	190.0	74.0	113.2	27.5	15.4	17.3	23.3	31.1
Average		262.9	247.5	132.2	81.5	45.2	43.2	41.7	187.5	75.3	110.9	26.8	14.9	17.1	23.3	30.0

Locality	No.															
C. l. occidentalis:																
Alberta—																
Edmonton	242907	276.7	248.1	146.3	81.0	45.3	50.8	44.8	194.6	79.0	111.3	27.6	13.9	18.3	23.9	30.3
Smith Landing	177370	274.0	250.0	146.8	82.5	50.3	51.5	44.9	196.5	85.1	110.7	25.5	15.3	13.4	21.8	28.5
Wood Buffalo Park[5]	98230	278.2	262.5	146.5	90.5	47.0	46.2	44.6	197.6	80.8	114.1	27.2	14.4	17.6	24.2	30.8
Wood Buffalo Park[5]	98225	274.2	258.8	146.0	84.9	50.7	46.1	43.2	199.0	82.8	115.4	28.5	15.6	18.0	25.2	33.6
British Columbia—																
Cache Creek, Peace River District[6]	4695	283.0	255.2	156.7	86.6	51.3	51.4	46.8	204.7	83.6	114.5	26.9	15.9	16.9	24.4	31.2
Mackenzie—																
Artillery Lake	262083	281.0	258.0	146.8	82.3	44.4	50.0	44.6		83.0	120.4	28.6	15.9	18.9	25.5	30.0
Aylmer Lake[8]	29040	272.0	245.3	146.4	81.1	43.3	50.7	46.0	191.7	81.0	100.8	27.2	14.1	17.9	24.2	31.0
Coronation Gulf	236104	278.5	256.0	146.2	83.3	45.6	49.0	46.1	198.3	84.3	118.7	27.7	13.4	19.2	24.7	30.6
Dease River	34443	265.3	240.8	156.5	85.2	43.0	51.4	44.1	186.5	85.3	108.7	25.3	13.4	16.3	24.0	29.9
Fort Simpson[7]	9001	292.8	266.0	156.5	85.4	50.1	53.2	44.9	204.8	82.5	116.4	30.6	17.1	18.8	24.8	33.8
Fort Simpson	9003	270.3	245.0	146.7	84.4	49.6	49.9	41.0	190.9	78.2	111.1	30.5	15.2	18.8	22.8	30.0
Fort Simpson[4]	134131	272.0	253.5	136.7	84.1	48.0	41.8	41.8	193.2		112.6	27.0	15.0	17.7	24.6	29.7
Yukon—																
Macmillan River (north fork)	134490	283.3	255.7	146.0	87.2	47.5	49.0	42.8	204.0	87.2	111.0	26.5	14.5	17.2	24.6	31.0
Pelly Lakes	214478	276.5	253.6	156.5	83.5	51.1	53.4	46.1	200.5	86.1	110.0	27.0	14.5	17.8	24.2	31.0
Pelly Lakes	214479	275.0	256.9	156.2	85.4	47.5	52.0	47.1	202.7	82.9	112.1	28.2	15.8	17.7	24.0	31.7
Pelly Lakes	214477	270.9	247.7	146.7	83.1	46.5	47.8	44.3	195.4	84.2	116.1	26.4	14.6	15.7	23.0	29.1
Pelly Lakes	214431	277.3	256.3	146.2	82.2	49.1	46.4	40.7	202.7	87.2	116.7	26.8	14.8	18.1	24.4	30.2
Average		276.5	253.5	146.7	84.3	47.7	49.4	44.1	197.7	83.0	112.7	27.3	15.0	17.7	24.1	30.7
C. l. hudsonicus:																
Keewatin—																
Cape Fullerton[5]	19493	260.0	240.7	146.1	80.5	46.4	46.0	38.8		73.7	111.8	27.3	16.0	18.7	25.9	30.0
Hudson Bay[5]	19348	254.0	233.2	136.4	78.1	46.2	46.1	37.3	183.1	73.7	107.8	26.9	14.6	18.5	24.2	30.0
Schultz Lake	180281	258.3	241.0	146.4	83.9	46.3	47.2	39.3	190.3	84.6	110.1	26.8	14.2	17.2	24.2	32.6
Schultz Lake	180232	262.1	237.7	146.5	80.2	44.2	47.0	38.8	186.3	75.1	107.2	25.5	14.0	17.6	22.1	28.8
Wager River[5]	22940	263.3	240.8	136.2	80.1	43.3	47.0	41.2	187.3	73.7	109.7	25.6	14.0	17.5	23.5	29.1
Average		259.5	238.7	146.4	80.0	45.3	46.8	39.6	186.8	76.8	109.2	26.4	14.7	17.9	24.0	30.1
C. l. arctos:																
Arctic America—																
Ellesmere Islands[5]	42119	264.7	236.9	136.7	79.4	46.0	45.6	40.4	186.8	76.1	108.6	26.4	15.3	17.6	23.0	30.1
C. l. labradorius:																
Labrador—																
Hopedale[3]	7409	262.2	243.5	146.5	78.8	49.5	46.6	46.9	189.6	81.8	110.1	25.7	13.7	17.1	23.3	29.4
Porcupine	210059	266.2	240.0	146.5	79.4	45.8	46.6	43.8	188.0	74.7	113.1	25.9	14.4	15.1	23.1	30.6
Quebec—																
Fort Chimo (near)[9]	23138	244.5	227.5	126.0	74.9	42.3	39.6	44.5	173.4	69.3	102.9	25.0	13.1	16.7	22.5	27.4
Average		257.6	237.0	136.7	77.7	45.8	44.3	45.1	183.7	75.3	108.7	25.5	13.7	16.6	23.0	29.1
C. l. beothucus:																
Newfoundland	264432	254.0	230.0	136.7	78.2	44.1	46.7	45.4	182.7	78.6	104.0	26.2	14.7	17.5	23.0	29.0

FOOTNOTES   [1] Subadult. [2] Type locality, Colo. Mus. Nat. Hist. [3] Roy. Ont. Mus. Zool. [4] Type locality, Young. [5] Amer. Mus. Nat. Hist. [6] Prov. Mus. [7] Type locality. [8] Mus. Comp. Zool. [9] Type locality. Subadult.

TABLE 4.—CRANIAL MEASUREMENTS OF ADULT MALES IN U. S. NATIONAL MUSEUM, UNLESS OTHERWISE INDICATED, OF *Canis lupus* GROUP—(Continued)

Species and locality	Number	Greatest length	Condylobasal length	Zygomatic breadth	Squamosal constriction	Width of rostrum	Interorbital breadth	Postorbital constriction	Length of mandible	Height of coronoid process	Maxillary tooth row, crown length	Upper carnassial, crown length (outer side)	Upper carnassial, crown width	First upper molar, antero-posterior diameter	First upper molar, transverse diameter	Lower carnassial, crown length
C. l. lycaon:																
Florida[1]	11179	250.2	224.5	128.2	75.4	38.9	43.8	43.7	172.1	73.5	100.1	25.0	12.7	16.3	20.9	27.4
Michigan—																
Calderwood	168820	259.3	237.8	132.5	75.7	41.4	44.9	41.4	183.5	69.7	105.3	25.0	14.0	16.3	22.4	27.3
Cusino	170692	244.2	230.4	128.0	76.4	40.1	43.8	40.2	176.2	76.1	96.5	24.1	14.1	15.8	21.3	27.4
Escanaba River	265071	248.5	234.0	139.3	74.6	43.2	50.0	44.2	179.5	69.9	104.6	25.0	13.4	15.9	23.4	29.3
Escanaba River	266072	249.2	225.0	134.9	77.4	41.3	50.6	41.7	177.2	76.5	104.6	24.1	13.4	16.0	22.9	28.7
Kenton	243395	239.5		134.1	75.9	41.3	41.6	42.6	175.0	66.6	99.8	21.8	13.4	16.0	21.8	27.7
Minnesota—																
Elk River	45561	257.3	236.5	136.5	78.6	41.6	46.8	42.6	180.3	74.9	106.5	24.3	12.9	15.7	21.7	27.7
Gunflint Lake[3]	1221	251.5	241.0	138.2	77.5	42.9	46.4	42.7	178.7	72.7	107.8	27.1	15.2	17.7	24.2	30.5
Gunflint Lake[3]	1349	256.8	236.0	136.0	78.2	44.5	46.0	41.0	183.0	75.7	109.3	25.4	13.0	17.3	22.8	29.5
New York—																
Adirondack Mts.	1804	233.0	219.3	127.9	76.9	36.7	43.0	41.8	168.6	69.0	95.6	24.0	13.0	16.9	22.3	27.1
Ontario—																
Brent, Algonquin National Park[3]	24-11-19-1	245.3	229.4	136.3	77.0	41.1	41.5	41.5	175.7	69.6	104.7	23.5	13.2	16.3	20.2	28.0
Mattawa (40 mi. NE)	140562	238.0	233.5	127.3	77.4	38.0	42.6	38.4	172.5	76.0	101.5	23.1	13.6	16.2	21.5	29.3
Mattawa (40 mi. NE)	140561	237.7	222.0	136.8	76.0	40.1	47.1	42.2	171.3	69.0	99.5	22.5	12.8	16.4	21.2	26.6
Whitney[4]	77344	246.0	231.3	138.0	75.4	41.1	48.7	41.2	181.2	71.3	106.3	23.9	12.7	16.7	21.5	26.6
Pennsylvania[5]	2261	234.2	221.0	122.4	73.5	35.7	43.5	41.2	165.5	65.2	101.0	24.2	12.9	16.8	21.6	28.8
Quebec—																
Lucerne[6]	77343	243.9	228.9	129.3	71.8	40.5	38.6	36.0	174.5	68.1	103.3	23.9	12.8	17.1	21.6	28.8
Montebello[6]	32-2-1-1	253.0	233.0	140.3	76.2	41.4	45.3	38.1	181.7	75.0	104.8	23.7	13.7	16.3	21.9	27.9
Montebello[6]	31-12-29-2	250.5	236.0	136.0	78.8	41.5	43.9	37.6	178.5	71.0	106.6	23.4	12.5	17.7	21.9	28.2
Wisconsin—																
Vilas Co. (near Mich. line)[7]	51772	267.3	247.7	140.7	79.6	43.4	48.4	45.5	194.4	76.5	113.1	26.0	15.2	18.2	23.4	30.3
	Average	247.7	231.5	133.8	76.4	40.8	45.2	41.2	177.3	71.5	103.7	24.6	13.3	16.7	22.0	28.2
C. l. nubilus:																
Colorado—																
Bent County	51434	261.5	239.8	133.2	82.3	43.9	46.5	42.2	179.3	75.9	106.2	25.4	13.5	16.0	23.4	29.4
Kansas—																
Gove County	139156	254.4	232.5	135.7	74.6	43.5	45.7	39.3	177.5	74.5	105.6	26.1	13.8	16.3	22.5	29.2

Locality	No.															
Montana—																
Kinsey	232866	264.5	244.5	14–1	80.2	48.8	50.2	43.7	189.5	76.1	112.1	25.4	14.1			27.4
Miles City	228133	258.2	244.2	14–0	80.7	46.7	47.6	56.7	188.8	81.1	110.0	25.2	13.4	15.9	22.5	28.9
Miles City	211143	254.4	238.9	13–5	78.0	46.2	45.6	39.2	183.2	78.8	107.5	25.2	13.2	16.2	21.7	28.3
Nebraska—																
Kearney	884	258.4	228.9	13–7	80.4	44.3	46.6	45.7	180.3	81.0	102.8	28.1	13.1	15.9	22.6	29.2
Kearney	1308	253.5	232.3	13–2	75.7	42.2	48.1	40.3	183.5	81.2	106.3	28.0	12.4	17.2	22.7	28.9
Kearney	1315	253.2	230.8	13–2	76.8	43.6	47.2	41.8	181.8	74.6	106.0	28.0	14.9	16.7	23.6	29.2
Kearney	1312	243.7	228.5	13–7	76.7	45.7	46.9	42.0	181.0	78.1	108.6	25.5	13.2	18.4	24.2	31.0
Kearney	1314	244.2	223.8	13–7	77.7	45.5	45.1	39.5	173.0	72.3	102.8	25.0	14.4	16.9	21.8	30.8
Platte River	2568	253.0	231.7	13–7	78.3	43.3	52.2	39.6	178.8	75.2	104.0	25.5	14.6	15.5	22.7	28.4
Platte River	3686	250.9	228.4	14–9	76.3	47.7	46.8	56.7	178.0	75.8	105.0	25.7	14.4	17.6	24.4	29.0
New Mexico—																
Santa Rosa (18 mi. south)	168344	259.1	240.5	13–5	80.2	46.1	51.4	41.4	186.1	76.1	112.1	25.9	16.1		23.1	29.2
North Dakota—																
Medora (20 mi. south)	60486	255.6	235.8	13–9	76.0	44.0	48.0	42.7	183.4	77.3	109.0	25.4	13.9	15.8	21.9	29.4
Oklahoma—																
Wichita Mountains	147703	256.4	233.4	13–4	75.8	42.2	44.8	35.0	175.7	75.7	108.7	26.7	15.1	17.1	24.8	30.4
South Dakota—																
Faith	227682	254.8	234.0	13–1	75.3	47.8	46.6	40.9	182.5	76.3	105.4	24.5	13.0	17.4	22.3	28.4
Folsom	223729	264.4	237.2	13–6	80.4	47.7	49.5	40.1	181.0	79.5	105.9	24.8	13.7	16.8	21.9	28.5
Wyoming—																
Douglas	227679	250.7	239.8	14–0	78.7	48.0	49.6	41.5	186.5	77.7	107.6	24.9	14.7	16.1	23.0	28.7
Douglas	227673	249.3	229.5	13–0	74.2	41.7	43.3	51.5	181.0	71.7	107.7	25.9	13.9	18.1	23.6	29.3
Average		254.7	234.4	13–4	77.8	45.2	47.5	39.5	181.6	76.8	107.0	25.5	14.0	16.7	22.9	29.2
C. l. irremotus:																
Alberta—																
Lethbridge (25 mi. southeast)	78120	265.9	249.2	14–0	80.7	44.9	46.4	39.6	189.8	73.6	109.7	26.2	13.7	17.0	23.0	28.9
Idaho—																
Argora, Clark Co.	227084	259.1	241.5	13–1	79.2	42.8	44.9	37.5	182.0	75.3	108.8	26.2	15.5	17.5	23.9	32.0
Leadore (10 mi. south)	215803	258.9	236.8	14–8	76.5	42.0	43.8	38.1	183.8	77.0	106.4	24.8	13.1	16.7	23.3	29.0
Soda Springs	233721	257.0	235.2	14–0	76.7	46.7	51.2	34.7	184.7	79.0	105.7	24.5	13.1	16.4	22.0	27.9
Soda Springs	234400	249.3	234.0	14–8	75.4	46.2	46.7	35.4	180.2	76.5	104.0	25.2	12.9	15.4	21.3	27.0
Tyhee, Bannock Co.	219405	251.7	234.8	13–4	77.4	44.2	45.2	34.4	182.0	72.9	106.2	25.0	13.7	16.7	21.0	28.5
Montana—																
Lame Deer	203802	253.4	236.5	14–6	84.6	44.8	43.9	39.6	183.5	75.4	106.0	26.2	14.1	16.6	23.1	30.1
Little Belt	156824	275.8	254.3	14–6	85.0	50.0	32.4	43.6	193.2	83.9	116.6	27.7	15.1	18.4	25.0	31.4
Powderville	58409	255.3	235.0	13–4	81.6	47.0	43.0	40.3	178.5	76.2	105.5	26.4	15.0	16.7	22.9	29.6
Powderville	58289	257.8	240.5	13–6	82.9	47.2	41.7	35.8	179.2	74.7	109.4	26.0	14.3	17.5	22.9	29.5
Powderville	57821	258.4	238.1	14–9	79.2	44.2	40.3	32.2	178.7	74.4	109.0	26.6	14.0	16.3	23.2	28.8
Red Lodge[8]	214869	259.2	237.0	14–7	81.1	47.7	34.7	34.7	186.0	74.4	105.7	25.7	13.9	17.6	20.2	28.5
Red Lodge[9]	214868	262.0	241.0	14–5	81.0	49.5	43.1	35.5	193.5	82.6	106.2	26.1	13.3	18.4	24.1	30.4
Three Forks[10]	271651	285.3	258.0	14–5	87.8	48.7	52.0	40.1	201.5	80.9	116.5	27.6	14.7	17.3	23.8	30.4
South Dakota—																
Belle Fourche	265070	260.0	240.0	14–0	83.0	46.4	46.9	38.4	184.7	77.3	107.3	25.2	13.8	17.7	23.2	29.7

FOOTNOTES: [1]Mus. Comp. Zool. [2]Minn. Mus. Nat. Hist. [3]Roy. Ont. Mus. Zool. [4]Mus. Vert. Zool. [5]Acad. Nat. Sci. Phila. [6]Roy. Ont. Mus. Zool. [7]Field Mus. Nat. Hist. [8]Type specimen. [9]Type locality. [10]Al Johnston.

TABLE 4.—CRANIAL MEASUREMENTS OF ADULT MALES IN U. S. NATIONAL MUSEUM, UNLESS OTHERWISE INDICATED, OF *Canis lupus* GROUP—(Continued)

Species and locality	Number	Greatest length	Condylobasal length	Zygomatic breadth	Squamosal constriction	Width of rostrum	Interorbital breadth	Postorbital constriction	Length of mandible	Height of coronoid process	Maxillary tooth row, crown length	Upper carnassial, crown length (outer side)	Upper carnassial, crown width	First upper molar, antero-posterior diameter	First upper molar, transverse diameter	Lower carnassial, crown length
C. l. irremotus—continued																
Wyoming—																
Barber, Johnson Co.	242148	264.5	245.6	141.5	78.6	46.5	52.6	42.7	192.2	79.3	110.4	26.5	14.2	17.0	24.7	29.7
Cora	147214	256.0	235.0	138.5	79.1	46.1	46.6	38.9	......	....	106.5	26.5	15.2	18.4	24.5	31.2
Elk	224475	256.8	239.5	139.2	74.8	45.8	45.7	40.4	181.5	71.8	110.7	26.1	13.7	16.9	23.9	29.8
Elk	227683	256.4	238.3	139.9	78.6	44.0	44.9	36.2	182.4	77.0	110.6	24.4	13.3	17.0	23.1	28.6
Lenore	224463	251.5	235.0	141.2	78.2	43.2	45.7	38.0	181.9	73.2	106.6	25.2	14.1	....	22.8	29.1
Manville	211643	278.5	257.0	142.3	83.2	48.8	47.3	36.5	200.0	83.7	106.5	27.5	15.0	16.6	24.3	30.3
Pinedale	148726	258.0	238.0	145.3	79.6	46.4	47.4	40.7	184.8	79.7		27.5	15.1	17.3	24.1	30.7
	Average	260.5	240.9	140.9	80.2	46.3	46.2	38.1	185.9	77.2	107.7	26.1	14.3	17.1	22.9	29.6
C. l. columbianus:																
British Columbia—																
Iskut Summit (60 mi. south Telegraph Creek)[1]	31043	288.9	268.0	155.0	86.2	50.8	52.3	45.4	206.4	89.5	114.5	28.3	14.2	18.0	23.6	31.4
Pemberton[2]	4656	265.7	249.0	144.1	82.1	46.0	43.9	43.4	199.6	82.5	113.5	24.8	14.2	17.8	24.8	31.2
Wistaria[3]	3559	272.9	260.0	148.4	82.5	46.0	48.8	45.7	196.2	75.0	112.1	27.1	13.8	17.3	24.1	31.1
Wistaria[4]	4264	263.9	244.4	147.7	80.8	45.0	48.1	38.3	193.0	80.9	107.3	26.8	14.0	16.4	22.9	29.5
	Average	272.9	255.4	148.8	82.9	47.1	47.0	43.2	198.8	82.0	111.9	27.5	14.0	17.4	23.9	30.8
C. l. ligoni:																
Alaska—																
Eleanor Cove, Yakutat Bay[5]	36.9.18.246	251.5	236.5	140.5	79.2	44.6	45.4	42.3	184.5	77.9	103.3	24.8	13.4	15.6	21.9	28.0
Kuiu Island	243332	254.0	245.6	143.2	78.4	45.6	47.0	42.6	193.3	70.9	111.9	24.8	13.6	17.9	24.1	30.2
Kupreanof Island[6]	243323	262.1	251.0	145.3	80.0	43.4	49.1	43.4	197.0	72.9	112.8	25.2	13.9	17.7	24.5	30.4
Kupreanof Island	244207	270.8	254.8	141.5	80.6	44.1	44.0	46.0	197.0	72.4	114.7	26.0	13.9	18.9	24.5	31.0
Prince of Wales Island	243574	262.5	239.4	142.2	81.4	44.1	48.0	45.1	191.4	74.1	108.7	24.6	14.3	15.4	21.1	28.0
Wrangell	244206	262.0	239.4	146.4	81.4	47.9	47.3	41.5	184.5	73.3	110.3	24.6	14.2	16.3	23.3	28.3
Zarembo Island	243329	261.5	241.2	144.0	80.5	42.6	43.7	43.3	183.7	74.0	107.5	25.0	14.5	16.2	23.9	28.4
Zarembo	243328	259.5	238.8	141.0	79.8	41.7	43.2	42.2	191.0	72.2	111.7	25.0	14.2	16.8	24.1	28.3
Zarembo	243333	255.8	235.0	140.4	78.9	44.8	45.7	40.6	190.5	75.4	106.9	24.9	13.7	16.2	23.9	30.0
	Average	260.0	242.9	142.7	80.4	44.3	46.0	42.7	190.3	73.7	109.8	25.0	13.9	16.8	23.5	29.2

Locality	Cat. no.	247.8	232.3	125.⊞	79.1	47.0	45.9	38.6	178.9	72.9	105.5	26.3	13.7	15.5	23.4	30.2
C. l. fuscus:																
California—																
Litchfield[4]	34228	247.8	232.3	125.⊞	79.1	47.0	45.9	38.6	178.9	72.9	105.5	26.3	13.7	15.5	23.4	30.2
Oregon—																
Cascadia	223530	256.5	235.5	127.⊞	78.8	45.0	47.8	44.3	187.0	85.0	109.1	25.6	14.2	16.8	22.0	30.1
Cascadia	243984	256.0	238.3	1⊞1.⊞	75.6	44.3	50.3	44.0	187.8	83.3	107.6	25.5	12.3	16.9	23.1	28.4
Clackamas River[7]	427	251.0	236.0	1⊞7.⊞	79.3	44.2	48.3	46.2	185.8	77.1	107.0	24.9	14.8	16.3	22.2	29.1
Estacada	228800	259.5	244.3	1⊞3.⊞	81.1	44.9	49.8	43.7	190.3	83.4	107.0	24.0	13.6	16.4	..	29.4
Glide (20 mi. NE)[7]	438	255.4	233.0	1⊞4.⊞	81.8	44.2	47.8	42.5	187.3	82.9	102.3	24.2	13.8	15.6	21.7	28.6
Molalla River[7]	422	255.2	237.8	1⊞1.⊞	79.9	45.0	56.0	49.5	188.3	85.0	105.7	24.2	14.1	15.8	23.3	27.0
Rogue River	243985	259.4	235.3	1⊞5.⊞	78.6	45.6	49.2	41.5	184.2	83.6	107.1	26.5	14.8	17.8	23.3	30.2
Silver Lake (30 mi. south)	247357	254.9	244.3	1⊞0.⊞	77.8	43.7	49.6	38.5	184.2	74.8	107.4	25.8	13.0	17.2	22.9	28.7
Tiller	223817	258.3	242.0	1⊞6.⊞	77.4	44.5	48.0	42.5	186.5	34.4	107.6	25.7	15.0	17.4	..	29.9
Washington—																
Puget Sound	3438	267.0	249.1	1⊞2.⊞	81.2	48.5	52.6	47.6	186.0	81.2	109.1	27.3	14.9	17.2	24.1	....
Average		257.3	238.9	1⊞8.⊞	79.1	45.2	49.8	43.5	186.0	81.2	106.8	25.6	14.0	16.7	22.9	29.2
C. l. crassodon:																
British Columbia—																
Vancouver Island[8]	137805	244.3	232.2	1⊞6.⊞	77.7	41.8	43.0	47.9	177.8	53.7	105.7	27.1	16.6	17.8	24.6	31.3
Vancouver Island[5]	12457	256.2	239.6	1⊞3.⊞	80.1	44.8	50.1	45.6	183.5	72.1	107.5	26.2	15.9	16.6	23.1	30.4
Vancouver Island[3]	3339	251.6	234.2	1⊞8.⊞	76.8	42.9	47.8	42.3	184.2	74.4	105.0	25.6	13.9	16.5	22.2	28.9
Average		250.7	235.3	125.⊞	78.2	43.2	47.0	45.3	182.1	70.1	106.6	26.3	15.5	17.3	23.3	30.2
C. l. youngi:																
California—																
Providence Mts.[1]	33389	252.1	232.3	150.⊞	80.0	44.9	49.0	44.9	186.2	82.6	107.4	25.9	15.1	17.1	22.7	30.1
Colorado—																
Salt Creek, Garfield County	210742	265.0	248.5	1⊞8.⊞	82.5	48.2	51.5	45.4	193.4	82.1	110.3	25.2	13.4	17.1	24.8	29.1
Sulphur, Rio Blanco County	224975	254.5	242.7	1⊞9.⊞	78.3	46.8	50.7	42.6	189.2	78.6	109.9	25.2	14.2	16.9	23.7	28.3
West Creek, Garfield County	224525	250.5	242.9	1⊞2.⊞	84.0	47.1	49.1	37.7	188.6	76.6	110.0	26.9	14.3	17.1	..	29.6
New Mexico—																
Abiquiu	223512	251.5	236.8	150.⊞	77.3	49.4	49.1	40.6	181.0	79.2	107.9	24.7	14.0	17.0	22.4	30.0
Utah—																
Duchesne	224457	260.4	248.5	1⊞2.⊞	82.6	48.0	47.9	41.7	194.5	83.2	111.7	25.8	14.2	16.4	22.5	29.4
Grouse Creek, Box Elder County	221961	265.4	242.2	144.⊞	81.8	49.7	47.8	43.6	190.5	78.9	112.3	25.2	14.0	16.7	23.1	29.9
Heart Draw, San Juan County[9]	224001	258.5	243.5	1⊞6.⊞	82.8	47.7	44.3	40.6	177.7	77.1	107.8	26.5	14.1	17.3	23.8	30.0
Heart Draw, San Juan County[9]	224000	254.0	235.0	1⊞6.⊞	80.2	44.4	44.1	39.3	186.0	76.1	108.4	26.4	14.1	16.9	20.1	30.2
La Sal (10 mi. SE)	221829	250.4	245.6	1⊞8.⊞	83.8	46.2	48.4	37.6	186.7	76.3	107.4	25.7	14.1	15.9	..	28.9
Wyoming—																
Federal	227684	252.0	231.7	1⊞7.⊞	77.2	46.6	46.7	42.2	178.4	75.2	103.6	25.0	13.7	16.4	22.8	29.2
Laramie	208508	232.0	246.6	1⊞7.⊞	79.9	45.8	46.2	39.0	191.3	77.2	110.6	26.1	14.9	16.7	22.7	29.5
Rock Springs	214813	230.0	240.5	1⊞8.⊞	79.1	48.8	50.5	41.2	187.4	77.8	108.2	25.7	14.9	16.2	23.2	29.4
Average		258.2	241.4	1⊞0.⊞	80.7	47.2	47.9	41.3	187.8	78.5	109.0	25.7	14.1	16.9	22.9	29.5

FOOTNOTES: [1] Mus. Vert. Zool. [2] B. C. Prov. Mus. [3] B. C. Prov. Mus. Type specimen. [4] B. C. Prov. Mus. Type locality. [5] Roy. Ont. Mus. Zool. [6] Type specimen. [7] Ore. Agric. College. [8] Subadult. [9] Type locality.

TABLE 4.—CRANIAL MEASUREMENTS OF ADULT MALES IN U. S. NATIONAL MUSEUM, UNLESS OTHERWISE INDICATED, OF *Canis lupus* GROUP—(Continued)

Species and locality	Number	Greatest length	Condylobasal length	Zygomatic breadth	Squamosal constriction	Width of rostrum	Interorbital breadth	Postorbital constriction	Length of mandible	Height of coronoid process	Maxillary tooth row, crown length	Upper carnassial, crown length (outer side)	Upper carnassial, crown width	First upper molar, antero-posterior diameter	First upper molar, transverse diameter	Lower carnassial, crown length
C. l. mogollonensis:																
New Mexico—																
Chloride	232445	258.4	235.0	142.1	79.7	44.2	47.3	38.9	184.8	80.5	104.1	24.9	13.9	16.1	22.7	28.8
Chloride	216250	257.4	235.4	136.9	79.5	45.1	47.6	38.0	182.9	75.6	99.7	25.6	14.4	18.2	23.4	30.8
Chloride	216249	259.8	236.1	142.6	81.7	42.8	47.6	38.6	184.0	81.5	106.5	26.0	13.1	16.5	23.0	29.6
Chloride	224516	255.0	237.5	137.4	79.7	46.4	44.2	39.6	181.0	77.3	107.0	25.3	14.9	15.4	22.5	28.1
Fairview	232451	253.5	231.5	144.5	83.4	46.1	45.7	41.4	184.0	79.4	102.0	24.3	14.1	15.8	21.3	28.8
Fairview	235088	252.0	229.8	142.6	82.1	43.6	45.7	42.2	182.5	80.9	107.1	24.2	13.5	16.4	23.9	27.0
Gila Nat. Forest	148976	257.5	234.8	141.8	82.1	45.9	51.0	42.2	183.2	73.0	105.7	27.7	15.0	17.4	23.3	31.5
Gila Nat. Forest	148971	255.0	231.9	133.7	76.9	46.8	46.0	38.9	181.0	76.9	105.0	26.0	14.9	17.9	23.2	31.1
Luna (10 mi. NW)[1]	224548	253.5	236.3	142.1	80.8	43.7	46.1	36.8	184.7	78.4	107.0	25.1	13.9	16.7	22.9	30.0
Magdalena	221655	253.2	228.0	133.8	80.3	44.7	46.1	37.9	177.9	77.3	104.5	25.0	16.0	16.7	22.6	28.6
Monticello	228264	258.5	234.0	149.5	83.2	47.8	46.1	40.7	184.4	81.8	106.5	25.6	16.0	15.6	22.7	28.5
Average		255.8	233.7	140.6	81.3	45.2	46.4	40.3	182.4	78.4	105.0	25.5	14.4	16.5	22.8	29.2
C. l. monstrabilis:																
New Mexico—																
Sacramento Mts.	159016	245.9	227.4	135.0	77.2	45.1	46.0	37.7	175.0	73.8	103.7	25.6	14.3	17.5	22.3	30.0
Sacramento Mts.	159020	255.3	232.7	131.2		44.6	42.9	38.3	177.6	73.4	102.6	24.1	12.3	15.7	21.1	27.3
Sacramento Mts.	159022	257.9	232.5	134.4	78.4	45.1	42.6	35.8	174.0	74.2	104.6	26.2	13.7	16.4	23.6	30.4
Texas—																
Guadalupe Mts.	110046	263.0	243.8	141.0	82.2	46.8	44.5	40.5	183.3	78.6	108.6	26.8	15.0	17.9	24.0	29.8
Ozona	227902	257.5	233.0	140.0	77.7	46.0	47.0	43.2	179.2	77.5	108.9	26.1	14.3	15.4	21.9	28.8
Ozona	227885	251.0	232.0	139.0	77.5	45.6	46.9	39.9	178.8	77.5	104.7	25.6	15.0	16.5	22.7	28.2
Rankin (10 mi. south)[1]	209497	260.0	236.8	137.5	80.4	43.7	45.4	39.5	184.4	83.9	103.8	24.7	14.3	15.1	22.5	28.0
Rankin (10 mi. south)	222090	255.5	237.8	131.5	74.7	46.2	46.9	40.7	178.2	79.1	106.7	25.8	14.8	17.1	24.2	30.0
Average		255.8	234.8	136.2	78.3	45.4	45.3	39.5	178.8	77.3	105.5	25.6	14.2	16.5	22.8	29.2

C. l. baileyi:

Arizona—															
Helvetia	226435	2±0.1	213.5	129 7	74.1	38.5	43.7	39.7	168.0	71.2	96.9	22.6	11.7	14.8	18.8	24.9
Santa Rita Mts.	251525	2±5.0	216.2	135 6	74.5	42.7	41.6	37.3	171.0	77.4	96.0	23.4	12.8	15.9	19.7	26.2
Chihuahua—															
Colonia Garcia[1]	98312	2±2.1	221.4	129 7	74.8	39.5	44.5	38.9	171.0	70.4	100.2	24.7	12.0	15.3	21.5	27.2
Colonia Garcia[3]	117059	2±6.5	231.5	144 7	82.8	43.4	46.2	44.8	183.0	77.8	104.2	25.1	14.6	15.9	22.2	27.0
Colonia Garcia[3]	98307	2±1.0	222.4	129 7	74.3	39.7	40.1	38.2	169.0	76.0	99.7	25.3	12.8	16.3	21.1	26.1
Colonia Juarez	98313	2±7.5	225.0	132 4	74.4	41.5	43.3	38.3	172.3	75.9	101.4	24.1	13.4	15.9	19.7	26.8
Gallego	170556	2±5.2	225.9	138 0	77.2	40.7	40.9	31.4	172.1	73.9	101.3	25.0	13.5	15.7	20.1	28.0
New Mexico—															
Animas (35 mi. SE)	234499	2±7.3	221.3	131 4	73.2	43.3	42.1	37.9	161.9	70.8	100.0	27.7	14.4	16.9	22.9	29.1
Animas Mts.	262129	2±9.8	226.0	140 1	83.6	41.8	45.3	41.7	176.3	74.8	100.2	25.3	13.4	15.3	22.0	27.7
Hachita	231324	2±0.2	224.8	132 3	76.2	42.1	42.5	36.3	173.1	77.5	103.3	25.4	13.7	16.1	21.4	27.6
Hachita	231320	2±6.8	217.5	136 4	73.7	38.9	43.0	36.4	166.4	74.6	96.0	24.7	13.0	15.3	20.7	26.8
Average		2±1.0	222.3	134 5	76.8	41.1	43.1	38.3	171.3	74.6	99.9	24.8	13.2	15.8	20.9	27.0

FOOTNOTES: [1] Type specimen. [3] Type locality.

497

TABLE 5.—CRANIAL MEASUREMENTS OF ADULT MALES IN U. S. NATIONAL MUSEUM, UNLESS OTHERWISE INDICATED, OF *Canis niger* GROUP

Species and locality	Number	Greatest length	Condylobasal length	Zygomatic breadth	Squamosal constriction	Width of rostrum	Interorbital breadth	Postorbital constriction	Length of mandible	Height of coronoid process	Maxillary tooth row, crown length	Upper carnassial, crown length (outer side)	Upper carnassial, crown width	First upper molar, antero-posterior diameter	First upper molar, transverse diameter	Lower carnassial, crown length
C. n. rufus:																
Arkansas—																
Boxley	243312	221.4	208.8	121.0	67.8	35.7	36.5	36.1	162.2	67.6	96.6	21.8	11.8	14.4	20.0	24.1
Oklahoma—																
Atoka	243317	218.2	202.3	118.7	65.7	35.0	41.1	37.0	156.0	66.5	93.6	20.1	10.5	13.9	19.2	23.2
Redfork	133233	228.5	212.4	120.0	67.2	32.4	39.3	36.1	161.3	64.4	97.8	20.8	11.6	15.3	19.4	24.1
Redfork	135748	217.2	204.0	111.1	63.0	31.1	34.9	36.2	156.5	60.5	92.1	20.3	11.3	13.8	18.1	22.5
Texas—																
Angleton	261753	218.7	202.5	114.5	63.6	32.3	33.7	31.9	155.5	62.8	93.4	21.3	10.0	14.3	18.4	24.6
Aransas Migratory Waterfowl Refuge, Aransas County	265645	220.3	205.8	111.3	67.6	32.7	34.9	36.3	156.4	60.8	90.6	20.9	10.1	13.7	19.2	23.2
Burnet	224531	221.6	208.0	109.5	67.4	33.1	36.7	36.8	155.5	66.2	92.8	21.9	11.7	15.0	19.6	24.1
Doole	224972	216.4	204.1	106.5	64.3	33.5	36.3	36.4	152.3	59.0	91.9	21.4	10.8	13.6	17.6	23.5
Edwards County	108680	216.9	204.7	113.2	63.9	32.6	36.5	33.7	160.2	63.2	91.0	21.8	10.8	14.4	19.7	25.3
Kerr County	146744	218.0	210.0	111.2	67.5	32.6	33.8	33.8	159.5	60.3	91.2	21.4	11.6	15.2	18.7	24.0
Llano	224003	225.0	207.8	117.5	68.7	34.6	36.4	36.0	161.0	61.1	94.2	22.4	11.6	14.2	18.7	24.6
Llano	224530	226.9	209.0	112.3	66.0	33.5	39.7	36.0	160.7	62.8	93.6	20.9	10.1	13.7	18.7	23.1
Llano	223589	210.0	201.6	108.0	65.4	31.6	34.8	34.5	148.5	60.5	94.6	21.4	10.6	13.2	18.0	23.1
Llano	214853	209.4	196.5	111.5	63.2	31.6	35.8	34.8	148.1	59.7	91.3	20.1	10.9	13.5	17.7	22.5
Llano	225366	209.5	196.5	105.5	60.7	32.8	36.9	34.2	157.2	59.1	92.3	21.0	10.9	13.0	18.7	22.4
Llano	224185	214.2	199.4	109.3	65.2	32.5	37.1	33.4	151.0	59.1	92.2	21.0	11.0	14.5	17.7	22.3
Llano	224529	222.0	206.7	114.0	65.0	32.5	36.7	39.9	160.0	69.2	94.4	22.5	11.0	14.7	18.7	23.3
Marble Falls	228239	222.5	207.0	103.2	68.8	30.0	36.7	37.3	157.8	57.6	96.9	21.7	10.7	14.8	19.9	24.2
Marble Falls	228069	214.5	202.3	105.9	63.3	32.3	32.5	37.3	155.0	57.6	93.7	21.2	10.2	13.9	18.3	24.2
Marble Falls	228517	208.0	197.1	111.4	63.2	34.6	36.5	38.6	150.7	60.3	91.0	21.7	10.5	15.2	19.3	24.0
Menard	213288	218.7	201.3	110.5	62.5	33.7	33.8	33.7	155.0	61.7	90.5	21.3	10.5	14.6	18.3	24.0
Port O'Connor	99719	235.0	221.5	121.9	70.1	34.7	40.3	33.7	167.0	69.0	96.0	22.7	12.3	14.9	20.2	24.6
Port O'Connor	99718	220.8	201.4	112.9	66.2	32.5	41.5	33.7	156.3	60.0	90.0	20.8	10.9	13.7	18.4	23.0
Sheffield	227900	208.3	200.8	107.5	62.3	33.2	35.8	33.2	150.7	63.2	91.2	21.8	10.8	14.4	18.9	25.3
	Average	218.4	204.7	112.0	65.3	32.9	36.6	35.5	156.4	62.6	93.5	21.5	11.0	14.3	19.0	23.8
C. n. gregoryi:																
Arkansas—																
Blue Ball	243432	219.5	206.4	119.5	67.3	36.8	37.9	38.9	156.7	63.3	96.0	24.6	13.5	16.1	21.0	26.5
Blue Ball	243434	223.0	198.5	122.5	70.4	36.4	41.5	38.7	153.5	65.9	91.0	23.2	11.7	14.7	19.7	26.2

Arkansas—continued

Locality	No.															
Egger	242586	244.6	221.8	120.5	68.8	36.1	40.1	36.3	169.0	64.7	100.9	24.0	11.7	15.9	21.2	25.8
Ferndale	243308	231.2	215.3	123.5	68.0	38.1	37.2	34.3	161.5	64.1	95.5	22.9	13.1	15.1	20.3	25.5
Ferndale	242576	229.5	217.5	123.8	68.8	37.5	41.6	37.2	163.5	64.2	95.3	22.8	13.0	15.1	20.2	25.4
Hollis	248720	242.8	223.3	126.7	75.4	39.4	43.5	39.0	171.7	66.9	98.5	23.6	13.1	15.8	22.2	25.8
Hot Springs	243430	236.3	221.2	131.3	74.7	41.6	47.9	39.9	173.4	68.1	102.7	23.6	13.4	15.4	20.8	26.8
Isaac	242583	240.4	221.4	131.7	72.9	41.5	42.2	40.6	173.8	74.0	101.5	25.2	13.0	16.5	22.2	26.9
Pinnacle	243593	248.0	225.4	137.5	74.8	41.6	46.2	42.1	174.8	73.8	99.9	24.2	13.0	15.3	21.1	27.9
Tallsville	236650	245.3	231.0	124.5	71.9	37.8	39.8	35.1	174.9	64.7	100.9	24.0	11.7	15.9	21.2	25.8
Illinois—Warsaw[1]	4609	220.5	208.4	115.5	68.3	34.5	38.2	36.5	158.4	64.3	92.0	22.4	10.4	14.6	19.0	24.2
Louisiana—Mer Rouge	132229	245.2	225.5	121.0	70.8	38.4	38.6	35.5	171.4	70.0	101.7	23.9	13.2	16.6	21.6	27.0
Tallulah (vicinity)[2]	136731	250.0	228.0	126.0	73.2	34.9	40.6	32.4	173.0	68.6	103.6	23.5	12.5	16.6	20.6	26.5
Tallulah (vicinity)	133687	249.5	230.7	124.7	75.4	35.0	42.6	36.7	176.0	67.8	104.0	24.9	12.0	16.1	22.6	26.8
Winn Parish	265475	242.4	221.0	126.7	69.8	35.1	37.0	34.5	170.7	74.0	101.2	22.1	12.7	14.9	20.2	25.1
Mississippi—Biloxi[3]	100225	234.5	219.9	122.0	70.6	33.6	38.9	34.5	168.0	68.9	98.0	23.2	12.0	15.2	20.7	24.9
Missouri[3]—Barren	244246	245.3	233.7	130.4	72.5	37.0	44.2	40.5	180.0	72.2	103.8	24.5	11.6	15.5	20.7	27.3
Barren	244247	234.5	221.7	122.3	69.0	35.1	39.1	37.6	169.2	67.7	102.8	23.8	13.6	14.7	20.7	27.3
Barren	244523	226.0	215.8	124.9	69.3	35.4	39.2	40.2	162.0	67.6	98.7	22.8	11.0	14.5	19.8	26.1
Barren	244299	218.5	207.4	123.9	67.8	32.1	36.1	34.4	154.0	68.0	91.1	22.0	11.9	14.5	20.0	25.5
Cook's Station	244301	226.4	208.2	119.1	67.3	32.9	40.4	36.4	160.0	67.3	96.1	21.8	11.7	15.2	19.9	25.3
Cook's Station	244424	226.8	225.0	124.4	67.3	36.1	40.7	41.0	164.8	64.8	98.8	22.5	11.6	15.2	20.1	26.4
Gatewood	244212	247.2	227.6	121.0	66.8	35.0	37.8	38.3	169.4	71.4	103.0	24.3	12.5	15.1	20.1	26.2
Gatewood	244213	238.8	226.2	115.2	66.9	35.0	38.5	36.0	169.9	69.2	103.1	23.2	12.0	15.5	20.7	26.5
West Plains	235435	228.8	219.0	121.4	67.6	39.4	40.0	36.0	166.4	70.7	99.1	24.2	11.5	15.5	20.8	27.5
West Plains	235436	233.8	215.0	125.3	72.2	36.1	38.3	34.9	169.8	62.3	97.4	22.0	12.8	14.8	19.2	24.8
Oklahoma—Broken Bow	234436	247.9	231.0	126.5	71.7	40.0	43.7	39.6	178.5	73.9	103.2	23.7	13.6	15.9	21.5	25.8
Broken Bow	234434	233.7	215.2	122.5	68.0	38.1	41.8	39.6	168.4	70.6	100.3	23.0	12.1	15.2	21.0	26.0
Broken Bow	232436	230.5	216.5	123.0	67.1	34.8	39.0	39.7	165.4	66.5	102.1	23.4	12.5	15.2	21.0	26.0
Broken Bow	232423	233.0	215.3	130.5	70.9	37.9	43.7	40.6	165.4	65.0	99.5	24.4	13.1	16.7	21.6	25.2
Page	234451	237.7	209.8	120.2	68.7	37.4	42.7	40.6	169.4	65.0	96.9	25.2	12.3	15.7	21.6	26.7
Sherwood	234437	236.0	219.5	121.2	68.5	37.0	37.1	38.7	169.5	67.8	99.8	24.9	12.8	15.4	21.3	26.7
Smithville	234437	239.0	224.4	120.5	67.9	38.0	41.0	39.7	176.0	71.5	100.9	23.4	10.7	15.4	21.8	27.3
Smithville	231538	228.0	209.4	116.5	67.8	35.0	34.2	33.3	156.7	64.0	91.0	23.0	11.3	16.4	21.8	25.2
Smithville	235499	228.0	209.4	122.5	71.8	35.2	42.2	39.3	163.0	73.4	93.3	23.0	11.3	16.4	21.4	26.3
Smithville	235497	232.0	222.0	115.5	67.9	35.9	36.1	33.1	165.0	68.4	98.2	24.6	12.1	15.2	21.4	26.3
Texas—Hardin County	262473	246.7	228.0	119.5	74.1	37.9	40.5	39.4	175.9	73.4	102.1	23.4	12.5	15.5	20.1	25.2
Polk County	250679	241.0	222.3	120.3	70.3	34.9	40.3	37.2	170.0	74.0	98.8	21.4	11.0	15.3	20.2	24.5
Polk County	250678	228.2	214.1	107.3	66.4	35.8	36.1	36.5	165.0	69.7	97.2	24.2	12.6	16.2	21.5	26.0
Average		236.1	219.3	122.9	70.0	37.0	40.2	37.5	167.9	68.5	99.2	23.6	12.4	15.5	20.9	26.1
C. n. niger: Alabama—Cherokee	223936	236.0	219.0	125.9	72.3	39.7	39.7	37.6	170.0	70.7	98.5	24.1	14.1	22.0	21.6	27.3

FOOTNOTES: [1] Subadult. Amer. Mus. Nat. Hist. [2] Type specimen. [3] Amer. Mus. Nat. Hist.

TABLE 6.—CRANIAL MEASUREMENTS OF ADULT FEMALES IN U. S. NATIONAL MUSEUM, UNLESS OTHERWISE INDICATED, OF *Canis lupus* GROUP

Species and locality	Number	Greatest length	Condylobasal length	Zygomatic breadth	Squamosal constriction	Width of rostrum	Interorbital breadth	Postorbital constriction	Length of mandible	Height of coronoid process	Maxillary tooth row, crown length	Upper carnassial, crown length (outer side)	Upper carnassial, crown width	First upper molar, antero-posterior diameter	First upper molar, transverse diameter	Lower carnassial, crown length
C. l. tundrarum:																
Alaska—																
Point Barrow[1]	4054	270.5	244.2	140.5	77.2	47.0	50.5	46.2	195.5	80.0	112.6	24.5	13.4	15.9	21.1	28.4
Point Barrow[2]	16748	258.7	242.2	138.5	76.1	43.2	47.3	41.9	188.1	74.7	110.6	25.9	15.0	17.7	24.7	30.5
	Average	264.6	243.2	139.5	76.7	45.1	48.9	44.1	191.8	77.4	111.6	25.2	14.2	16.8	22.9	29.5
C. l. pambasileus:																
Alaska—																
Eagle	265983	254.8	243.2	134.4	79.0	43.5	46.4	42.8	181.5	72.9	105.7	26.5	14.4	17.1	23.6	29.1
Fairbanks	264420	265.9	245.5	133.0	74.9	44.6	44.3	40.7	191.3	71.6	111.9	25.4	14.8	17.5	23.8	28.7
Little Delta River	261121	260.0	240.1	142.8	75.7	44.9	47.2	43.1	190.5	79.0	110.1	25.3	13.5	16.5	23.5	29.8
Tanana	218342	269.0	246.8	129.4	79.8	44.1	46.1	40.5	191.1	74.6	111.0	25.7	14.5	17.0	23.2	27.7
Yukon—																
White River[3]	33-9-20-4	261.7	245.8	131.7	78.0	41.8	39.5	37.0	189.0	73.5	109.8	25.6	14.8	16.7	23.7	30.6
	Average	262.3	244.3	134.3	77.5	43.2	44.7	40.8	188.6	74.3	109.7	25.7	14.4	16.9	23.4	29.2
C. l. alces:																
Alaska—																
Kachemak Bay[3]	147471	280.5	263.5	141.3	82.2	47.4	49.0	44.3	201.3	79.1	118.5	25.5	12.8	17.1	22.3	30.3
Kachemak Bay[4]	147472	272.0	253.2	141.4	81.8	46.6	45.9	42.1	194.3	82.0	112.3	24.5	13.0	17.1	22.3	29.1
	Average	276.3	258.4	141.4	82.0	47.0	47.5	43.2	197.8	80.6	115.4	25.0	12.9	17.1	22.3	29.7
C. l. occidentalis:																
Alberta—																
Wood Buffalo Park[5]	130266	257.3	237.5	143.0	83.1	44.6	42.3	45.0	185.5	76.4	104.8	25.8	14.2	17.0	23.4	29.7
Wood Buffalo Park[5]	92227	265.8	244.7	140.5	84.3	44.5	42.5	38.8	188.7	75.2	110.1	25.0	13.9	16.3	23.4	29.2
Wood Buffalo Park[5]	98232	256.0	245.5	134.0	81.8	44.4	41.7	42.6	184.4	76.3	107.6	26.3	13.1	16.9	23.4	28.7
Wood Buffalo Park[6]	130170	256.5	243.5	131.4	80.5	44.9	41.9	41.5	185.5	76.6	106.7	25.2	13.4	16.3	21.9	29.7

Locality	Cat. No.	1	2	3	4	5	6	7	8	9	10	11	12	13	14	15
Mackenzie—																
Fort Anderson	6508	257.8	241.9	150.5	81.3	45.9	44.6	39.5		74.0	110.0	26.1	15.1	17.8	23.5	
Fort Smith	134781	249.5	233.2	163.0	79.7	40.5	40.0	37.2	183.2	70.1	102.7	24.4	13.4	16.1	21.8	26.9
Great Bear Lake[4]	34447	249.5	239.0	165.4	79.8	42.7	43.2	36.0	176.7		106.6	26.5	14.2	18.0	24.1	29.0
Great Slave Lake[5]	121469	255.5		157.4	73.8	41.0	44.5	40.0	182.4	77.0	105.9	24.6	13.3	15.7	22.8	27.8
Yukon—																
Macmillan River (north fork)	134497	254.0	233.7	156.0	77.7	42.7	42.8	42.8	180.8	78.9	102.0	23.9	13.8	15.4	22.2	27.4
Average		255.8	239.1		80.4	43.5	42.8	40.4	183.4	75.6	106.3	25.3	13.8	16.6	22.9	28.6
C. l. hudsonicus:																
Keewatin—																
Schultz Lake[3]	180283	251.0	228.8	154.8	77.4	42.4	44.4	43.2	181.9	75.4	104.1	24.5	13.8	17.4	22.6	27.6
C. l. orion:																
Arctic America—																
Greenland[5]	42084	242.4	227.5	152.8	74.7	39.6	42.1	33.8	173.4	71.0	102.6	24.5	13.8	16.2	22.0	28.0
C. l. labradorius:																
Labrador—																
Hopedale[5]	3020	237.8	223.8	150.4	71.4	39.7		44.0	173.4	68.7	101.9	25.0	13.2	17.5	23.4	28.5
Quebec—																
Fort Chimo (near)	23135	247.1	222.7	152.7	73.0	41.7	43.5	43.9	175.5	73.8	98.4	25.0	12.4	15.3	21.3	28.1
Average		242.5	223.3	151.6	72.2	40.7	43.5	43.5	174.5	71.3	100.2	25.0	12.8	16.4	22.4	28.3
C. l. lycaon:																
Michigan—																
Marquette (30 mi. NW)	242289	234.4	217.6	112.2	69.1	38.4	43.6	42.5	167.7	64.3	98.8	22.5	11.8	15.0	21.0	26.1
Marquette (30 mi. NW)	242290	233.7	217.2	113.3	72.2	36.9	43.6	37.9	169.3	66.9	96.8	22.5	11.7	13.3	20.9	26.0
Marquette County[7]	21207	250.8	223.3	125.5	75.1	40.5	48.9	41.7	177.7	68.7	104.2	23.1	13.1	14.5	22.0	25.7
Randville	168349	244.0	226.4	113.7	76.5	41.2	43.3	39.5	173.8	72.0	99.2	23.4	12.7	15.8	19.5	26.1
Walsh[8]	.....	267.0	248.8	112.0	79.4	42.5	43.0	39.9	190.8	79.4	110.0	24.7	14.1	13.8	22.3	27.2
Ontario—																
Algonquin Nat. Park	178452	230.3	208.5	116.3	71.9	35.9	38.5	38.8	157.7	61.0	94.4	22.6	11.4	15.0	19.4	26.0
Silver Islet, Thunder Bay[3]	11281	230.3	221.8	126.7	74.5	39.8	35.5	35.5	165.5	71.1	98.9	24.0	12.7	15.3	23.2	27.6
Pennsylvania—[1]	2262	234.8	215.8		75.7	37.1	37.6	41.6	167.2	67.9	98.1	23.7	12.5	15.3	20.8	26.4
Quebec—																
Lucerne[9]	77342	234.7	222.6	131.2	71.7	39.5	40.8	34.6	169.0	72.2	98.1	22.9	11.7	15.6	20.6	27.1
Lucerne[9]	31-3-12-2	226.9		113.7	70.2	35.0	37.2	34.0			94.0	21.9	12.3	16.1	20.8	
Montebello[3]	31-12-29-1	213.6	203.3	116.7	69.6	34.4	35.8	30.4	155.0	62.5	91.0	22.5	12.0	15.8	19.5	25.8
Montebello[3]	31-12-29-4	224.7	211.4	115.3	70.2	35.3	37.2	33.8	157.7	65.8	94.5	21.8	12.4	15.8	21.0	25.9
Montebello[3]	31-12-29-3	225.2		112.5	69.3	37.1	42.4	35.0	163.8	65.8	96.2	21.8	11.8	15.1	20.6	25.9
Wisconsin—																
Eagle River	150421	254.0		130.6	74.7	41.8	45.3	42.7	178.0	71.0	103.2	24.2	13.6	15.6	21.7	28.3
Vilas County (near Michigan line)[7]	51773	258.7	242.3	136.0	79.5	40.3	47.8	41.2	189.5	78.8	108.4	23.5	14.2	16.9	22.1	28.5
Average		237.5	222.3	120.0	73.3	38.4	41.6	37.4	170.2	69.1	99.0	23.0	12.5	15.9	21.0	26.6

FOOTNOTES: [1] Type locality, Colo. Mus. Nat. Hist. [2] Type specimen. [3] Type locality. [4] Amer. Mus. Nat. Hist. [5] Mus. Comp. Zool. [6] Roy. Ont. Mus. Zool. [7] Field Mus. Nat. Hist. [8] Stanley P. Young. [9] Acad. Nat. Sci. Phila. [10] Mus. Vert. Zool.

501

TABLE 6.—CRANIAL MEASUREMENTS OF ADULT FEMALES IN U. S. NATIONAL MUSEUM, UNLESS OTHERWISE INDICATED, OF *Canis lupus* GROUP—(Continued)

Species and locality	Number	Greatest length	Condylobasal length	Zygomatic breadth	Squamosal constriction	Width of rostrum	Interorbital breadth	Postorbital constriction	Length of mandible	Height of coronoid process	Maxillary tooth row, crown length	Upper carnassial, crown length (outer side)	Upper carnassial, crown width	First upper molar, antero-posterior diameter	First upper molar, transverse diameter	Lower carnassial, crown length
C. l. nubilus:																
Colorado—																
Bent County	51435	225.8	213.0	124.6	72.0	43.4	40.0	39.5	162.5	68.8	97.0	24.3	13.3	17.0	22.1	28.3
Montana—																
Meredith	222040	245.8	228.0	128.4	78.0	42.3	41.8	41.6	178.8	74.2	104.5	24.6	13.5	16.4	21.8	27.6
Miles City	224443	241.9	226.8	130.0	75.2	46.2	49.6	41.6	172.5	69.9	103.8	24.6	13.8	16.8	22.0	27.3
Miles City	224442	244.0	223.4	131.1	74.3	43.7	43.7	38.2	172.5	66.9	102.1	25.0	13.1	17.3	23.1	28.3
Mizpah	223691	222.0	212.8	129.2	72.3	42.4	46.9	42.4	168.7	65.9	101.0	23.3	13.3	16.1	21.3	27.0
Nebraska—																
Kearney	3343	228.7	210.7	119.4	70.6	38.7	38.9	34.8	161.7	66.5	99.5	24.1	12.8	16.9	23.2	27.8
Platte River	3575	231.0	212.5	130.5	71.4	40.9	40.3	38.0	165.5	71.4	96.2	23.4	14.1	15.5	20.2	28.0
Platte River	2611	233.5	212.9	126.2	73.0	38.1	37.3	35.3	167.0	66.3	.....		11.6	14.8	20.0	25.6
New Mexico—																
Santa Rosa (18 mi. south)	168345	250.5	230.8	135.1	74.5	42.0	44.9	37.8	180.7	75.7	106.1	26.1	14.3	16.3	22.3	27.9
South Dakota—																
Dewey	221852	241.3	223.8	134.6	72.9	43.3	43.6	38.6	171.4	73.7	103.9	26.1	13.5	17.2	21.9	29.5
Fort Randall, Gregory County	12907	228.3	210.5	123.7	71.0	41.6	42.8	38.2	164.0	65.7	94.3	23.0	13.2	15.5	20.0	24.9
Imlay	11268 / 210683	249.3	229.0	131.1	75.9	45.5	43.8	37.3	179.7	78.5	103.8	25.1	13.2	17.1	22.7	29.6
Wyoming—																
Douglas	212919	226.7	218.5	129.1	73.4	39.2	41.6	37.7	165.0	66.0	99.2	24.2	13.7	15.9	21.8	28.5
Average		236.1	219.4	128.7	73.4	42.1	42.7	37.0	170.0	70.0	101.0	24.4	13.3	16.3	21.8	27.7
C. l. irremotus:																
Alberta—																
Gleichen[1]	7657	238.7	222.0	124.5	71.6	41.4	38.5	35.9	169.9	66.8	101.4	25.0	14.0	17.1	23.5	29.5
Idaho—																
Alridge	215247	242.3	224.9	128.8	74.4	42.6	43.5	34.9	174.9	73.0	99.5	24.9	14.3	17.7	23.7	29.8
Alridge	214904	242.5	225.9	128.0	73.8	41.3	38.9	33.5	175.0	74.6	102.9	23.9	12.8	17.0	22.7	27.4
Leadore	236102	233.4	219.0	121.6	70.3	40.3	41.6	39.1	167.5	67.8	99.6	23.6	13.7	16.4	21.4	28.2
Pocatello (10 mi. east)	234228	235.2	221.5	120.5	68.8	38.5	39.3	36.0	167.6	67.6	100.2	22.6	11.9	16.5	22.7	27.5
Soda Springs	234700	233.3	216.2	124.4	71.2	40.7	44.9	36.0	165.8	67.8	98.9	23.0	12.2	14.7	21.0	25.6
Soda Springs	231437	232.8	219.3	127.7	74.2	42.7	46.7	40.2	165.4	69.9	97.7	24.1	13.4	15.2	20.6	26.1
Soda Springs	234701	241.3	221.9	119.7	73.2	42.7	40.2	36.7	170.4	71.3	100.3	24.0	13.2	15.9	20.9	27.0
Soda Springs (20 mi. NE)	227671	237.5	221.0	117.0	70.6	41.7	36.6	36.6	169.7	67.7	101.7	23.9	13.0	15.4	21.3	26.7
Tybee, Bannock Co.	214893	237.4	222.9	126.7	71.1	41.5	43.9	38.1	166.0	68.7	99.4			15.1	21.8	28.3

Cranial measurements table (continued). Columns are skull/cranial measurements (column headings not reprinted on this page).

Locality	Number														
Montana—															
Beaverhead Mts.	228351	239.0	225.0	71.3	39.3	43.0	39.0	172.4	68.3	102.0	23.8	14.4	15.6	22.7	28.5
Beaverhead Mts.	228518	241.4	226.2	73.5	39.5	41.5	34.7	173.2	69.7	102.3	24.2	14.7	17.6	22.6	27.8
Belt	223432	248.0	230.7	76.5	40.2	45.0	42.3	174.7	70.3	103.4	24.9	13.3	16.5	22.3	28.0
Dillon	222667	254.5	237.1	76.8	42.3	41.7	39.7	179.4	73.5	102.3	25.2	14.8	16.8	22.9	30.3
Dillon	225227	244.5	225.5	69.1	40.8	41.7	36.9	173.0	70.6	105.3	25.0	13.4	16.4	23.7	28.0
Ingomar	224164	242.3	225.0	74.5	40.3	39.5	36.4	175.0	73.0	101.6	23.4	13.2	15.0	21.3	27.0
Kruger	228135	242.5	221.4	74.5	40.5	42.0	37.8	169.7	70.5	101.5	24.0	12.6	16.2	21.3	27.3
Little Belt Mts.	156837	237.0	219.3	70.4	38.7	41.7	37.1	168.0	69.6	103.4	24.0	12.7	16.9	21.5	27.6
Powderville	57723	238.5	223.0	72.9	41.7	41.7	40.1	170.5	70.5	103.4	24.0	12.7	16.2	21.4	27.6
Riceville	228132	241.8	223.4	75.0	40.0	40.1	39.1	171.0	70.3	102.7	24.8	12.1	16.0	21.8	27.7
Wyoming—															
Arvada	223505	241.5	225.8	75.7	42.1	41.1	35.9	173.0	66.2	103.9	22.6	12.4	15.1	20.4	25.3
Barber, Johnson Co.	242147	248.0	231.0	76.7	46.5	49.1	33.0	179.5	73.0	105.7	24.7	13.4	16.8	23.1	28.0
Cokeville	178738	239.5	225.4	77.0	40.5	40.8	36.8	168.0	70.5	100.7	23.8	12.7	17.0	23.2	27.0
Kelly	230700	238.2	220.5	72.7	40.1	34.3	34.1	172.2	70.5	99.7	22.4	11.4	15.5	21.7	26.5
Lost Springs	227675	244.5	230.0	72.5	39.9	42.9	36.7	170.8	67.3	103.0	24.4	13.6	16.5	21.7	27.2
Split Rock	234729	247.7	234.2	77.8	43.1	44.3	36.9	181.2	73.5	108.2	25.8	12.9	17.1	24.6	28.2
Split Rock	212926	246.3	230.4	74.6	43.9	45.4	40.8	180.0	73.4	104.4	25.2	13.1	16.5	23.6	29.4
Average	4672	241.1	224.7	73.3	41.2	42.5	40.3	172.0	70.1	102.3	24.2	13.1	16.3	22.2	27.7
C. l. columbianus:															
British Columbia—															
Chezacut[2]	31042	254.8	235.4	77.7	43.1	45.7	29.7	184.1	69.5	108.1	24.7	13.0	16.7	22.0	28.4
Iskut Summit, six mi. south of Telegraph Creek[3]	4282	259.0	242.5	79.5	41.2	42.2	39.7	193.3	78.6	110.5	25.7	12.7	17.2	23.8	30.9
Wistaria[4]	4283	262.2	235.8	79.3	45.4	46.8	44.6	185.3	73.6	105.8	25.6	12.9	16.7	23.0	29.0
Wistaria[4]		266.5	246.4	79.5	43.1	42.7	57.0	188.7	73.0	108.4	24.7	13.4	17.1	23.2	28.2
Average		260.6	240.0	79.0	43.2	44.4	40.3	187.6	73.7	108.2	25.2	13.0	16.9	22.4	29.1
C. l. ligoni:															
Alaska—															
Baker Island	243334	246.7	227.3	79.1	41.3	47.6	46.3	182.5	73.8	103.3	23.3	13.7	15.1	21.9	28.0
Baker Island	243335	258.0	233.0	79.2	43.0	45.5	43.0	186.8	81.2	105.1	24.3	14.1	16.1	22.5	28.7
Dry Bay, Alsek River[5]	36-9-18-280	249.5	232.5	78.5	41.5	46.5	40.1	177.7	75.4	101.8	23.3	13.5	14.8	21.0	27.8
Ketchikan	264901	249.5	231.0	76.9	43.2	40.9	41.5	183.0	74.4	106.1	23.0	13.6	15.7	22.5	29.1
Ketchikan	264990	251.7	231.0	76.2	43.8	44.3	41.4	186.3	71.9	108.3	24.6	14.2	16.1	21.6	29.1
Kuiu Island	243331	229.0	233.4	77.4	43.8	44.0	41.6	178.5	66.7	104.6	22.8	12.8	16.1	23.5	28.0
Kuiu Island	264195	250.0	233.4	74.5	40.6	41.9	39.8	182.2	70.6	107.9	23.8	12.3	17.1	24.3	29.5
Kuiu Island	264193	251.2	234.2	75.8	40.8	40.7	40.0	183.8	74.1	104.8	26.0	14.3	16.4	22.9	28.7
Kupreanof Island	243324	250.0	232.2	76.1	42.4	41.2	56.4	185.3	73.4	106.1	23.9	12.9	16.4	21.2	27.6
Prince of Wales Island	243576	240.8	227.2	76.7	40.5	40.9	42.7	178.8	71.3	104.3	23.0	13.6	15.4	20.8	26.3
Prince of Wales Island	243573	240.0	222.4	73.2	39.4	59.0	40.1	175.0	68.5	100.1	23.1	12.7	14.3	21.2	26.3
Zarembo Island	243330	237.0	223.9	74.8	41.3	42.9	41.3	178.0	69.0	102.1	22.2	13.4	14.6	21.1	26.5
Zarembo Island	243326	243.4	223.2	74.8	40.1	42.9	42.4	181.4	69.0	106.5	23.2	13.4	17.1	22.1	26.5
Average		247.0	230.0	76.5	41.3	42.9	41.3	181.5	72.3	104.7	23.4	13.5	15.7	22.1	27.9

FOOTNOTES: [1] Field Mus. Nat. Hist. [2] B. C. Prov. Mus. [3] Mus. Vert. Zool. [4] B. C. Prov. Mus. Type locality. [5] Roy. Ont. Mus. Zool.

TABLE 6.—CRANIAL MEASUREMENTS OF ADULT FEMALES IN U. S. NATIONAL MUSEUM, UNLESS OTHERWISE INDICATED, OF *Canis lupus* GROUP—(Continued)

Species and locality	Number	Greatest length	Condylobasal length	Zygomatic breadth	Squamosal constriction	Width of rostrum	Interorbital breadth	Postorbital constriction	Length of mandible	Height of coronoid process	Maxillary tooth row, crown length	Upper carnassial, crown length (outer side)	Upper carnassial, crown width	First upper molar, antero-posterior diameter	First upper molar, transverse diameter	Lower carnassial, crown length
C. l. fuscus:																
Oregon—																
Cascadia	235515	239.8	218.5	128.3	75.4	44.0	45.0	41.7	170.5	72.8	98.6	21.9	12.9	15.1	21.3	26.3
Cascadia	236528	237.5	220.8	131.8	72.0	40.6	46.8	43.0	172.4	71.8	101.4	22.8	13.1	15.0	20.8	26.4
Estacada	227740	245.0	220.7	130.4	75.8	40.3	43.3	42.3	175.3	76.1	101.4	23.3	14.1	14.3	20.3	26.6
Glide (40 mi. E)	226432	240.2	223.	123.2	75.1	39.5	41.6	38.2	173.7	73.6	99.9	23.1	13.3	15.3	20.9	27.8
Glide (15 mi. NE)	224002	240.8		127.4	75.6	42.9	48.3	42.3	178.0	74.2	103.4	23.3	13.9	15.9	21.1	26.9
Rogue River	243986	250.4	229.8	128.7	74.8	42.8	48.2	42.4	180.5	77.2	103.1	24.4	12.9	16.7	22.0	27.2
Washington—																
Ashland (25 mi. NE)	233248	253.5	235.3	137.0	78.7	43.3	46.8	40.9	184.7	80.6	103.1	24.5	13.0	16.0	22.0	26.8
	Average	243.9	192.9	129.5	75.3	42.4	44.7	41.1	176.4	75.2	101.6	23.3	13.1	15.5	21.2	26.9
C. l. crassodon:																
British Columbia—																
Alberni[1]	1862	249.5	231.0	135.4	75.5	44.3	47.0	42.3	182.0	70.0	105.7	25.2	14.5	15.9	22.2	28.0
Vancouver Island	135451	241.9	222.1	132.0	79.0	40.8	43.4	43.0	170.8	70.1	101.8	24.9	14.6	17.2	21.7	28.8
Vancouver Island	137806	247.8	230.5	134.0	76.4	41.0	46.8	44.4	178.4	66.3	106.4	25.1	14.9	17.2	23.5	28.7
	Average	246.4	227.9	133.8	77.0	42.0	45.7	43.2	177.1	68.8	104.6	25.1	14.7	16.8	22.5	28.5
C. l. youngi:																
Colorado—																
Glade Park, Mesa County	223710	238.2	223.5	127.2	77.0	40.8	42.0	38.9	169.7	69.4	101.1	24.7	13.1	16.2	21.7	27.6
Piceance	210906	244.5	228.7	130.9	73.2	42.7	43.2	39.0	175.8	70.6	104.0	24.6	12.7	16.1	22.0	28.0
Piceance	216355	242.8	226.5	128.8	72.5	40.0	44.1	39.0	172.2	70.1	104.7	24.5	13.4	15.3	22.1	27.8
Turman's Creek, Rio Blanco Co.	216354	234.5	218.5	131.4	74.3	40.3	39.7	36.0	171.6	73.1	99.9	23.1	12.0	15.1	21.0	28.4
West Creek, Garfield County	224526	242.8	231.4	131.7	74.3	42.9	49.7	39.1	180.5	75.3	106.4	25.1	13.8	16.6	22.9	28.9
New Mexico—																
Canjilon	231344	240.0	222.5	125.0	75.9	44.0	40.3	36.7	167.2	73.7	102.2	24.4	14.1	16.0	21.7	28.9
Wyoming—																
Federal	221850	237.1	211.3	128.0	77.7	43.6	37.8	37.8	162.2	73.1	99.5	23.1	12.3	15.8	21.3	27.6
Laramie	235504	233.7	214.4	131.8	72.1	43.5	43.0	37.7	171.3	69.9	102.5	....	13.0	....	....	....
	Average	239.2	223.4	129.4	74.5	42.2	42.5	38.1	171.3	71.9	102.8	24.2	13.1	15.9	21.8	27.9

C. l. mogollonensis:

Locality	Cat. No.															
Arizona—																
Escudilla Mts.	157627	235.3	219.0	129.7	73.5	42.1	41.1	39.8	168.7	68.0	96.1	23.9	13.5	16.0	21.6	27.4
Escudilla Mts.	205745	232.7	213.7	122.5	74.8	38.1	39.8	37.1	165.5	69.2	98.2	24.0	13.7	16.1	21.3	26.5
Heber	224173	247.3	224.4	141.4	81.1	44.0	44.2	37.4	175.3	76.5	102.7	25.0	14.7	16.8	22.3	29.2
New Mexico—																
Chloride	224167	245.5	222.8	124.4	76.1	41.5	47.4	41.8	173.2	72.6	102.8	23.9	13.5	16.4	21.5	27.4
Chloride	224584	236.8	218.0	134.7	76.6	45.2	44.9	43.3	169.6	73.7	98.9	24.8	14.5	15.6	21.8	28.2
Fairview	235067	242.5	225.5	131.6	80.1	43.6	41.3	39.1	178.0	79.0	103.0	24.6	13.9	15.7	21.8	27.5
Gila Nat. Forest	148979	240.2	222.4	134.2	75.6	41.5	39.2	38.5	167.0	67.4	102.2	24.1	14.3	16.5	22.4	28.3
Luna	226434	240.2	222.4	133.4	75.2	44.1	46.0	42.3	174.0	78.7	101.3	24.7	14.3	16.4	22.0	27.8
Magdalena	221655	241.2	221.6	133.4	77.8	44.7	40.0	38.6	173.0	73.0	99.8	22.9	12.7	14.5	20.2	26.3
Average		240.5	221.1	133.2	76.8	42.8	42.7	39.8	171.6	73.1	100.6	24.2	13.9	16.0	21.7	27.6

C. l. monstrabilis:

Locality	Cat. No.															
New Mexico—																
Elk	223563	236.4	212.3	124.2	69.2	39.3	40.5	39.1	168.4	68.4	96.5	23.7	12.9	14.8	21.1	27.3
Sacramento Mts.	159021	233.8	217.0	124.0	73.1	39.3	43.3	42.1	166.8	67.4	96.0	21.0	11.9	15.1	20.9	25.4
Texas—																
Big Lake	224165	252.3	228.8	123.3	74.0	40.6	43.3	38.4	173.0	73.5	102.2	23.6	13.3	15.4	21.1	27.8
Monahans	118990	242.5	225.3	122.5	75.3	42.3	44.5	42.3	172.0	67.8	103.3	24.5	13.5	16.5	22.4	27.8
Rankin	209408	250.4	231.3	125.9	78.1	45.3	45.3	40.3	178.8	73.5	103.3	23.8	13.8	17.1	22.1	28.0
Rankin	215361	232.3	216.9	122.9	75.2	39.6	45.0	42.2	166.2	68.3	95.9	24.8	12.9	14.8	20.9	27.0
Rankin	211242	251.7	228.1	123.4	74.3	39.3	45.1	40.3	171.3	69.2	104.2	24.2	13.8	17.0	22.5	27.7
Rankin	215360	246.8	226.0	124.1	75.3	38.7	42.4	39.4	170.5	73.3	99.3	23.7	13.8	15.2	20.9	26.4
Average		243.3	223.8	124.7	74.3	40.6	43.7	40.5	170.9	70.2	100.2	23.8	13.2	15.7	21.5	27.1

C. l. baileyi:

Locality	Cat. No.															
Arizona—																
Santa Rita Mts.	251526	231.2	211.8	124.7	75.6	39.4	42.2	38.3	160.9	67.8	97.8	23.4	12.9	16.3	19.8	25.3
Chihuahua—																
Colonia Garcia³	99608	224.4	209.5	120.1	74.1	37.9	43.1	42.8	165.0	69.0	95.4	24.5	12.2	15.1	20.4	26.3
Colonia Garcia³	98311	234.2	215.5	130.9	74.6	38.1	40.0	40.3	168.0	69.0	99.3	23.4	12.1	15.5	19.5	24.9
Durango—																
El Salto	94728	231.5	210.0	124.6	70.3	38.3	42.8	39.7	159.7	66.2	98.3	25.2	13.0	16.0	20.5	27.7
New Mexico—																
Hachita	231536	232.9	209.9	128.8	73.0	40.1	43.8	42.7	163.0	69.8	93.2	22.8	12.0	14.4	19.5	25.4
Hachita	231323	233.3	217.0	131.6	75.9	41.7	45.4	41.2	163.8	73.8	95.7	24.0	12.3	15.5	21.0	26.4
Texas—																
Fort Davis (16 mi. NW)	266563	231.0	212.5	127.5	74.9	37.3	42.7	42.1	162.5	67.5	96.7	23.9	12.7	15.1	19.1	25.4
Average		231.2	212.4	124.7	74.1	39.1	42.9	41.0	163.3	69.0	96.6	23.9	12.5	15.4	20.0	25.9

FOOTNOTES: ¹ B. C. Prov. Mus. ³ Type locality

TABLE 7.—CRANIAL MEASUREMENTS OF ADULT FEMALES IN U. S. NATIONAL MUSEUM, UNLESS OTHERWISE INDICATED, OF *Canis niger* GROUP

Species and locality	Number	Greatest length	Condylobasal length	Zygomatic breadth	Squamosal constriction	Width of rostrum	Interorbital breadth	Postorbital constriction	Length of mandible	Height of coronoid process	Maxillary tooth row, crown length	Upper carnassial, crown length (outer side)	Upper carnassial, crown width	First upper molar, antero-posterior diameter	First upper molar, transverse diameter	Lower carnassial, crown length
C. n. rufus:																
Arkansas—																
Boxley	243321	202.5	190.9	111.0	64.1	31.2	34.3	35.5	146.0	60.7	88.5	21.1	10.6	13.8	19.4	23.5
Hector	266420	202.7	191.3	108.5	63.1	32.2	36.9	36.8	144.3	57.3	86.9	21.0	9.6	13.4	18.4	23.5
Oklahoma—																
Redden	261766	209.5	201.5	106.4	64.7	32.4	37.3	39.3	155.0	59.8	93.4	21.8	10.9	14.9	18.0	24.1
Tahlequah	251059	210.5	196.4	105.0	62.8	34.7	34.7	36.0	151.6	56.6	94.8	20.5	10.0	13.5	18.6	23.7
Texas—																
Click	228089	210.4	195.0	110.5	64.6	32.6	35.8	35.2	146.2	60.3	88.6	21.6	9.5	14.5	17.8	23.8
Llano	214852	207.3	191.6	110.2	63.1	31.7	33.9	39.1	151.2	60.6	89.0	21.6	10.6	14.7	18.7	23.2
Llano	223713	200.9	193.7	106.0	63.0	29.9	39.7	40.0	149.0	61.1	87.1	19.4	9.8	12.4	17.3	20.0
Llano	223649	198.5	190.6	100.3	63.0	29.8	34.7	32.2	143.0	57.1	91.8	19.1	9.3	12.4	17.7	21.8
Llano	224580	212.0	197.2	103.5	63.6	28.6	32.1	33.2	152.5	57.9	90.6	20.9	10.4	13.8	19.4	22.8
Port O'Connor	99720	203.2	187.5	105.4	62.0	31.3	33.0	33.0	141.6	55.4	82.4	20.0	9.3	13.8	19.8	21.5
Average		205.8	193.6	105.7	63.5	31.3	35.2	36.3	148.0	58.7	88.5	20.7	10.0	13.8	18.4	22.8
C. n. gregoryi:																
Arkansas—																
Blue Ball	243433	222.8	206.8	112.3	65.7	34.9	35.5	33.2	159.5	65.4	95.7	21.3	11.8	14.8	19.1	24.0
Blue Ball	243431	218.5	204.0	108.2	64.9	32.7	36.1	37.1	156.0	58.9	90.2	20.7	9.8	13.9	18.1	22.8
Ferndale	242574	222.9	120.2	108.0	67.0	36.5	33.9	37.5	158.0	63.7	89.6	21.6	11.7	15.2	20.5	25.0
Isaac	242584	213.5	202.0	116.0	67.4	36.5	37.2	35.0	154.0	61.3	94.3	21.6	10.1	15.0	19.2	23.8
Isaac	242582	216.2	206.0	119.2	65.3	33.2	36.2	36.1	157.3	60.6	90.9	24.8	13.4	16.3	22.5	26.7
Isaac	242580	209.3	195.5	100.6	62.1	33.5	35.4	34.5	148.6	56.1	90.4	23.7	14.4	16.4	19.4	24.1
Pinnacle	243594	221.6	203.3	112.5	69.1	34.7	38.7	39.6	157.3	62.2	93.6	22.6	15.7	15.7	21.0	25.8
Solo	243306	224.6	211.3	117.5	64.8	33.8	33.8	40.7	159.3	64.4	95.9	23.7	12.7	15.7	20.5	25.4
Stillwater	244226	228.2	215.8	125.5	70.4	36.2	41.5	39.0	166.0	65.3	99.6	24.7	12.1	16.0	21.8	27.8
Wye	224228	204.9	204.9	103.4	65.2	35.0	35.5	33.4	147.9	63.8	87.2	22.4	11.2	13.8	19.8	25.1
Indiana—																
Wabash[1]	112	232.0	.....	117.0	70.2	34.3	35.4	39.6	161.8	66.1	94.0	22.0	12.1	14.6	20.6	25.1
Louisiana—																
Sabine River	248333	216.8	198.5	113.6	68.4	33.9	37.3	35.9	151.9	64.2	90.7	21.5	11.1	15.2	19.9	24.8
Sikes	265134	218.5	207.7	114.5	68.7	32.6	40.2	37.5	157.7	66.8	93.1	20.1	11.0	14.8	19.0	23.4
Tallulah (vicinity)	136105	222.7	202.5	114.2	67.9	38.0	35.6	31.0	156.7	68.6	91.2	22.6	11.7	15.1	20.0	24.7

Locality	No.															
Missouri—																
Arcadia	245738	226.4	213.5	117	66.2	35.6	37.5	38.7	162.2	67.2	97.0	22.0	11.8	15.5	20.2	25.6
Barren	244298	225.8	210.4	112.2	66.8	33.5	36.7	34.8	168.2	69.1	98.1	22.1	12.8	15.7	20.1	25.4
Cook's Station	244300	225.6	212.1	120.5	70.0	33.8	38.5	38.7	139.4	65.0	94.8	21.9	11.6	14.7	19.6	25.8
Cook's Station	244490	229.5	206.5	115.0	70.0	30.7	35.0	36.0	156.5	66.0	91.1	22.0	10.8	14.9	19.5	25.4
Cook's Station	244302	230.7	207.8	113.4	68.9	31.4	33.4	32.0	159.4	65.0	94.3	22.8	10.7	15.3	19.3	24.6
Gatewood	243214	250.0	214.9	118.0	64.0	37.3	35.1	36.8	161.1	66.3	96.8	23.0	12.6	14.5	19.3	25.3
Stone County	244224	222.5	206.3	115.0	65.1	30.0	38.1	35.9	158.1	65.6	94.5	21.4	9.5	13.2	18.3	24.3
Stone County	242215	221.7	203.8	114.0	67.0	34.0	32.2	34.5	154.2	65.0	91.0	22.0	11.0	14.3	18.8	24.7
Tyrone	244526	222.3	208.5	118.5	69.0	35.0	35.4	39.8	156.4	64.0	93.6	22.1	11.6	15.0	19.0	25.1
Upalika	244528	230.5	212.5	121.0	66.7	35.4	37.2	36.9	163.5	63.6	95.6	28.8	12.1	15.8	20.1	26.6
Oklahoma—																
Broken Bow	234431	225.0	212.8	120.0	70.4	38.1	37.3	35.3	162.8	66.4	94.9	23.9	11.8	15.5	20.7	26.6
Broken Bow	232422	226.5	202.4	119.0	66.5	36.4	44.9	36.3	156.0	67.8	89.8	23.4	11.0	15.4	20.1	25.5
Broken Bow	233433	224.5	201.2	113.0	67.3	31.3	34.0	35.0	157.0	64.1	93.0	21.6	10.4	15.0	18.8	23.7
Page	234450	222.1	204.5	114.2	63.9	34.4	36.2	38.8	156.7	65.4	91.9	23.6	11.1	15.2	19.3	25.0
Sherwood	234426	250.0	215.2	118.5	66.8	36.2	37.4	36.0	165.5	66.5	100.3	23.2	11.7	16.2	21.1	25.5
Sherwood	234429	227.0	203.5	116.3	66.1	34.1	34.7	36.1	157.0	63.3	92.1	22.7	11.3	14.8	19.4	23.6
Sherwood	234428	222.4	197.6	111.9	67.3	34.2	37.2	39.0	151.0	63.3	90.9	20.1	11.3	13.9	18.4	22.7
Smithville	231540	219.4	206.0	115.0	68.1	33.9	44.4	33.3	155.5	64.5	94.1	24.3	12.5	15.9	21.5	25.4
Smithville	234416	227.4	205.5	115.0	66.0	33.3	35.3	36.4	156.0	65.8	92.9	22.3	11.6	15.0	19.9	23.8
Smithville	232416	223.0	198.9	114.4	67.1	32.4	35.7	41.5	156.4	63.5	87.7	22.0	11.0	15.2	20.0	23.8
Texas—																
Kountze	147701[1]	222.3	208.4	115.0	67.5	34.4	37.5	37.2	158.4	60.3	96.9	22.3	12.7	15.3	20.4	24.9
Average		220.5	209.4	115.6	67.1	34.4	37.0	36.3	157.3	64.3	93.6	22.6	11.5	15.1	19.9	24.9
C. n. niger:																
Florida—																
St. Johns River	39488 / 19376	......	......	122.2	67.2	36.1	43.2	38.9	158.9	65.5	......	23.2	12.8	15.3	21.7	25.6

FOOTNOTE: ¹ Subadult. Amer. Mus. Nat. Hist.

XVII

REFERENCES AND SELECTED BIBLIOGRAPHY

ABERNATHY, JOHN R.
  1936. Catch 'em alive Jack. Reissue with extensive variations in text of the author's In Camp with Theodore Roosevelt. 224 pp. New York Association Press. 1933.
ABERT, J. W. (LT.)
  1848. Report of Lt. J. W. Abert of his examination of New Mexico in the years 1846-1847. U. S. House Executive Documents No. 41, 30th Cong., 1st sess., 1847-1848, pp. 417-548, with map; also as Senate Doc. No. 23, 30th Cong., 1st sess., pp. 1-132.
ADAMS, A. LEITH
  1873. Field and Forest rambles, with notes and observations on the natural history of eastern Canada. 333 pp., illus. London.
ALASKA GAME COMMISSION
  1938. Game and fur conditions [in Alaska]. Fourteenth Ann. Rept. to the Secretary of Agriculture, 1937-38. 25 pp. mimeog.
ALBERT, G. D.
  1882. History of the county of Westmoreland. 727 pp. L. H. Everts & Co., Philadelphia.

ALDOUS, CLARENCE M.
  1939. Coyotes in Maine. Jour. Mamm. 20 (1): 104-106. February.
ALLEN, GLOVER M.
  1920. Dogs of the American Aborigines. Bull. Mus. Comp. Zool. 63 (9): 431-517, illus. March. Cambridge, Mass.
  1942. Extinct and vanishing mammals of the Western Hemisphere . . . Amer. Comm. for International Wildlife Prot., Special Publication No. 11, pp. XV plus 620, illus. December 11.
———————, and BARBOUR, THOMAS
  1937. The Newfoundland wolf. Jour. Mamm. 18 (2): 229-234, illus. May. New: *Canis lupus beothucus*.
ALLEN, HENRY T.
  1895. Hunting in Many Lands. Wolf hunting in Russia. A book of the Boone and Crockett Club. 447 pp., illus. New York.
ALLEN, J. A.
  1869. Catalogue of the mammals of Massachusetts; with a critical revision of the species. Bull. Mus. Comp. Zool. 1 (8): 143-252.
  1871a. Notes on the mammals of Iowa. Proc. Boston Soc. Nat. Hist. 13: 178-194. December 15, 1869. (Also published separately, 18 pp.)
  1871b. On the mammals and winter birds of east Florida . . . . Bull. Mus. Comp. Zool. 2 (3): 161-450. April. Cambridge, Mass.
  1874a. Notes on the mammals of portions of Kansas, Colorado, Wyoming, and Utah. Bull. Essex Inst. 6 (3): 43-52; 6 (4): 53-66. March and April. Salem, Mass.
  1874b. Notes on the natural history of portions of Montana and Dakota . . . . Proc. Boston Soc. Nat. Hist. 17: 33-91.
  1876a. Description of some remains of an extinct species of wolf and extinct species of deer from the lead region of the Upper Mississippi. Amer. Jour. Sci. (3d ser.) 11: 47-51.
  1876b. Former range of some New England carnivorous mammals. Amer. Nat. 10: 708-715.

1876c. Geographical variations among North American mammals. . . . Bull. U. S. Geol. and Geog. Survey Terr. 2 (4): 309-344. July 1. Washington, D. C. Amer. Nat. 10: 625-627, October.

1876d. The extirpation of the larger indigenous mammals of the United States. The Penn Monthly 7 (82): 794-806.

1876e. The American bisons living and extinct. Memoirs Geol. Survey Kentucky 1 (pt. 2): 1-246, with 12 pls. and map. Cambridge, Mass.; also Mem. Mus. Comp. Zool. 4 (10): 1-246.

1877.   History of the American bison, Bison americanus. *In* Hayden, 9th Ann. Report U. S. Geol. & Geog. Survey Terr. 1875, pp. 443-587.

1895a. List of mammals collected in the Black Hills· region of South Dakota and in western Kansas by Mr. Walter W. Granger, with field notes by the collector. Bull. Amer. Mus. Nat. Hist. 7 (art. 7): 259-274. August 21.

1895b. On collection of mammals from Arizona and Mexico made by Mr. W. W. Price, with field notes by the collector. Bull. Amer. Mus. Nat. Hist. 7 (art. 6): 193-258. June 29.

ALLEN, LEWIS F.
1868.   American cattle: Their history, breeding, and management. 528 pp. New York.

ALLEN, PAUL
1814.   History of the expedition under command of Captains Lewis and Clark to the sources of the Missouri; thence across the Rocky Mountains and down the river Columbia to the Pacific Ocean. Performed during the years 1804-5-6. By order of the Government of the United States. 2 vols., illus., Phila., Bradford and Inskeep; and A.B.M.H. Inskeep, New York. J. Maxwell, Printer, Vol. 2, pp. 114, 122.

ALMIRALL, LEON V.
1926.   Coyote coursing. 64 pp., illus. December 12. Denver, Colo.

1941.   Canines and coyotes. 150 pp., illus. Caldwell, Idaho.

ALTSHELER, BRENT
　1936.　Natural history index-guide, sec. 2, div. 1, 311 pp. Nat.
　　　　Hist. Pub. Co., Louisville, Ky.
AMES, A. E.
　1874.　Mammalia of Minnesota. Bull. Minn. Acad. Nat. Sci.
　　　　1: 68-71.
ANDERSON, R. M.
　1934.　Mammals of eastern Arctic and Hudson Bay. Pp. 67-
　　　　108. Canada's Eastern Arctic, Dept. Interior, Ottawa.
　1938.　Mammals of the province of Quebec. Pp. 68-69. Pre-
　　　　pared for the Provancher Soc. of Nat. Hist. of Can-
　　　　ada, Quebec.
　1943.　Summary of the large wolves of Canada, with descrip-
　　　　tion of three new Arctic races. Journ. Mamm. 24
　　　　(3): 386-393. August.
ANGELL, HOMER D.
　1940.　Champoeg—Oregon's shrine to civil government. Exten-
　　　　sion of remarks in the House of Representatives,
　　　　Monday, May 27. Cong. Record Appendix 86
　　　　(105): 10, 740.
ANONYMOUS
　1800.　A brief state of the Province of Quebec . . . written in
　　　　the year 1787. Mass. Hist. Soc. Coll. for 1799, vol.
　　　　6, pp. 48-63.
　1852.　Children suckled by wolves. Chamber's Journal, 17
　　　　(n.s.): 122-123.
　1853.　The wolf as an object of superstition. Chamber's Edin-
　　　　burgh Journal (n.s.) 20: 27-30.
　1854.　Wolf nurses in India. Harper's New Monthly Maga-
　　　　zine, 9 (50): 199. July.
　1856a.　Fur hunting in Oregon. Harper's New Monthly Maga-
　　　　zine 12 (69): 340-346. February.
　1856b.　Israel Putnam. Harper's New Monthly Magazine 12
　　　　(71): 579-580. April.
　1869.　Wolf-hunting in Chicago. Appleton's Journal 2: 230-
　　　　231.
　1871.　A full-page illustration, engraved from a sketch by artist
　　　　W. M. Gray, showing buffalo bulls guarding a herd
　　　　against a wolf pack. Harper's Weekly 15: 724-725.

1875. Some wild animals of Newfoundland. Forest and Stream
       4 (25): 390. July 29.

1882. Wolf children. Chamber's Journal, 59: 597-599.

1885a. History of Crawford County, Pa. Warner, Bears & Co.,
       Chicago. P. 529.

1885b. Wolf hunting with the Sibley hounds. American Field
       24 (23): 535. December 5.

1885c. Wolves in Maine. Forest and Stream 24: 429. June 25.
       Timber wolf said to have attacked a man at Pittston,
       Maine.

1886. An Adirondack wolf. Rome (New York) Sentinel. Feb-
       ruary 10. Also Forest and Stream 26: 71. February
       18.

1887. The gray wolf eating watermelons. Forest and Stream
       29: 403. December 15.

1888a. Texas wolves. Forest and Stream 29: 504. January 19.

1888b. Wolves in France. The Field, the Farm, the Garden,
       71 (1): 14. January. London.

1897. History of Tioga County, Pa. P. 44, illus. R. C. Brown
       & Co., Harrisburg, Pa.

1908. The wolf hunter. Rod and Gun and Motor Sports in
       Canada 10 (7): 603. December.

1910a. Wolf bounty frauds (Ontario). Rod and Gun in Canada
       11 (12): 1218. May.

1910b. A relation of Maryland. Ann. Dom. 1635. Narratives of
       Early Maryland, 1633-1684: 63-112. New York.

1910c. A Parry Sound wolf hunt. Forest and Stream 74: 338,
       February 26.

1911. Wolves and big game. Rod and Gun in Canada 12 (10):
       1352. March.

1913a. The cunning of the wolf. Outdoor World and Recreation
       48 (6): 342. May.

1913b. Wolves in Ontario-Canada. Forest and Stream 80: 142,
       February 1.

1914a. The timber wolf in Oregon. Forest and Stream 82: 54-
       55.

1914b. The wolf in Maine. Forest and Stream 82 (16): 514.
       April.

1915. White wolf killed. Forest and Stream 84: 101, February.

1926. Wild animals that think. Literary Digest 88 (10): 71-75. March 6.

1927. Combatting the wolves in northern Canada. Natural Resources Canada, Canadian Dept. of the Interior 6 (3): 3. Ottawa. March.

1927a. Wolf children of India. Living Age, 332 (4307): 1021-1022. June 1.

1927b. India's wolf children found in caves. Literary Digest, 95: 54-56. October 8.

1934. Treatment of rabies is preventive rather than cure. Hygeia 12 (8): 765. August.

1939a. Trained timber wolves. Outdoor Life 83 (7): 65.

1939b. The Oregon trail. P. 63. Compiled and written by the Federal Writers' Project of WPA. Sponsored by Oregon Trail Memorial Association, Inc. American Guide Series. New York.

1940a. From Ketchikan to Barrow. Alaska Sportsman 6 (7): 21. July. Comment re wolf depredations on reindeer.

1940b. The animal kingdom. The Pierpont Morgan Library, New York. P. 70.

1943. Indiana fur value shown in invoice left by Vigo [Francis] of Vincennes three lifetimes ago. Outdoor Indiana 10 (10): 3, 15. November.

ANTHONY, H. E.
1928. Field book of North American mammals. G. P. Putnam's Sons, New York, p. 254.

ARNOLD, BRIDGEWATER
1927. A dictionary of fur names. Nat. Assoc. Fur Industry, New York: 22.

ARNOLD, SAMUEL GREENE
1859. History of the state of Rhode Island. 2 vols. New York.

ARTHUR, STANLEY C.
1928. The fur animals of Louisiana. State of Louisiana Department of Conservation, Bull. No. 18, pp. 1-433.

ASH, EDWARD C.
1927. Dogs, their history and development. 2 vols. London.

AUBREY, CHARLES
    1908.   Memoirs of an old buffalo hunter. Forest and Stream
         71: 133-134, 172, 216-217.

AUDUBON, JOHN JAMES, and BACHMAN, JOHN
    1851-54. The quadrupeds of North America. 3 vols. New
         York. New: *Canis lupus* var. *rufus* (= *C. niger
         rufus*).

AUGHEY, SAMUEL
    1880.   Sketches of the physical geography and geology of Ne-
         braska. 326 pp. Omaha.

B., F. M.
    1899.   A Pennsylvania Putnam and a wolf. Forest and Stream
         52: 405. May 27.

B., J. A.
    1884.   A hunt with the Comanches. Forest and Stream 23: 163-
         164.

BACK, GEORGE (CAPTAIN)
    1936.   Narrative of the Arctic land expedition to the mouth of
         the Great Fish River, and along the shores of the
         Arctic Ocean in the years 1833, 1834, 1835. Zool.
         App. by John Richardson. 663 pp. London, Paris,
         Brussels, Leipzig, Frankfort, Philadelphia.

BAILEY, VERNON
    1905.   Biological survey of Texas. U. S. Dept. Agr., Bur. Biol.
         Survey. North Amer. Fauna 25: 1-222, illus. Oc-
         tober 24.
    1907a. Directions for the destruction of wolves and coyotes. U.
         S. Dept. Agr., Bur. Biol. Surv. Circ. 55: 1-6.
    1907b. Destruction of deer by the northern timber wolf. U. S.
         Dept. Agr., Bur. Biol. Surv. Circ. 58: 1-2, illus.
         May 4.
    1907c. Wolves in relation to stock, game, and the national for-
         est reserves. U. S. Dept. Agr., Forest Serv. Bull. 72:
         1-31, illus.
    1908.   Destruction of wolves and coyotes—results obtained dur-
         ing 1907. U. S. Dept. Agr., Bur. Biol. Surv. Circ.
         63: 1-11, illus.
    1909.   Key to animals on which wolf and coyote bounties are
         often paid. U. S. Dept. Agr., Bur. Biol. Surv. Circ.
         69: 1-3, illus. May.

1918. Wild animals of Glacier National Park. U. S. Dept. of the Interior, Natl. Park Service, 210 pp. Mammals, pp. 1-102.

1926. A biological survey of North Dakota. U. S. Dept. Agr., Bur. Biol. Survey. North Amer. Fauna 49: 1-226.

1928. Animal life of the Carlsbad Cavern. Monograph Amer. Soc. Mammalogists 3: 1-195, illus. Baltimore.

1930. Animal life of Yellowstone National Park. 241 pp. Springfield, Ill.

1931. Mammals of New Mexico. U. S. Dept. Agr., Bur. Biol. Survey. North Amer. Fauna 53: 1-412.

1936. The mammals and life zones of Oregon. U. S. Dept. Agr., Bur. Biol. Survey. North Amer. Fauna 55: 1-416, illus.

1940. The home life of the big wolves. Natural History 46 (2): 120-122, illus. September.

BAIN, JAMES

1901. Travels and adventures in Canada and the Indian territories between the years 1760-1776 by Alexander Henry, fur trader. 347 pp. Boston.

BAIRD, SPENCER F.

1857-59. The mammals of North America. General report on North American mammals. 764 pp. Philadelphia.

1859. Mammals of the U. S. and Mexican boundary survey 2 (pt. 2): 1-62, illus.
   Refers to *Canis torquatus*, a manuscript name of Berlandier's which can not be satisfactorily assigned.

BALL, V.

1873. Notes on children found living with wolves in the northwestern provinces and Oudh. Proc. Asiatic Soc. Bengal: 8, 128-129. January-December.

BALLANTYNE, ROBERT MICHAEL

1859. Hudson Bay, or everyday life in the wilds of North America. 322 pp., 3rd Ed. London and New York.

BANCROFT, HUBERT HOWE

1882-90. The works of Hubert Howe Bancroft. 39 vols. Vol. 29, History of Oregon, 1834-1848. 1886. San Francisco.

BANGS, OUTRAM
  1898a. The land mammals of peninsular Florida and the coast
    region of Georgia. Proc. Boston Soc. Nat. Hist. 28
    (7): 157-235.
  1898b. A list of the mammals of Labrador. Amer. Nat. 32: 489-
    507. July.
BANNISTER, H. M.
  1869. The Esquimaux dog. Amer. Nat. 3 (10): 522-530. De-
    cember.
BARNES, CLAUDE T.
  1927. Utah mammals. Univ. of Utah Bull. 17 (12): 1-183.
    Salt Lake City.
BARNES, WILL C.
  1915. Fighting predatory animals on the western ranges.
    Breeders' Gazette 67: 705-706, illus.
  1921. How a den of wolves was exterminated. Breeders' Ga-
    zette 80: 923-924, 956-957, illus.
BARROWS, WILLARD
  1863. History of Scott County, Iowa. Annals Iowa State Hist.
    Soc. (1st ser.) 1: 11-176.
BARTLETT, G. W.
  1909. How shall we destroy the wolves? Rod and Gun and
    Motor in Canada 11 (3): 240-242. August.
BARTLETT, JOHN RUSSELL
  1856-65. Records of the colony of Rhode Island and Providence
    plantations in New England. 10 vols. Vol. 1. Printed
    by order of Legislature, 1636 to 1663. Providence,
    Rhode Island.
BARTON, BENJAMIN SMITH
  1803. On Indian dogs. Alexander Tillock's Philosophical
    Magazine 15: 1-9, 136-142. London.
  1805. Some accounts of the different species and varieties of
    native American or Indian dogs. Phila. Medical and
    Physical Journal 1 (pt. 2, sec. 1): 3-31.
BARTRAM, WILLIAM
  1928. The travels of William Bartram. 414 pp. Edited by
    Mark Van Doren. New York.

BATTY, JOSEPH H.
1874. Notes from the plains. The American Sportsman 5 (1): 1.
1882. How to hunt and trap. 226 pp. New York.
1884. A hunt with the Comanches. Forest and Stream 23: 163-164. Sept. 25.

BAYNES, ERNEST HAROLD
1923. Timber wolves—wild and tame. Nature Magazine 2 (6): 333-338, 356.

BEALS, CHARLES EDWARD
1916. Passaconaway in the White Mountains. 343 pp. Boston.

BEARD, D., CAHALANE, V. H., JACKSON, H. H. T., LINCOLN, F. C., and THOMPSON, BEN.
1942. Fading trails. A story of endangered wildlife. Pp. XV plus 279. The Macmillan Co., New York.

BEATTY, RICHARD CROOM
1932. William Byrd of Westover. 233 pp. Boston and New York.

BEDDARD, FRANK EVERS
1902. Mammalia. 605 pp. London and New York. Also The Cambridge Nat. Hist., vol. 10.

BEEBE, VICTOR L.
1934. History of Potter County, Pennsylvania. 280 pp. Potter County Hist. Soc., Coudersport.

BEEBE, WILLIAM
1943. Our zoo's former inhabitants. Four mammals and a bird that were driven from our grounds long before the Zoological Society took possession. Animal Kingdom, 46 (5): 111-116, illus. September-October. N. Y. Zool. Soc.

BEECHEY, F. W. (CAPTAIN)
1839. The zoology of Capt. Beechey's voyage . . . . 1825-28. Mammalia by J. Richardson. Pp. VIII plus 180. London.
        New: *Canis lupus* var. *fusca* (= *Canis lupus fuscus*).

BELL, HERBERT CHAS., Ed.
1890. History of Venango County, Pennsylvania. 1164 pp. Brown, Runk & Co., Chicago.

BELL, WILLIAM BONAR
  1920. Hunting down stock killers. U. S. Dept. Agr. Year-
       book, pp. 289-300, illus. Also Separate No. 845.
       Washington, D. C.
  1926. Wolf and coyote control. The Producer 7 (9): 3-4; 7
       (10): 6-8. February and March. Denver, Colo.

BENNITT, RUDOLF, and NAGEL, WERNER O.
  1937. A survey of the resident game and fur-bearers of Mis-
       souri. Univ. of Missouri Studies 12 (2): 1-215,
       illus. April 1. Columbia, Mo.

BENSON, ADOLPH B.
  1937. The America of 1750—Peter Kalm's travels in North
       America. 2 vols., illus. Vol. 1, pp. 1-380; vol. 2, pp.
       1-797. The English version of 1770 revised from the
       original Swedish.

BENT-PROWERS COUNTY CATTLE AND HORSE
GROWERS' ASSOCIATION
  1938. Minutes of annual meetings, 1870-1938. 386 pp. Las
       Animas, Colo.

BERLANDIER, L.
  1851. On the species of Mexican wolves; with preliminary re-
       marks by a committee of the Academy of Natural
       Sciences of Philadelphia. Proc. Acad. Nat. Sci. Phila.
       5: 156-157. February.

BERNARD, WILLIAM
  1906. Westport and the Santa Fe trade. Kansas Hist. Col-
       lections 1905-1906 9: 552-565. Topeka.

BEVERLY, ROBERT
  1705. The history and present state of Virginia. In four parts,
       illus. 104, 40, 64, 83 pp.
  1707. Histoire de la Virginie. 433 pp., illus. French transla-
       tion. Publ. Thomas Lombrail, Amsterdam.

BEWICK, THOMAS
  1804. A general history of quadrupeds. 531 pp. First American
       edition. New York.

BIBLE, HOLY
       Old Testament, II Samuel, Ch. 23, vs. 20.

BILLINGS, E.
  1856.   The natural history of the wolf (*Canis lupus*), and its
          varieties. The Canad. Nat. and Geol. 1 (3): 209-215.
          Montreal.
BLACK, J. D.
  1936.   Mammals of northwestern Arkansas. Jour. Mamm. 17
          (1): 29-34. February.
  1937.   Mammals of Kansas. 30th Biennial Rept. Kansas State
          Bd. Agr. 1935-36, pp. 116-217, illus.
BLACKMAN, EMILY C.
  1873.   History of Susquehanna County, Pennsylvania, 640 pp.
          Clayton, Remsen, and Hoffelfinger, Philadelphia.
BLISS, ISLEY, and RICHARDS, W. M.
  1936.   Four centuries in Kansas. P. 18. Wichita.
BOLE, B. P., JR., and MOULTHROP, PHILIP NELSON
  1942.   The Ohio recent mammal collection in the Cleveland
          Museum of Natural History. Cleveland Mus. Nat.
          Hist. Sci. Pub. 5 (6): 83-181. September 11.
BONNYCASTLE, SIR RICHARD HENRY
  1842.   Newfoundland in 1842. 2 vols. A sequel to The Can-
          adas in 1841. London.
BOWLEGS, BILLY
  1923.   Coursing in the good old days. Outdoor Life 52 (2):
          93-98, illus. August.
BRACKENRIDGE, H. M.
  1904.   Journal of a voyage up the river Missouri in 1811. Early
          Western Travels 6: 21-166. Edited by Reuben Gold
          Thwaites. Cleveland.
BRADBURY, JOHN
  1904.   Travels in the interior of America in the years 1809,
          1810, and 1811. . . . Early Western Travels, vol. 5,
          p. 118. Edited by Reuben Gold Thwaites. Cleveland.
BRADSBY, H. C.
  1891.   History of Bradford County, Pennsylvania. 1320 pp.
          S. B. Nelson & Co., Chicago.
BRAINARD, DAVID L.
  1940.   Six came back—the Arctic adventure of David L. Brain-
          ard. 305 pp. Edited by Bessie Rowland James. In-
          dianapolis and New York.

BRANCH, EDWARD DOUGLAS
1929. The hunting of the buffalo. 240 pp. D. Appleton & Co., New York and London; pp. 7-8, 11, 16, 107.

BRECK, LLOYD
1908. In wild Wisconsin. Forest and Stream 71: 297. August 22.

BREHAUT, ERNEST
1912. An encyclopedist of the Dark Ages, Isidore of Seville. 274 pp. Also Studies in History, Economics, and Public Law 48 (1): 225. Edited by the faculty of Political Science, Columbia Univ. Whole No. 120. New York.

BREWER, WILLIAM H.
1930. Up and down California in 1860-1864. 601 pp. New Haven, Connecticut.

BRIGHAM, JOHN B.
1859. Louisa [County]. 5th Ann. Rept. Iowa State Agr. Soc., 1858. Pp. 364-373.

BRISTOW, ARCH, and DUTTON, CHARLES J.
1939. Last stand of the lobo. Hunter-Trader-Trapper Outdoorsman 79 (2): 23-24, illus. August.

BRITISH COLUMBIA, PROVINCE OF
1895. Animal pests. Fourth report of the Dept. of Agr. of the Province of British Columbia, 1894. Pp. 1126-1131. Victoria.
1897. Noxious animals and animal pests. Fifth report of the Dept. of Agr. of the Province of British Columbia, 1895-96. Pp. 1167-1177. Victoria.
1910. Game animals, birds, and fishes of British Columbia. Bureau of Provincial Information Bull. 17: 27. 6th edition.

BROOKS, ALLAN
1926. Past and present big-game conditions in British Columbia and the predatory animal question. Jour. Mamm. 7: 37-40.
1944. Do predators eradicate disease? Rod & Gun, 45 (8): 13, 29; illus. January.

BROOKS, FRED ERNEST
1911. The mammals of West Virginia. Report of West Va. State Board of Agr. 20: 9-30. (For quarter ended Dec. 30, 1910.)

BROWN, C. EMERSON
1936. Rearing wild animals in captivity, and gestation periods. Jour. Mamm. 17 (1): 10-13. February.

BROWN, R. C., Ed.
1895. History of Butler County, Pennsylvania. R. C. Brown Co. 1360 pp. Harrisburg.

BROWN, THOMAS POLLOK
1934. California names. An alphabetical list of geographical place names in California. A pamphlet of 28 unnumbered pages issued by the American Trust Company, San Francisco.

BROWNING, MESHACH
1928. Forty-four years of the life of a hunter. 400 pp. Philadelphia.

BRYANT, EDWIN
1885. Rocky Mountain adventures. 452 pp. New York.

BUCHANAN, ANGUS
1920. Wild life in Canada. John Murray, Pub. London, 264 pp., illus.

BUCK, S. J. and E. H.
1939. The planting of civilization in western Pennsylvania. 565 pp. Univ. Pittsburgh Press, Pittsburgh.

BUDD, THOMAS
1902. Pennsylvania and New Jersey. Burrows Brothers Co., Cleveland, p. 73.

BUFFON, GEORGES LOUIS LECLERC
1750-1804. Histoire naturelle, generale, et particuliere, avec la description du cabinet du roy, 44 vols. Vol. 9, 375 pp., illus. Paris, 1761. Description of the "loup noir," pp. 362-370, and plate 41. The plate was copied and reproduced as plate 89 of Schreber (1775) over the name *Canis lycaon* (= *C. l. lycaon*).

BULLOCK-WEBSTER, FRANK
1909. Wolves in British Columbia. Rod and Gun in Canada 11 (7): 611. December.

BURT, WILLIAM HENRY
　　1938. Faunal relationships and geographic distribution of
　　　　　mammals in Sonora, Mexico. Univ. Mich., Mus. of
　　　　　Zool. Misc. Publ. 39: 1-77, 26 maps.
BUSHNELL, DAVID I., JR.
　　1938. Drawings by George Gibbs in Far Northwest, 1849-
　　　　　1851. Smithsn. Misc. Coll. 97 (8): 1-28, illus.
BYERS, O. P.
　　1912. Personal recollections of the terrible blizzard of 1886.
　　　　　Kansas Historical Collections 1911-1912 12: 99-117.
BYRD, COL. WM.
　　1901. The writings of Colonel William Byrd, of Westover in
　　　　　Virginia, 1728. 461 pp. Edited by John Spencer
　　　　　Bassett, New York.
CABOT, WILLIAM B.
　　1920. Labrador. 354 pp., illus. Boston.
CAGE, DUNCAN S.
　　1890. The big-game of North America. Coursing the gray
　　　　　wolf. 581 pp., illus. Ed. by G. O. Stiles, Chicago
　　　　　and New York.
CAHN, ALVIN R.
　　1937. The mammals of the Quetico Provincial Park of On-
　　　　　tario. Jour. Mamm. 18 (1): 19-30.
CAMERON, JENKS
　　1929. The Bureau of Biological Survey—its history, activities,
　　　　　and organization. Service Monograph of the U. S.
　　　　　Government 54: 46. Brookings Institution, Wash-
　　　　　ington, D. C.
CAMPANIUS, HOLM TOMAS
　　1834. A short description of the province of New Sweden. Now
　　　　　called, by the English, Pennsylvania in America. Me-
　　　　　moirs Pa. Hist. Soc. v. 3 (pt. 1), 166 pp. Philadelphia.
CANADA, DEPT. OF THE INTERIOR
　　1923. Canadian Nat. Parks Branch. J. B. Harkin, Commis-
　　　　　sioner. Report of the Commissioner of Canadian Nat.
　　　　　Parks, Ottawa, 1922, pp. 41-47. App. 4-5.
　　1924. Canadian Nat. Parks Branch. J. B. Harkin, Commis-
　　　　　sioner. Report of the Commissioner of Canadian Nat.
　　　　　Parks, Ottawa, 1923, pp. 1-36.

1927. Combatting the wolves in northern Canada. Natural Resources of Canada 6 (3): 3. Ottawa.

1934. National Parks of Canada. Nat. Parks, Branch, J. B. Harkin, Commissioner. Report of the Commissioner, 1933, pp. 1-51. Ottawa.

CANADA, DEPT. OF MINES AND RESOURCES
1937. Report of lands, parks, and forests. Pp. 56, 63, 86. R. A. Gibson, Director, Ottawa.

CARHART, ARTHUR HAWTHORNE
1939. World champion wolfer. Outdoor Life 84 (3): 22-23, 74-75, illus.

————, and YOUNG, STANLEY P.
1929. The last stand of the pack. 295 pp., illus. New York.

CARL ————
1886. Montana wolves and panthers. Forest and Stream 26: 508-509.

CARL, G. CLIFFORD, and HARDY, GEO. A.
1942. Report on a collecting trip to the Lac La Hache Area, British Columbia. Rept. Prov. Mus. Nat. Hist.; Prov. of British Columbia, Canada. Victoria, pp. 25-49.

CARMAN, EZRA AYERS, and others
1892. Special report on the history and present condition of the sheep industry of the United States. Bur. Anim. Ind., U. S. Dept. Agr. 1,000 pp. Washington, D. C.

CARNEY, EMERSON
1902. The gray wolf. Forest and Stream 58 (5): 84. February 1.

CARSON, LAWRENCE
1939a. Black wolves of Revillagigedo. The Alaska Sportsman 5 (1): 8-9, 25-29, illus. January.

1939b. Some wolves get away. The Alaska Sportsman 5 (10): 18-20, 22-26, illus. October.

CARTER, E. D.
1898. Wolves in Iowa. Forest and Stream 50 (18): 345. April.

CARTWRIGHT, DAVID W.
1875. Natural history of western wild animals and guide for hunters, trappers and sportsmen. 280 pp. Toledo, Ohio.

CARY, MERRITT
  1911. A biological survey of Colorado. U. S. Dept. Agr., Bur.
          Biol. Survey. North Amer. Fauna 33: 1-256, illus.
CASSIN, JOHN
  1858. United States exploring expedition during the years
          1838, '39, '40, '41, '42 under the command of
          Charles Wilkes. Ed. 2, Vol. 8, Mammalogy and
          Ornithology, pp. 1-466, 2 illus. and folio atlas. Phila-
          delphia.
CATESBY, MARK
  1743 or 1771. The natural history of Carolina, Florida, and the
          Bahama Islands. 2 vols. London.
CATLIN, GEORGE
  1848. Catlin's notes of eight years' travels and residence in
          Europe with his North American Indian collection.
          2 vols., 3d Ed. London.
  1913. North American Indians. Modern edition. 2 vols.
          Philadelphia.
CHAPMAN, CHARLES H.
  1907. Taking of wolves by trap, poison, and dogs. Pp. 1-3.
          Michigan State Dept. of Fish and Game. Sault Ste.
          Marie.
CHAPMAN, H. H.
          1938. Wolf packs. Journal of Forestry, p. 1158.
          November.
CHASE, STUART
  1936. Rich land, poor land. A study of waste in the natural
          resources of America. Pp. i-x; 1-361; illus.; Whit-
          tlesey Hounse, New York; London, McGraw-Hill
          Book Co., Inc., pp. 178-191.
CHITTENDEN, HIRAM MARTIN
  1935. The American fur trade of the far West. 2 vols. New York.
CLAPP, HENRY
  1868. Notes of a fur hunter. American Naturalist 1 (12): 652-
          666. February.
CLARK, AUSTIN H.
  1943. Iceland and Greenland. Smithsn. Inst., War background
          studies No. 15, Pub. 3735, pp. IV plus 103, illus. Au-
          gust 19.

CLARK, WILLIAM, and LEWIS, MERIWETHER
1904-05. Original journals of the Lewis and Clark expedition, 1804-1806. 8 vols. Edited by Reuben Gold Thwaites. New York.

CLARKE, C. H. D.
1940. A biological investigation of the Thelon Game Sanctuary, with remarks on the natural history of the interior barren lands. Canada Dept. of Mines and Resources, Mines and Geology Branch, Nat. Mus. of Canada Bull. 96, Biol. Ser. 25: 1-135. Ottawa.

CLAYTON, JOHN
1844. A letter from Mr. John Clayton rector of Crofton at Wakefield and Yorkshire to the Royal Society May 12, 1688. Tracts and Other Papers Relating to the Colonies of North America, vol. 3, 45 pp. Collected by Peter Force.

CLYMAN, JAMES
1928. The adventures of a trapper and covered wagon emigrant as told in his reminiscences and diaries, 1792-1881. Edited by Charles L. Camp. San Francisco Historical Society.

COCKERELL, T. D. A.
1927. History of Colorado. Natural History, vol. 1, pp. 139-200. Colo. State Hist. and Nat. Hist. Soc. Denver.

COCKING, MATTHEW
1908. Journal of Matthew Cocking from York factory to Blackfeet country, 1772-73. Edited with introduction and notes by Laurence J. Burpee. Trans. Royal Soc. Canada, sec. II, pp. 106-110. Ottawa.

COLBERT, EDWIN H.
1939. Wild dogs and tame—past and present. Natural History 43 (2): 90-95, illus.

COLLINS, GRENOLD
1937a. Excerpt from Alaska Game Commission report. February 26, Juneau, Alaska. In files of Fish and Wildlife Service, Washington, D. C.
1937b. Report of Arctic patrol and inspection trip, pp. 24-26. In files of Fish and Wildlife Service.

COLORADO LIVE STOCK RECORD
    1884.   April 18. Denver.
COMEAU, NOEL
    1940.   Notes preliminaires sur la presence du *Canis tundrensis
            ungavensis*, n. ssp. dans la province de Quebec. Ann
            l'Acfes, Montreal, 6: 121-122.
CONNELLY, WILLIAM ELSEY
    1915.   The Lane trail. Kansas Hist. Collections 1913-1914
            13: 268-279. Topeka.
COOPER, COURTNEY RYLEY
    1926.   High country—the Rockies yesterday and today. 294
            pp. Boston.
COOPER, J. G., SUCKLEY, G., and GIBBS, G.
    1860.   The natural history of Washington Territory, with much
            relating to Minnesota, Nebraska, Kansas, Oregon,
            and California. . . . 1853-1857, 3 pts. in 1 vol. Pac.
            R. R. Repts., vol. 12, Book 2, 399 pp.
COOPER, JOHN M.
    1938.   Snares, deadfalls, and other traps of the northern Algon-
            quins and northern Athabaskans. The Catholic Univ.
            America Anthropological Series 5, p. 144, illus.
            Washington, D. C.
COOPER, WILLIAM
    1810.   A guide in the wilderness—history of the first settle-
            ments in the western counties of New York, p. 23.
            Dublin. 1897 Ed., 41 pp. Rochester.
COOS COUNTY (OREGON)
    1887.   Coos County Court Journal 4: 1.
COPE, E. D.
    1879.   On the genera of Felidae and Canidae. Proc. Acad. Nat.
            Sci. Phila., pp. 168-194.
    1880.   On the zoological position of Texas. U. S. Natl. Mus.
            Bull. 17: 1-51.
    1883.   On the extinct dogs of North America. The Amer. Nat.
            17 (3): 235-249, illus. March.
CORBIN, BEN
    1900.   Corbin's advice, or, the wolf hunter's guide. 76 pp.,
            illus. Bismarck, North Dakota.

CORNEY, PETER
  1896. Voyages in the northern Pacific. 138 pp. Honolulu.
CORNISH, CHARLES JOHN
  1907. Animal artisans and other studies of birds and beasts.
          Longmans, Green & Co., London, New York, Bombay, and Calcutta. 274 pp., illus.
CORNISH, CHARLES J., et al
  1906. Library of natural history—living animals of the world.
          5 vols. New York.
CORY, CHARLES B.
  1896. Hunting and fishing in Florida, including a key to the
          water birds known to occur in the state. 304 pp.
          Boston.
  1912. The mammals of Illinois and Wisconsin. Field Mus.
          Nat. Hist. Publ. 153, Zool. Ser. 11: 1-505. Chicago.
COUES, ELLIOTT, U. S. A.
  1867. The quadrupeds of Arizona. Amer. Nat. 1 (6): 281-
          292; 1 (7): 351-363; 1 (8): 393-400; 1 (10): 531-
          541.
  1873. The prairie wolf or coyote, Canis latrans. Amer. Nat. 7
          (7): 384-389. Salem, Mass.
  1876. An account of the various publications relating to the
          travels of Lewis and Clarke, with a commentary on
          the zoological results of their expedition. U. S. Dept.
          of the Interior, Geol. and Geog. Survey Terr. Bull.
          (ser. 2) 1: 417-444. February 8.
  1877. Fur-bearing animals. A monograph of the North American Mustelidae. U. S. Dept. of the Interior, Geol.
          Surv. Terr. Misc. Publ. No. 8, pp. 1-348. Washington, D. C.
  1893. History of the Expedition under the Command of Lewis
          and Clark. 4 vols. F. P. Harper. New York.
  1897. Manuscript journals of Alexander Henry and David
          Thompson, 1799-1814. 3 vols. New York.
          See Henry, Alexander, and Thompson, David.

————————, and YARROW, H. C.
1875.   Report upon the collections of mammals made in por-
        tions of Nevada, Utah, California, Colorado, New
        Mexico, and Arizona, during the years 1871, 1872,
        1873, and 1874. Geog. and Geol. Explor. and Sur-
        veys west of 100th Mer. 5: 37-129.

COUPIN, HENRI EUGENE VICTOR
1904.   Animals that hunt. Smithsn. Inst. Ann. Rept. for 1903,
        pp. 567-571, August 29. Washington, D. C. A trans-
        lation from Revue Scientifique (Paris), pp. 274-277.

COWAN, IAN McTAGGART
1939.   The vertebrate fauna of the Peace River district of
        British Columbia. B. C. Prov. Mus., Occas. Papers
        No. 1, pp. 1-102. Victoria, British Columbia.

COWIE, ISAAC
1913.   The company of adventurers; a narrative of seven years
        of the Hudson's Bay Company during 1867-1874 on
        the great buffalo plains. . . . 515 pp. Toronto.

COX, ROSS
1831.   Adventures on the Columbia River 1811-1817. 2 vols.
        London.

COYNER, DAVID H.
1847.   The lost trappers—a collection of interesting scenes and
        events in the Rocky Mountains. 255 pp. Cincinnati.

CRABB, E. D.
1924.   The gross weight of Woodhouse's wolf. Jour. Mamm.
        5 (3): 199-200.

CRANE, JOCELYN
1931.   Mammals of Hampshire County, Massachusetts. Jour.
        Mamm. 12 (3): 267-272.

CRIDDLE, NORMAN
1925.   The habits and economic importance of wolves in Can-
        ada. Dom. of Canada Dept. of Agr. Bull. (n.s.) 13:
        1-24.

CRILE, GEORGE W.
1941.   Intelligence, power, and personality. 347 pp., illus.
        New York and London.

CROOK COUNTY (OREGON)
1885.   Crook County Commissioners' Journal 1: 334.

CROSS, E. C.
1940.   Arthritis among wolves. The Canad. Field-Nat. 54 (1): 2-4, 4 illus. January. Ottawa.
CROSS, OSBORNE (MAJOR)
1850.   A report in the form of a journal to the quartermaster general of the march of the regiment of mounted riflemen to Oregon from May 18 to October 5, 1849. U. S. War Dept. Rept. 1849-50. Printed for Senate 1850, Doc. No. 3, Report Quartermaster General, App. A, pp. 126-244. Washington, D. C.
CUMING, SIR ALEXANDER
1928.   Journal of a journey to the Cherokee Mountains. Samuel Cole Williams' Early Travels in the Tennessee Country. 540 pp. Johnson City, Tenn.
CUMING, F.
1904.   Sketches of a tour to the western country, 1807-1809. Ed. by Reuben Gold Thwaites in Early Western Travels. Vol. 4, 377 pp. Arthur H. Clark Co., Cleveland.
CUSTER, ELIZABETH B.
1890.   Following the Guidon. 341 pp., illus. New York.
DALRYMPLE, BUD
1919.   The gray wolf of South Dakota. 31 pp. Altoona, Pa.
1923.   The value of the tame wolf as a decoy. Outdoor Life 52 (3): 188.
D'ARTAGUETTE, DIRON
1928.   Journal of a journey from New Orleans to the Illinois country, 1722-1723, p. 75. Johnson City, Tenn.
DARWIN, CHARLES
1874.   The descent of man, and selection in relation to sex. 797 pp., illus. 2nd Ed.
DAVIS, CLYDE B.
1928.   Wolf pursues deer into water. Outdoor Life—Outdoor Recreation 62 (4): 86. October.
DAVIS, DUKE
1939.   More on habits of wolves. Field and Stream 44 (2): 12-13. June.

DAVIS, STELLA M.
   1929.   The last wolf in Portland (Me.). Maine Naturalist 9
           (2): 73. June.
DAVIS, WILLIAM B.
   1939.   The recent mammals of Idaho. 400 pp., 2 pls., 33 figs.
           The Caxton Printers, Ltd., Caldwell, Idaho. April 5.
DAVIS, WM. W. H.
   1876.   History of Bucks County, Pennsylvania. 875 pp. Demo-
           crat Book and Job Office Print, Doylestown.
DAWKINS, W. BOYD
   1874.   Cave hunting. Researches on the evidence of caves re-
           specting the early inhabitants of Europe. Pp. i-xxiv;
           1-455, illus.; London, Macmillan Company; pp. 76,
           79, 81, 131, 146, 400, 401.
DAWSON, W. M.
   1937.   Heredity in the dog. U. S. Dept. Agr. Yearbook. Pp.
           1314-1349. Also Separate No. 1601. Washington,
           D. C.
DAY, ALBERT M.
   1932.   Handbook for hunters of predatory animals. U. S. Dept.
           Agr., Bureau of Biological Survey. Pp. 1-52, illus.
DEARBORN, NED
   1919.   Trapping on the farm. Yearbook, U. S. Dept. Agric.:
           451-484, illus.; 468. Yearbook Separate 823.
   1932.   Foods of some predatory fur-bearing animals in Michi-
           gan. School of Forestry and Conservation, Univ.
           Mich. Bull. 1: 1-52, illus; 50; Ann Arbor.
DEGERBOL, MAGNUS
   1927.   Uber prahistorische, dänische Hunde. Vidensk. Medd.
           Dansk naturh. Foren. Kobenhavn, Bind 84: 17-71,
           illus.
                 Includes remarks on wolves of Greenland and
           Ellesmere Island.
DEKAY, J. E.
   1842.   The natural history of New York. Zoology, pt. 1, 146
           pp., illus. Albany.
DELLINGER, S. C., and BLACK, J. D.
   1940.   Notes on Arkansas mammals. Jour. Mamm. 21 (2):
           187-191. May.

DELMONT, JOSEPH
1931.   Catching wild beasts alive. 285 pp. London. Remarks
        and observations on the dingo as compared to the
        wolf.
DENNY, CECIL (SIR)
1943.   Down the Peace (River) in a dug-out. The Beaver, Out-
        fit 273, pp. 10-13, illus. March. Hudson's Bay Co.,
        Winnipeg, Manitoba, Canada.
DENVER, CITY AND COUNTY
1927.   Municipal facts 10 (5 and 6): 14. Publ. by City and
        County of Denver, Colo. May and June.
DE SMET, P. J. (FATHER)
1847.   Oregon missions and travels over the Rocky Mountains
        in 1845-46. 408 pp. New York.
DE TONTY, HENRY
1917.   Memoir on LaSalle's discoveries, sent in 1693 to Count
        Pontchartrain. P. 302. New York.
DE WITT, LEONARD C.
1940.   Vanquishes her foe in battle to the death. Western
        Sportsman 4 (2): 6, 7, 25, illus. January.
DICE, LEE R.
1927.   Manual of recent wild mammals of Michigan. Univ.
        Mich. Handbook Series, No. 2; pp. 39. Ann Arbor.
DICK, EVERETT
1928.   The long drive. Kansas Historical Collections 1926-
        1928 17: 27-97.
DICKINSON, JOHN P.
1939.   Range cattle days in old Colorado. The American Cattle
        Producer 21 (3): 9-10. August.
DILLIN, JOHN G. W.
1924.   The Kentucky rifle. 124 pp. plus index, illus. Publ. Na-
        tional Rifle Association, Washington, D. C.
DIONNE, C. E.
1902.   Les mammiferes de la province de Quebec. 285 pp.,
        illus. Quebec.
DIXON, JOSEPH S.
1916.   The timber wolf in California. California Fish and
        Game 2 (3): 125-129.

1934.   Mother wolf carries food for twelve miles to her young. Jour. Mamm. 15 (2): 158.

1938.   Birds and mammals of Mount McKinley National Park, Alaska. U. S. Dept. Int. Natl. Park Service, Fauna Ser. No. 3: 1-236.

DODDRIDGE, JOSEPH (REV.)

1824.   Notes on the settlement and Indian Wars of the western parts of Virginia and Pennsylvania from the year 1763 until the year 1783. 316 pp. Wellsburgh, Va.

1876a. Notes on the settlement and Indian wars of the western parts of Virginia and Pennsylvania from the year 1763 until the year 1783. 331 pp. Albany, N. Y.

1876b. Western Virginia and Pennsylvania. P. 99.

DODGE, RICHARD IRVING

1876.   The Black Hills. 151 pp. New York.

1877.   The plains of the great West and their inhabitants. . . . 448 pp. New York.

DONALDSON, THOMAS

1887.   The George Catlin Indian Gallery in the U. S. National Museum (Smithsonian Institution), with memoirs and statistics. U. S. Government Printing Office, Washington, D. C. Pp. vii plus 939, illus.

DONHAM, C. R., SIMMS, B. T., and MILLER, F. W.

1926.   So-called salmon poisoning in dogs (Progress Report). Jour. Veterinary Medical Assoc. (n.s. 21) 68 (6): 701-715, illus.

DONHAM, C. R., and SIMMS, B. T.

1927.   Coyote susceptible to salmon poisoning. Jour. Amer. Veterinary Medical Assoc. (n.s. 24) 71 (2): 215-217.

DORR, HENRY C.

1885.   The Narragansetts. R. I. Hist. Soc. Coll. 7: 135-237. Providence.

DOUGLAS, DAVID

1914.   Journal kept by David Douglas during his travels in North America 1823-27. 364 pp. Publ. under the direction of the Royal Horticultural Society. London. Describes collecting a "new species" of *Canis* (= *C. l. fuscus*).

DOUGLAS, NORMAN
  1938.   Old Calabria. 498 pp. Oxford University Press. New
          York and London.
DUFRESNE, FRANK
  1935.   Estimated value of Alaska wildlife. The Daily Alaska
          Empire, Progress ed., 3rd sec., pp. 1-8. March. Ju-
          neau, Alaska.
  1942.   Mammals and birds of Alaska. U. S. Dept. Interior,
          Fish and Wildlife Service Circ. 3: 1-37, illus. Wash-
          ington, D. C.
  1943.   Grizzly fight (Wolves vs. grizzly bears). Field &
          Stream, 48 (6): 22-23, 64, 1 illus. (drawn). October.
DUIS, E.
  1874.   The good old times in McLean County, Illinois. 865 pp.
          Bloomington, Ill.
DUNNE, A. L.
  1939.   Report on wolves followed during February and March
          1939. The Canad. Field-Nat. 53 (8): 117-118. Ot-
          tawa.
DU PRATZ, LE PAGE
  1774.   The history of Louisiana. 387 pp. Transl. from the
          French ed. publ. in 1758. London.
  1928.   History of Louisiana. Samuel Cole Williams' Early
          Travels in the Tennessee Country. P. 110. Johnson
          City, Tenn.
DURANT, SAMUEL W.
  1877a. History of Lawrence County, Pennsylvania. 228 pp.
          L. H. Everts & Co., Philadelphia.
  1877b. History of Mercer County, Pennsylvania. 156 pp. L.
          H. Everts & Co., Philadelphia.
DUTCHER, WILLIAM
  1887.   Old-time natural history. Forest and Stream 28 (6):
          105-106. March 3.
EASTMAN, CHARLES ALEXANDER
  1904.   Red Hunters and the animal people. 248 pp. Harper &
          Bros. New York and London.
ECKELS, RICHARD PRESTON
  1937.   Greek wolf lore. 88 pp. Univ. of Pennsylvania, Phila-
          delphia.

EDITOR
  1938. Trains wolves for sled team. The Outdoorsman 77 (4):
         6. October.
EDWARDS, STACY
  1922. An unusual timber wolf. Outdoor Life 50 (5): 383-
         384, illus. November.
ELLIOT, DANIEL GIRAUD
  1904. The land and sea mammals of Middle America and the
         West Indies. Field Columbian Mus., Publ. 95, Zool.
         Ser. 4 (pt. 2): 441-850. Chicago.
  1905. A check list of mammals of the North American conti-
         nent, the West Indies, and the neighboring seas. Field
         Columbian Mus., Publ. 105, Zool. Ser. 6: 1-761.
         Chicago.
ELLIS, FRANKLIN, and EVANS, SAMUEL
  1883. History of Lancaster County, Pennsylvania. Everts &
         Peck, Philadelphia. 1101 pp.
ELTON, CHARLES
  1931. Epidemics among sledge dogs in the Canadian Arctic
         and their relation to disease in the Arctic fox. Canad.
         Jour. of Research 5 (6): 673-692. December.
ELY, ALFRED, ANTHONY, H. E., and
  CARPENTER, R. R. M.
  1939. North American big game. A Book of the Boone and
         Crockett Club, New York. 533 pp.
EMMART, EMILY WALCOTT
  1940. The Badianus Manuscript. (Codex Barberini, Latin
         241.) Vatican Library. An Aztec herbal of 1552.
         341 pp., illus., 118 plates reproduced; 2 figs. and 4
         pls. Baltimore.
EVANS, ESTWICK
  1819. A pedestrious tour of four thousand miles through the
         western states and territories, during the winter and
         spring of 1818. 256 pp. Concord, N. H. (Thwaite's
         Early Western Travels 8: 91-364, 1904.)
FARLEY, FRANK L.
  1925. Changes in the status of certain animals and birds during
         the past fifty years in Central Alberta. Canad. Field
         Nat. 39 (9): 200-202. December.

FAVOUR, ALPHEUS HOYT
1936. Old Bill Williams—mountain man. 229 pp. Chapel Hill, N. C.

FERRIS, WARREN ANGUS
1940. Life in the Rocky Mountains. Edited by Paul C. Phillips. 365 pp., illus. Denver.

FETTERLY, ROBERT
1943. Frontispiece. Alaska Sportsman, 9 (9). September.

FEUILLEE-BILLOT, MME. A.
1932. Les derniers loups de France. La Nature 60 (2): 551-559.

FISHER, SYDNEY GEORGE
1900. The making of Pennsylvania. J. B. Lippincott & Co., Philadelphia. 364 pp.

FLINT, DR. THOMAS
1924. Diary of Dr. Thomas Flint. California to Maine and return, 1851-55. 78 pp. Los Angeles.

FLOWER, MAJOR STANLEY S.
1929. Mammals. List of the vertebrate animals exhibited in the gardens of the Zool. Soc. of London, 1828-1927 1: 1-419. London.
1931. Contributions to our knowledge of the duration of life in vertebrate animals. Proc. Zool. Soc. London 5 (pt. 1): 145-234.

FLOWER, WILLIAM HENRY, and
LYDEKKER, RICHARD
1891. An introduction to the study of mammals, living and extinct. 763 pp. London.

FORREST, EARLE R.
1926. History of Washington County, Pennsylvania. S. J. Clarke Pub. Co., Chicago. 3 vols.

FOUQUET, L. C.
1925. Buffalo days. Kansas Hist. Collections 1923-1925, vol. 16, pp. 341-352.

FOWLER, JACOB
1898. The journal of Jacob Fowler, narrating an adventure from Arkansas through the Indian Territory, Oklahoma, Kansas, Colorado, and New Mexico, to the sources of Rio Grande del Norte, 1821-22. 183 pp. New York. Edited with notes by Elliott Coues.

FOX, HERBERT
    1923.   Diseases in captive wild mammals and birds. 665 pp.,
            illus. J. B. Lippincott Company. Philadelphia, Lon-
            don, and Chicago.
FREEMAN, FREDERICK
    1858-62. The history of Cape Cod: the annals of Barnstable
            County including the district of Mashpee. 2 vols.
            Boston.
FREMONT, JOHN CHARLES
    1887.   Memoirs of my life. 655 pp., 1 vol. Chicago and New
            York.
FREUCHEN, PETER
    1935a. Arctic adventure—my life in the frozen North. 467 pp.
            New York and Toronto.
    1935b. Report of the fifth Thule expedition, 1921-24, the Dan-
            ish expedition to Arctic North America in charge of
            Knud Rasmussen 2 (4 and 5), Mammals, Pt. 2, Field
            Notes and Biological Observations. Copenhagen.
FRYXELL, F. M.
    1926.   An observation on the hunting methods of the timber
            wolf. Jour. Mamm. 7 (3): 226-227. August.
FULLER, A. R.
    1885.   Dog-wolf hybrid. Forest and Stream 25: 507. July 23.
FUNKHOUSER, WILLIAM DELBERT
    1925.   Wild life in Kentucky. Ky. Geol. Surv., Frankfort, 385
            pp., illus.
GABRIELSON, IRA NOEL
    1941.   Wildlife conservation. 250 pp., illus. New York.
GARMAN, H.
    1894.   A preliminary list of the vertebrate animals of Kentucky.
            Bull. Essex Inst. 26 (1-3): 1-63. January, Febru-
            ary, March.
GARRARD, LEWIS H.
    1850.   Wah-to-yah and the Taos Trail. 349 pp. Cincinnati and
            New York.
GARRETSON, MARTIN S.
    1938.   The American bison. 254 pp. New York.

GASS, SERGEANT PATRICK
  1904.   Gass's Journal of the Lewis and Clark expedition. 298
          pp. Reprint of the edition of 1811. Chicago.
GERSTELL, RICHARD
  1937.   The Pennsylvania bounty system. Research Bull. 1: 3.
          Harrisburg.
GESELL, ARNOLD
  1941.   Wolf child and human child. 107 pp. New York.
GIBSON, W. HAMILTON
  1881.   Camp life in the woods and the tricks of trapping and
          trap making. 300 pp., illus. New York.
GIDLEY, JAMES W., and GAZIN, C. LEWIS
  1938.   The Pleistocene vertebrate fauna from Cumberland
          Cave, Maryland. U. S. Nat. Mus. Bull. 171: 1-99,
          illus.
GILLMORE, PARKER
  1874.   Prairie and forest. A description of the game of North
          America, with personal adventures in their pursuit.
          Harper Bros., New York. 378 pp., illus.
GILPIN, J. BERNARD
  1870.   On the mammalia of Nova Scotia. Nova Scotian Inst.
          Nat. Sci. Proc. and Trans. 2 (4) pt. 2: 58-69.
GLASER, FRANK
  1934.   Letter to Alaska Game Commission sent from Healy
          Forks, Alaska, to Juncau, Alaska, dated December
          26. In files of Fish and Wildlife Service, Washing-
          ton, D. C.
GODMAN, JOHN D.
  1846.   American natural history. 2 vols. in 1. 3d ed. Philadelphia.
GOLDMAN, EDWARD A.
  1937.   The wolves of North America. Jour. Mamm. 18 (1):
          37-45. February 14.
              New: *Canis lupus labradorius, C. l. ligoni, C. l.
          youngi, C. l. irremotus, C. l. monstrabilis, C. l. mo-
          gollonensis,* and *C. rufus gregoryi.*
  1941.   Three new wolves from North America. Proc. Biol. Soc.
          Wash. 54: 109-114. September 30.
              New: *Canis lupus alces, C. l. columbianus,* and
          C. l. hudsonicus.

GOLDSMITH, OLIVER
1818. Natural history. Pp. 76-78. Pub. by Benjamin Warner.

GOODRICH, A. T.
1837. The Territory of Florida: Civil and Natural History. P. 63. New York.

GOODWIN, GEORGE GILBERT
1935. Mammals of Connecticut. Conn. State Geol. & Nat. Hist. Survey Bull. 53: 1-221.
1936. Big game animals in the northeastern United States. Jour. Mamm. 17 (1): 48-50.

GOOLD, WILLIAM
1889. All about wolves. Portland, Maine Daily Press. December 14.

GORDON, W. R.
1942. I tamed a wolf for my dog team. The Alaska Sportsman 8 (10): 10-11, 29-31, illus. October.

GRAHAM, ALBERT ADAMS (COMPILER)
1883. History of Fairfield and Perry counties, Ohio. 1186 pp., 2 maps. Chicago.

GRAHAM, GIDEON
1939. Animal outlaws. 256 pp., illus., 2d edition. Collinsville, Oklahoma.

GRANT, MADISON
1908, 1910. Condition of wild life in Alaska. New York Zool. Soc. 12th Ann. Rept. (1907): 125-134. Or Publ. 1976, Smithsonian Inst. Ann. Report for 1909: 521-529, 1 plate. Washington, D. C.

GRANT, ULYSSES SIMPSON
1885-86. Personal memoirs of U. S. Grant. 2 vols. New York.

GREAT BRITAIN
1749. House of Commons. Report from Committees of the House of Commons. From the Committee on the state of the Hudson's Bay Company 2: 263-266.

GREELEY, HORACE
1860. An overland journey from New York to San Francisco in the summer of 1859, pp. 93-94. New York, San Francisco.

GREELY, ADOLPHUS W.
1888.   Report on the proceedings of the United States expedi-
         tion to Lady Franklin Bay, Grinnell Land. 2 vols.,
         v. 1, 545 pp.; v. 2, 738 pp. Washington, D. C.
GREEN, JACOB
1822.   Curious instinct of the common hog (*Sus scrofa* Linn.).
         American Journal of Science 4 (2): 309-310.
GREEN, R. G., and EVANS, C. A.
1940.   A deficiency disease of foxes. Science 92 (2381): 154-
         155. August 16.
GREGG, JOHN
1943.   The strange "dog" of Fort Selkirk. The Beaver, Outfit
         273. Hudson's Bay Co., Winnipeg, Manitoba, Can-
         ada, p. 31, illus.
GREGG, JOSIAH
1905.   Commerce of the prairies; or the journal of a Santa Fe
         trader 1831-39. Early Western Travels, vols. 19
         and 20. Edited by Reuben Gold Thwaites. Cleve-
         land.
GREGORY, TAPPAN
1935.   The black wolf of the Tensas. Chicago Acad. Sci. Pro-
         gram Activities 6 (3): 1-68, illus.
1936.   Mammals of the Chicago region. Chicago Acad. Sci.
         Program Activities 7 (2-3): 1-75. July.
1939.   Eyes in the night. Timber Wolves. 243 pp., illus. New
         York.
GREGORY, WILLIAM K.
1933.   Nature's wild dog show. Bull. New York Zool. Soc. 36
         (4): 83-96, illus.
GRENFELL, WILFRED T., et al
1913.   Labrador, the country and the people. 529 pp. New
         York.
GRINNELL, GEORGE BIRD
1892.   Blackfoot lodge tales. 310 pp. New York.
1893.   Pawnee stories and folk tales. P. 246. New York.
1896.   About wolves and coyotes. Forest and Stream 47: 511-
         512. December 26.
1897a. Various trapping methods. How wolves were caught.
         Forest and Stream 49 (20): 382. November 13.

1897b. Trail and Campfire. Wolves and wolf nature. 353 pp.
       A book of the Boone and Crockett Club. New York.
1904.   American big game in its haunts. A book of the Boone
       and Crockett Club. 497 pp. New York.
1907.   Dog-wolf partnership. Forest and Stream 69 (20): 772.
       November.
1911.   When antelope were plenty. Forest and Stream 77 (16):
       582-583, 600-601. October.
1914.   The wolf hunters. 303 pp. New York.
1924.   A letter to Audubon. Jour. Mamm. 5 (4): 223-230.

GRINNELL, J. B.
1863.   Sheep on the prairies. Report of the Commissioner of
       Agr. for the year 1862. 37th Cong., 3d sess., Ex.
       Doc. No. 78, pp. 300-312.

GRINNELL, JOSEPH
1933.   Review of the recent mammal fauna of California. Univ.
       Calif. Publ. Zool. 40 (2): 71-234, September.
       Berkeley.

————, DIXON, JOSEPH S., and LINSDALE, JEAN M.
1937.   Fur-bearing animals of California. . . . Contributions
       from Univ. of Calif. Mus. Vert. Zool. 2 vols.
       Berkeley.

GUBERNATIS, ANGELO DE
1872.   Zoological mythology, or the legends of animals. 2 vols.
       London.

HAFEN, LE ROY R., and YOUNG, FRANCIS MARION
1938.   Fort Laramie and the pageant of the West, 1834-1890.
       429 pp. Glendale, Calif.

HAHN, WALTER LOUIS
1909.   The mammals of Indiana. 33rd Ann. Rept. Indiana De-
       partment of Geology and Natural Resources. Pp.
       417-663. Indianapolis.

HALL, ARCHIBALD
1861.   On the mammals and birds of the District of Montreal.
       The Canad. Nat. and Geol. 6 (4): 284-309.

HALL, E. RAYMOND
1932.   Remarks on the affinities of the mammalian fauna of
       Vancouver Island, British Columbia, with descrip-

tions of new subspecies. Univ. Calif. Publ. Zool. 38 (12): 415-423. November 8.
New: *Canis occidentalis crassodon* (= *C. lupus crassodon*).

1942.   Fur Bearers and the War. Trans. 7th North Amer. Wildlife Conference, Amer. Wildlife Inst., Toronto, Canada. Pp. 472-480.

HALLIDAY, W. E. D.
1940.   Predatory animals in the national parks (Canadian). Forest and Outdoors 36 (9): 277-278, 292-293; 36 (10): 317-318, 324-326, 329, illus. Montreal. September and October.

HALLOCK, CHARLES
1880.   The sportsman's gazetteer and general guide. 700 pp. and appendix 208 pp., illus. New York.

HAMILTON, W. J.
1939.   American mammals, their lives, habits, and economic relations. 434 pp., illus. New York and London.

HARDING, A. R.
1923.   Wolves timber and prairie. Outdoor Life 51 (1): 52. January.

HARGRAVE, JAMES
1938.   The Hargrave correspondence, 1821-1843. 472 pp. Publ. by Champlain Society. Toronto.

HARLAN, RICHARD
1825.   Fauna Americana, being a description of mammiferous animals inhabiting North America. 318 pp. Philadelphia.

HARMON, DANIEL WILLIAMS
1820.   A journal of voyages and travels in the interior of North America between the 47th and 58th degrees of north latitude. 432 pp. Andover, New York. 1903.

HARPER, FRANCIS
1927.   The mammals of the Okefenokee Swamp region of Georgia. Proc. Boston Soc. Nat. Hist. 38 (7): 191-396. Also issued as a reprint March 1927.

1932.   Mammals of the Athabaska and Great Slave Lakes region. Jour. Mamm. 13 (1): 19-36.

1942.   The name of the Florida wolf. Journ. Mamm. 23 (3): 339.

HARPSTER, JOHN W.
   1938.   Pen pictures of early western Pennsylvania. Univ. Pitts-
            burgh Press. 337 pp.
HARRIS, LEO D.
   1940.   The unruly gangsters of the Badlands. North Dakota
            Outdoors 2 (12): 4, illus. June. Bismarck, North
            Dakota.
HARRY, JOSEPH EDWARD
   1936.   Dog and dogs. 315 pp. New York and London.
HARTING, JAMES EDMUND
   1880.   British animals extinct within historic times. 258 pp.
            Boston.
HARTMANN, GEORGE
   1907.   Wooed by a sphinx of Azatlan; the romance of a hero of
            our late Spanish-American War. . . . 125 pp. Prescott,
            Arizona.
HARTSEL, SAMUEL
   1916.   Personal narrative. Denver Record-Stockman, p. 6.
            Historical Review Edition. January.
HARVARD CLASSICS, THE—Elliott
   1910.   The story of the Volsungs and Niblings 49: 268 (foot-
            note). New York.
HARVEY, OSCAR JEWELL
   1927.   A history of Wilkes-Barre. 3 vols. Wilkes-Barre, Pa.
HASTINGS, LANSFORD WARREN
   1932.   The emigrants' guide to Oregon and California. 157 pp.
            Reproduced in facsimile from the original edition of
            1845. Princeton, New Jersey.
HATFIELD, DONALD M.
   1940.   Animal populations and sunspot cycles. Chicago Nat. 3
            (4): 105-110; 107. December.
HATTON, JOHN H.
   1939.   Livestock albums. American Cattle Producer 21 (6):
            5-6, illus. November.
HAWN, LAURENS
   1878.   Death struggle of a buffalo. Western Homestead. Pp.
            190-191. November. Leavenworth, Kansas.

HAYDEN, FERDINAND VANDIVEER
  1862.   On the ethnography and philology of the Indian tribes
          of the Missouri Valley. Trans. Amer. Philos. Soc. 12
          (n.s.), pt. 2, art. 3; 231-461. Philadelphia.
  1863.   On the geology and natural history of the Upper Mis-
          souri. Trans. Amer. Philos. Soc. 12 (n.s.), pt. 1, art.
          1: 1-218, map.
  1875.   Report of the U. S. Geological Survey. P. 556.
HAYS, W. J.
  1871.   Notes on the range of some of the animals in America at
          the time of the arrival of the white men. Amer. Nat.
          5: 387-392.
HAZARD, SAMUEL
  1828-35. Hazard's register of Pennsylvania. 16 vols. Phila-
          delphia.
  1850.   Annals of Pennsylvania, 1609-1682. 664 pp. Philadel-
          phia.
HEARNE, SAMUEL
  1911.   A journey from Prince of Wales's Fort in Hudson's Bay
          to the northern Ocean in the years 1769-72. 437 pp.
          Edited by J. B. Tyrrell. Toronto.
HEIN, EDWARD N.
  1943.   The forest balance. Wisc. Conser. Bull. 7 (9): 10-11.
          Wisc. Conser. Dept., Madison.
HENDERSON, ARCHIBALD
  1920.   The conquest of the old Southwest; the romantic story
          of the early pioneers into Virginia, the Carolinas, Ten-
          nessee, and Kentucky, 1740-1790. 395 pp., illus. The
          Century Company, New York.
HENDERSON, JUNIUS, and CRAIG, ELBERTA L.
  1932.   Economic mammalogy. 397 pp. Springfield, Ill., and
          Baltimore, Md.
HENING, WILLIAM WALLER
  1810-1823. The statutes at large; being a collection of all the
          laws of Virginia. 13 vols. Richmond.
HENRY, ALEXANDER
  1901.   Travels and Adventures in Canada and the Indian Terri-
              tories—Alexander Henry. Fur Trader, 1760-1776.
          Pp. 273-274. Boston.

HENRY, ALEXANDER, and THOMPSON, DAVID
  1897.   New light on the early history of the greater Northwest.
           Manuscript journals of Alexander Henry and of
           David Thompson, 1799-1814. 3 vols. Edited by
           Elliott Coues. New York.
HERNANDEZ, FRANCISCO
  1651.   Rerum medicarum novae hispaniae thesaurus; sev. plan-
           tarum animalium mineralium Mexicanorum historia.
           950 pp., illus.
                  The "Xoloitzcuintli," p. 479, became the basis
           for *Canis mexicanus* Linnaeus, believed to be a wolf
           until shown by Allen (1920, p. 478) to apply to Mex-
           ican "hairless' dog.
HERRICK, C. L.
  1892.   Mammals of Minnesota. Geol. and Nat. Hist. Survey
           of Minn. Bull. 7: 1-299, illus. Minneapolis.
HEVERLY, C. F.
  1885.   History of Monroe Township and Borough, 1779-1885.
           209 pp. Reporter-Journal Printing Co., Towanda,
           Pennsylvania.
  1926.   History and geography of Bradford County, 1615-1924.
           Bradford Co. Hist. Soc. Towanda, Pennsylvania.
HEWITT, C. GORDON
  1916.   The conservation of our northern mammals. Seventh
           annual report of Commission of Conservation, Otta-
           wa, Canada. 283 pp., illus. Montreal.
  1921.   The conservation of the wild life of Canada. XX plus
           344 pp., illus.
HICHENS, WILLIAM (CAPTAIN)
  1930.   Unwanted animals—a world problem. Discovery,
           Monthly Jour. Knowl. 2 (124): 133-136. April.
           London.
HILL, N. N., JR. (COMPILER)
  1881.   History of Licking County, Ohio. 822 pp., also numer-
           ous figs. Newark, Ohio.
HILTON, WILLIAM
  1911.   Narratives of Early Carolina, 1650-1708. A relation of
           a discovery lately made on the coast of Florida—
           1664. 388 pp. New York.

HOARE, W. H. B.
    1930. Conserving Canada's musk-oxen. 53 pp. North West
            Terr. and Yukon Branch, Dept. of Interior, Ottawa,
            Canada.
    1939. Sanctuary. The Beaver, a magazine of the North, Out-
            fit 270 (1): 38-41, illus. June. Winnipeg.
HOCHMEYER, ERNEST
    1885. Were-wolves and wolf-children. American Field 24
            (1): 8. July 4.
HOFFMAN, CHARLES FENNO
    1835. A winter in the West. 2 vols. New York.
HOFFMAN, W. J.
    1878. List of mammals found in the vicinity of Grand River,
            D. T. Proc. Boston Soc. Nat. Hist. 19: 95-102.
            March.
HOLLIS, BURR
    1885. Hybrid wolves. Forest and Stream 25: 467. July 9.
HOLLISTER, H.
    1869. History of Lackawanna Valley [Pennsylvania]. 442 pp.,
            2d Ed. New York.
HOLLISTER, N.
    1913. Mammals of the Alpine Club expedition to the Mount
            Robson region. Canadian Alpine Journal, Special
            number, 44 pp., 13 pls. February 17.
    1923. Report on the National Zoological Park. Smithsonian Inst.
            Annual Report 1922: 88-103. Washington, D. C.
HOPE, JOHN ARTHUR
    1909a. The wolf hunt in northern Ontario. Rod and Gun and
            Motor Sports in Canada 10 (10): 946-947. March.
    1909b. The winter wolf hunt in northern Ontario. Rod and Gun
            in Canada 11 (1): 3-6, illus. June.
    1909c. Wolf hunting in Quebec. Rod and Gun in Canada 11
            (6): 633. November.
HORMELL, ROBERT S.
    1940. Notes on the history of rheumatism and gout. The New
            England Journal of Medicine 223 (19): 754-760.
            November 7.
                Discusses use by ancient Greeks of hot wolf oil to
            cure arthritis.

HORNADAY, WILLIAM TEMPLE
    1889.   The extermination of the American bison, with a sketch
           of its discovery and life history. U. S. Natl. Mus.,
           Ann. Rept. 1887: 367-548, pls. 1-22.
    1913.   Our vanishing wild life. 411 pp. New York.
HOWELL, ARTHUR H.
    1921.   A biological survey of Alabama. U. S. Dept. Agr., Bur.
           Biol. Survey. North Amer. Fauna 45: 1-76.
    1936.   A revision of the American Arctic hares. Jour. Mamm.
           17 (4): 315-337.
HUGHES, J. C.
    1883.   Mammals. American Naturalist 17 (11): 1192. No-
           vember.
HUME, EDGAR ERSKINE
    1942.   Ornithologists of the United States Army Medical
           Corps. 36 biographies, with foreword by Alexander
           Wetmore: i-xxv; 1-583; 235.
HUMPHREYS, DAVID (COLONEL)
    1818.   An essay on the life of the Hon. Major General Israel
           Putnam . . . . with an appendix containing an histori-
           cal and topographical sketch of Bunker Hill battle by
           S. Swett. 276 pp. Boston.
HUTYRA, F., MAREK, J., and MANNINGER, R.
    1938.   Special Pathology and Therapeutics of the Diseases of
           Domestic Animals. 4th English ed. Chicago.
ILJIN, N. A.
    1941.   Wolf-dog genetics. Jour. Genetics 42 (3): 360-414,
           illus. July.
INGERSOL, ERNEST
    1906.   The life of animals. 555 pp. New York.
INGHAM, THOMAS J.
    1899.   History of Sullivan County, Pennsylvania. 3 pts. in 1
           vol. Chicago.
INMAN, HENRY
    1899a. Buffalo Jones' forty years of adventure. 469 pp. Topeka,
           Kansas.
    1899b. The old Santa Fe trail. 493 pp. Topeka, Kansas.
    1917.   Tales of the trail—short stories of western life. 280 pp.,
           5th ed. Topeka, Kansas.

IOWA:
   THE HISTORY OF APPANOOSE COUNTY
      1878. 624 pp. Chicago.
   THE HISTORY OF FAYETTE COUNTY
      1878. 758 pp. Chicago.
   THE HISTORY OF FREMONT COUNTY
      1881. 778 pp. Des Moines.
   THE HISTORY OF KEOKUK COUNTY
      1880. 822 pp. Des Moines.
   THE HISTORY OF MARSHALL COUNTY
      1878. 696 pp. Chicago.
   HISTORY OF MONTGOMERY COUNTY
      1881. p. 451.
   THE HISTORY OF PAGE COUNTY
      1880. P. 374. Des Moines.
   THE HISTORY OF WARREN COUNTY
      1879. 743 pp. Des Monies.
   THE HISTORY OF WOODBURY AND
   PLYMOUTH COUNTIES
      1890-1891. 1022 pp. Chicago.
IOWA, STATE OF
   1857a. Journal of Iowa House of Representatives of the Sixth
          general assembly of the State of Iowa 1856. 664 pp.
   1857b. Journal of Iowa Senate of the Sixth general assembly of
          the State of Iowa 1856: 631 pp.
   1860. Journal of the House of Representatives 1859. Pp. 188,
          270, 271, 377, 378, 591, 623.
IRVING, WASHINGTON
   1855. Astoria; or, anecdotes of an enterprise beyond the Rocky
          Mountains. 519 pp. New York.
   1895. The adventures of Captain Bonneville, U. S. A., in the
          Rocky Mountains. 2 vols. New York.
JACKSON, C. F.
   1922. Notes on New Hampshire mammals. Jour. Mamm. 3
          (1): 13-15.
JACKSON, HARTLEY H. T.
   1908. A preliminary list of Wisconsin mammals. Bull. Wis.
          Nat. Hist. Soc. 6 (1-2): 13-34, illus. April.

JACKSON, SHELDON
    1900. Ninth annual report on introduction of domestic rein-
          deer into Alaska. Govt. Print. Office, Wash., D. C.:
          1-261; illus.

JACKSON, W. H.
    1942. Three unlucky wolves. Alaska Sportsman 8 (7): 8-9,
          29-30, illus. July. Ketchikan, Alaska.

JAMES, EDWIN, and LONG, STEPHEN H.
    1823. Account of an expedition from Pittsburgh to the Rocky
          Mountains, performed in the years 1819 and 1820.
          2 vols. Philadelphia.

JAMES, JAMES ALTON
    1942. The first scientific exploration of Russian America and
          the purchase of Alaska. Northwestern University;
          pp. i-xii; 1-276; map, 6 illus.

JARDINE, JAMES T.
    1908. Preliminary report on grazing experiments in a coyote-
          proof pasture, with an introduction by Frederick V.
          Coville. U. S. Dept. Agr., Washington, D. C. For-
          est Service Circ. 156: 1-32, illus.

JENNISON, GEORGE
    1937. Animals for show and pleasure in ancient Rome. 209
          pp., illus. Manchester, England.

JENSEN, A. S.
    1928-29. Greenland. Pub. by Comm. for Direction of Geol. and
          Geog. Invest. in Greenland, Copenhagen. 3 vols.,
          illus.

JEWETT, STANLEY G.
    1914. Oregon timber wolf. Oregon Sportsman 29 (5): 7-10,
          illus. May.
    1923. *Canis gigas* in the Blue Mountains of Oregon. Jour.
          Mamm. 4 (1): 54.

JOHNSON, CHARLES EUGENE
    1921. A note on the habits of the timber wolf. Jour. Mamm.
          2 (1): 11-15.
    1922. Notes on the mammals of northern Lake County, Min-
          nesota. Jour. Mamm. 3 (1): 33-39.

JOHNSON, FREDERICK CHARLES
  1887-1908. The Historical Record of Wyoming Valley. 14
      vols. Wilkes-Barre, Pennsylvania.
JOHNSON, SIR HARRY HAMILTON
  1903. British mammals. 405 pp. London.
JONES, DANIEL W.
  1890. Forty years among the Indians. 400 pp. Salt Lake City,
      Utah.
JONES, PAUL A.
  1937. Coronado and Quivira. 242 pp., illus. Lyons, Kansas.
JOSSELYN, JOHN
  1672. New England Rarities. London. Reprinted Boston,
      1865. Pp. 47, 50, 51.
JUDSON, KATHARINE B.
  1911. Myths and legends of Alaska. P. 127. Chicago.
KALM, PETER
  1937. The America of 1750, Peter Kalm's Travels in North
      America. The English version of 1770. Revised
      from original Swedish, edited by Adolph B. Benson,
      with a translation of new material from Kalm's diary
      notes. 2 vols. New York.
KANNER, LEO (M.D.)
  1928. Folklore of the teeth. 316 pp. New York.
KANSAS STATE HISTORICAL SOCIETY
  1896. Governor Medary's administration. Trans. Kans. State
      Hist. Soc. 5: 561-633. Topeka.
  1928. The life of George W. Brown. Kans. Hist. Soc. Coll.
      1926-28 17: 98-134.
KEATING, WILLIAM H.
  1825. Narrative of an expedition to the source of St. Peter's
      River, Lake Winnipeg, Lake of the Woods, Etc.,
      performed in the year 1823. 2 vols. London.
KEIM, DE B. R.
  1924. On the border with Sheridan's troopers. The Pioneer
      West—Narratives of the Westward March of Em-
      pire. 386 pp. Selected and edited by Joseph Lewis
      French, with a foreword by Hamlin Garland.
KELLER, OTTO
  1887. Thiere des classichen Alterthums. P. 158. Innsbruck.

KELLOGG, REMINGTON
    1937.   Annotated list of West Virginia mammals. Proc. U. S.
          Natl. Mus. 84 (3022): 443-479.
    1939.   Annotated list of Tennessee mammals. Proc. U. S. Natl.
          Mus. 86 (3051): 245-303.

KENDALL, GEORGE WILKINS
    1844.   Narrative of the Texan Santa Fe expedition comprising a
          description of a tour through Texas. 2 vols. New
          York.

KENDRICK, JOHN B., SENATOR
    1931.   Control of Predatory Animals. Hearings before the
          Committee on Agriculture and Forestry, U. S. Sen-
          ate, 71st Cong., 2nd and 3rd sess., on S. 3483. Pp. 6,
          7, 47. May 8, 1930, and January 28 and 29, 1931.

KENNICOTT, ROBERT
    1855.   Catalogue of animals observed in Cook County, Illinois.
          Trans. Illinois State Agricultural Society 1: 577-612.
          Springfield.

KIMBALL, GERTRUDE SELWYN
    1900.   Pictures of Rhode Island in the Past, 1642-1833. Com-
          piled by Gertrude Selwyn Kimball. 175 pp. Provi-
          dence.
             "A Short Account of the Present State of New
          England."

KINGSTON, C. S.
    1923.   Introduction of cattle into the Pacific Northwest. The
          Washington Historical Quarterly 14 (3): 165-185.
          July.

KNOX, M. V. B.
    1875.   Kansas Mammalia. Trans. Kans. Acad. Sci. 4: 18-22.

KUMLIEN, LUDWIG
    1879.   Contributions to the natural history of Arctic America
          made in connection with the Howgate Polar Expedi-
          tion 1877-78. U. S. Natl. Mus. Bull. 15: 1-179.

KUNKEL, G. M.
    1930.   Report of case of tularemia contracted from a coyote
          (*Canis lestes*) in New Mexico. Public Health Re-
          ports 45 (9): 439-440. February 28. Reprint No.
          1356 from Public Health Reports, pp. 1-2.

KURZ, RUDOLPH FRIEDERICK
  1937. Journal of Rudolph Kurz. Smithsonian Inst. Bull.,
         Amer. Ethnology No. 115, pp. 1,382, illus.
LA FLECHE, E. R.
  1909. The wolves in Algonquin Park. Rod and Gun in Can-
         ada 11 (1): 12-15. June.
LAIDLAW, C. M.
  1922. The destruction of wolves. Monteith Demonstration
         Farm Circular, pp. 1-3, 6-7. Ontario Dept. Agr. May.
LAING, IIAMILTON M.
  1939. Leave it to lobo. Field and Stream 44 (3): 36-38, 63.
         July.
  1944. Wolf at the crossing. Field and Stream 48 (11): 28-29,
         73-74; illus. March.
LANE, BOB
  1941. Wolves are queer devils. The Alaska Sportsman 7 (1):
         10-11, 32-34, illus. January.
LANMAN, CHARLES
  1848. A tour to the River Saguenay in lower Canada. 231 pp.
         Philadelphia.
  1854. Adventures in the wilds of North America. 300 pp.
         Edited by Charles Richard Weld. London.
  1885. Farthest north, or, the life and explorations of Lieut.
         James Booth Lockwood of the Greely Arctic expedi-
         tion. 333 pp., illus. New York.
LANTZ, D. E.
  1908. Bounty laws in force in the United States July 1, 1907.
         Yearbook, U. S. Dept. Agr., 1907: 560-565.
LARPENTEUR, CHARLES
  1898. Forty years a fur trader on the Upper Missouri River,
         1833-1872. 2 vols. Edited by Elliott Coues. New York.
LASCELLES, TONY
  1939a. You were asking: Food habits of timber wolf? Forest
         and Outdoors 35: 49-50. February.
  1939b. Do wolves hunt in packs? Can a deer escape wolves?
         Forest and Outdoors 35 (3): 83, 84. Montreal.
  1939c. The nature album. Why don't Huskies bark like domes-
         tic dogs? Forest and Outdoors 35 (12): 354-356.
         December. Montreal.

LAUT, AGNES C.
 1921. The fur trade of America. 341 pp., illus.
LAWSON, JOHN
 1714. The history of North Carolina. 258 pp. London. Edited
  by Francis Latham Harriss and reissued 1937. Richmond.
LEAVITT, SCOTT
 1929. Discourse on the grey wolf, in course of discussion on
  Agriculture Appropriation bill. Cong. Record, pp.
  679-683. December 14. 71st Cong., 2nd sess., from
  December 2 to December 21, U. S. House of Repre-
  sentatives.
LECHFORD, THOMAS
 1642. Plain dealing, or newes from New England. 280 pp.
  London.
LEE, D., and FROST, J. H.
 1844. Ten years in Oregon. 344 pp. New York.
LEESON, MICHAEL A.
 1890. History of the counties of McKean, Elk, Cameron, and
  Potter (Pennsylvania). 1261 pp. J. H. Beers Co.,
  Chicago.
LEINWEBER, MARTIN
 1944. Stumbling stampeders. Alaska Sportsman 10 (3)
  March: 10-11, 27-32; illus.
LEONARD, ZENES
 1904. Leonard's Narrative Adventures of Zenes Leonard, Fur
  Trader and Trapper, 1831-1836. Reprinted from the
  rare original of 1839, edited by W. F. Wagner,
  M.D., with maps and illustrations. The Burrows
  Bros. Co., Cleveland. 282 pp., 6 illus.
LEOPOLD, ALDO
 1936. Game management. Chas. Scribner's Sons, New York
  and London: i-xxi; 1-481; illus.; 35, 36, 86, 247,
  251.
LETT, WILLIAM PITTMAN
 1890. The Big Game of North America. The wolf. Pp. 453-
  473, illus. Ed. by G. C. Stiles. Chicago and New
  York.

LEWIS, MERIWETHER, and CLARK, WILLIAM
1904-05. Original journals of the Lewis and Clark expedition, 1804-1806. 8 vols. Edited by Reuben Gold Thwaites. New York. Edition on Van Gelder handmade paper; 200 copies only printed.

LIGON, J. STOKLEY
1917. Sexes and breeding notes. Excerpt from report to Biological Survey from Albuquerque, New Mexico, August 22. In files of Fish and Wildlife Service, Washington, D. C.

1926. When wolves forsake their ways. Nature Magazine 7: 156-159. March.

1927. Wild life of New Mexico. New Mexico State Game Commission, 212 pp., illus. Santa Fe.

LINDSAY, W. LAUDER
1880. Mind in the lower animals, in health and disease. 2 vols. New York.

LINN, JOHN BLAIR
1877. Annals of Buffalo Valley, Pennsylvania. 620 pp. Harrisburg.

1883. History of Centre and Clinton Counties, Pennsylvania. 672 pp. Philadelphia.

LINNÉ (LINNAEUS), CARL
1766. Systema naturae, vol. 1, 532 pp., 12th ed.
(Canis) mexicanus, p. 60, based on the "Xoloitzcuintli" of Hernandez (1651, p. 478), and believed to be a wolf until shown by G. M. Allen (1920, p. 478) to be a Mexican "hairless" dog.

LINSEY, JAMES H. (REV.)
1842. A catalogue of the mammals of Connecticut. Amer. Jour. Sci. 43: 345-354. New Haven.

LITTLE, JAMES A.
1890. From Kirtland to Salt Lake City. 260 pp. Salt Lake City, Utah.

LLOYD, T. W.
1929. History of Lycoming County, Pennsylvania. Vol. 1, p. 565. Hist. Pub. Co., Topeka and Indianapolis.

LOMAX, ALFRED L.
  1928.   History of pioneer sheep husbandry in Oregon. Oregon
          Hist. Quarterly 29 (2): 99-143. June.
LONG, STEPHEN H., and JAMES, EDWIN
  1823.   Account of an expedition from Pittsburgh to the Rocky
          Mountains performed in the years 1819 and 1820.
          2 vols. Philadelphia.
LOOMIS, F. B., and YOUNG, D. B.
  1912.   On the shell heaps of Maine. Amer. Jour. Sci. 34 (4th
          ser., art. 3): 17-42, illus. July.
LOPEZ, CARLOS M., and LOPEZ, CARLOS
  1911.   Caza Mexicana. Pp. XIX plus 629, illus.
          General account of the wolf in Mexico.
LORD, JOHN KEAST
  1866.   The naturalist in Vancouver Island and British Colum-
          bia. 2 vols., illus. Vol. 1, 358 pp., vol. 2, 375 pp.
          London.
LORING, J. ALDEN
  1905.   The Wichita buffalo range. New York Zool. Soc. 10th
          Ann. Rept., pp. 181-200, illus. New York.
LOWERY, GEORGE H., JR.
  1936.   A preliminary report on distribution of the mammals of
          Louisiana. Proc. Louisiana Acad. Sci. 3 (1): 1-39,
          illus. March.
  1943.   Check-list of the mammals of Louisiana and adjacent
          waters. Occas. Papers, Mus. Zool., Louisiana State
          Univ., 13: 234. Baton Rouge, November 22.
LUDLOW, WILLIAM
  1876.   Report of a reconnaissance from Carroll, Montana Terri-
          tory, on the Upper Missouri, to Yellowstone National
          Park, and return, made in summer of 1875. Pp. 1-
          155. Govt. Printing Office, Washington, D. C.
LUMMIS, CHARLES F.
  1920.   The Spanish pioneers. 8th ed. 292 pp., illus. Chicago.
LUTTIG, JOHN C.
  1920.   Journal of a fur trading expedition on the Upper Mis-
          souri, 1812-1813. 192 pp. Edited by Stella M.
          Drum. Missouri Hist. Society. St. Louis.

LYON, MARCUS W., JR.
  1936. Mammals of Indiana. Amer. Midland Nat. 17 (1):
          1-384, January.
MacFARLANE, RODERICK ROSS
  1905. Notes on mammals collected and observed in the north-
          ern Mackenzie River district, Northwest Territories
          of Canada . . . . Proc. U. S. Natl. Mus. 28 (1405):
          673-764.
MAILLIARD, JOSEPH
  1927. The birds and mammals of Modoc County, California.
          Proc. Calif. Acad. Sci., 4th ser., 16 (10): 261-359.
          April 27. San Francisco.
MANN, ALBERT G.
  1899. An ancient bear trap. Proc. Worcester Soc. Antiquity
          Collections, 1897-99, 16: 405. Worcester, Mass.
MANN, WALTER G., and LOCKE, S. B.
  1931. The Kaibab deer—a brief history and recent develop-
          ments. Mimeographed report with colored map. 67
          pp. Prepared by Forest Service, U. S. Dept. Agr.
          Summary of wolves removed from Kaibab National
          Forest 1911-1930.
MANNING, T. H.
  1943. Notes on the mammals of South and Central Baffin
          Island. Jour. Mamm. 24 (1): 47-59. February.
MARCY, RANDOLPH B.
  1853. Exploration of the Red River of Louisiana in the year
          1852. 33rd Cong., 2nd sess., Senate Ex. Doc. 54: 320
          pp. Washington, D. C.
  1888. Big game hunting in the wild West. Wolves. Outing
          Magazine 11 (4): 291-299, illus. January.
MARION COUNTY (OREGON)
  1887. Marion County Commissioners' Journal 9: 424.
  1892. Marion County Commissioners' Journal 12: 434.
MARTIN, HAYES F., and HOLLAND, BEULAH F.
  1939. The zoologic distribution of intraoral cancer. Sci.
          Monthly 49 (3): 262-266. September.
              Discussion of occurrence of cancer in domestic and
          wild animals, including the wolf.

MARTIN, JOHN HILL
    1877.   Chester (and its vicinity) Delaware County in Pennsyl-
            vania; with Genealogical Sketches of Some Old Fam-
            ilies. 530 pp. Philadelphia.
MASON, OTIS T.
    1902.   Traps of the American Indians—a study in psychology
            and invention. Smithsonian Inst. Annual Report
            1901: 461-473.
MASSACHUSETTS
    1853-54. Records of the Governor and Company of the Massa-
            chusetts Bay in New England. 5 vols. in 6. Boston.
            Edited by N. B. Shurtleff.
    1860.   The Massachusetts Code (Law), Ch. 18: 158. Bounty
            legislation.
    1882.   The Massachusetts Code (Law), Ch. 27: 227. Bounty
            legislation.
MATHER, KIRTLEY F.
    1940.   The future of man as an inhabitant of the earth. Sci.
            Monthly 50 (3): 193-203. March.
MATHIASSEN, THERKEL
    1931.   Contributions to the physiography of Southampton Is-
            land. Report of the Fifth Thule Expedition 1921-
            24 . . . . 1 (2): 1-31. Copenhagen.
MATTHEW, W. D.
    1930.   The phylogeny of dogs. Jour. Mamm. 11 (2): 117-
            138. May.
MATTSON, EDWIN H.
    1939.   Bounty trapping in Michigan. Fur, Fish, and Game
            (Harding Magazine) 69 (3): 8-10, illus. March.
MAXIMILIAN, PRINCE OF WIED
    1906.   Travels in the interior of North America 1830. Early
            Western Travels, vols. 22, 23, 24. Edited by Reuben
            Gold Thwaites, Cleveland.
MAXWELL, HU
    1898.   The history of Randolph County, West Virginia. 531
            pp., illus. Morgantown.
            Bounties on wolves.

MAYNARD, C. J.
   1872.   Catalogue of the mammals of Florida, with notes on
             their habits, distribution, etc. Bull. Essex Inst. 4
             (9-10): 135-150.

McATEE, W. L.
   1907.   A list of the mammals, reptiles, and batrachians of Mon-
             roe County, Indiana. Proc. Biol. Soc. Wash. 20: 1-
             16. February 25.
   1918.   A sketch of the natural history of the District of Co-
             lumbia. Bull. Biol. Soc. Wash. 1: 1-142.

McCLEERY, E. H.
   1929.   The lone killer. 35 pp. Pittsburgh, Pa.

McCLURE, JAMES R.
   1904.   Taking the census and other incidents in 1855. Trans.
             Kansas State Hist. Soc., 1903-1904, 8: 227-250.
             Topeka.

McCLURE, S. W.
   1914.   The wolf at the stockman's door. The Country Gentle-
             man 79 (46): 1845-1846, illus. November 14.

McGEHEE, JAMES STEWART
   1910.   Fremont's fourth expedition, '48-'49. The narrative of
             Micajah McGehee. Outdoor Life 25: 471-485.
             May.

McGEHEE, MICAJAH
   1891.   Rough times in rough places—a personal narrative . . . .
             The Century Magazine 41 (5): 771-780. March.

McGOWAN, DAN
   1936.   Animals of the Canadian Rockies. Pp. 27-31. New
             York.

McINTYRE, WILLIAM
   1904.   Rosengarten and sons. Amer. Jour. Pharmacy 76 (7):
             303-304.
                  On date of early manufacture of strychnine in
             United States. July.

McKNIGHT, W. J.
   1881.   Pioneer notes of Jefferson County, Pennsylvania. 670
             pp. Philadelphia.

McLEAN, JOHN
  1932. Notes of a twenty-five years' service in the Hudson Bay
        territory. P. 276. Edited by W. S. Wallace. To-
        ronto.
McWHORTER, LUCULLUS VIRGIL
  1915. The border settlers of northwestern Virginia from 1768
        to 1795, 509 pp., illus. Hamilton, Ohio.
MEAD, JAMES R.
  1899. Some natural-history notes of 1859. Trans. Kans. Acad.
        Sci. for 1897-1898 16: 280-281. Edited by the Li-
        brarian. Topeka. June.
  1906. The Saline River country in 1859. Trans. Kansas State
        Hist. Soc. 1905-1906 9: 8-19.
MEADER, STEPHEN W.
  1936. Trap lines north—a true story of the Canadian woods.
        268 pp., illus. New York.
MEARNS, EDGAR ALEXANDER
  1907. Mammals of the Mexican boundary of the United
        States. U. S. Natl. Mus. Bull. 56: 1-530.
MEINTAEFEL, P. A.
  1937. Wolf myth exploded. Christian Science Monitor. P. 5.
        July 7. Re wolves seldom if ever attacking humans.
MENAULT, ERNEST
  1870. The intelligence of animals, with illustrative anecdotes.
        368 pp., illus. New York.
          From the French of Ernest Menault.
MERRIAM, C. HART
  1882. The vertebrates of the Adirondack region, northeastern
        New York. Trans. Linnaean Society 1: 9-107. New
        York.
  1897a. Revision of the coyotes or prairie wolves, with descrip-
        tions of new forms. Proc. Biol. Soc. Wash. 2: 19-33.
        March 15.
          All of the coyotes listed are treated as distinct
        species.
  1897b. Suggestions for a New Method of Discriminating be-
        tween Species and Subspecies. Science (n.s.) 5 (122):
        753-758. May 14.

Discussion involving wolves, in reply to Roosevelt (1897).

1923. Wolf attack on humans denied. Outdoor Life 51 (6): 493. June.

MERRIAM, JOHN CAMPBELL
1912. The fauna of Rancho La Brea. 2 vols., illus. Mem. Univ. Calif. Berkeley.

MICHIGAN, STATE OF
0000. Department of Conservation, 10th Biennial Report; Game Division Separate, p. 50. Lansing.
Michigan Senate Documents for 1839. p. 128. Lansing.
Journal of the Senate for 1840. Vol. 1: 101. Lansing.

MILES, BENJAMIN C.
1895a. A letter. Forest and Stream 45 (9): 182. August 31.
1895b. The gray wolf of Tennessee. Forest and Stream 45 (9): 182.

MILLER, GERRIT S., JR.
1899. Preliminary list of New York mammals. New York State Mus. Bull. 6 (29): 271-290. October. Albany.
1912a. The names of the large wolves of northern and western North America. Smiths. Misc. Coll. 59 (15), (publ. 2093: 1-5. June 8.
1912b. The names of two North American wolves. Proc. Biol. Soc. Wash. 25: 93-96. May 4.
Name *Canis lycaon* is fixed for eastern wolf, and *Canis floridanus* is described.
1920. (Review) Lönnberg, Einar. Remarks on some South American Canidae. Arkiv för Zoologi 12 (13): 1-18, figs. 1-4. September 3, 1919. Stockholm. Jour. Mamm. 1 (3): 149-150.

MILLS, ENOS A.
1932. Watched by wild animals. 243 pp., illus. Boston and New York.

MINER, JACK
1908. How I missed a moose and deer and shot a wolf. Rod and Gun and Motor Sports in Canada 10 (6): 547-552. November.

MIVART, ST. GEORGE
   1890. Dogs, jackals, wolves, and foxes. Monograph of the
          Canidae. 216 pp. London.
MOHLER, JOHN R.
   1923. Rabies or hydrophobia. U. S. Dept. Agr., Farmers'
          Bull. 449: 1-23. Washington, D. C.
MONTAGU, M. F. ASHLEY
   1943. (Review) J. A. L. Singh and Robert Zingg, Wolf chil-
          dren and feral man. Harper and Bros., New York,
          XLI+379 pp. 1942. Amer. Anthropologist (n.s.)
          45 (3): 462-472. July-September.
MOORE, ELY
   1908. A buffalo hunt with the Miamis in 1854. Kansas Hist.
          Collections, 1907-1908 10: 402-409.
MOORE, E. G.
   1932. Alaska sheep and wolves, a timely talk. Outdoor Life
          70 (1): 16-17, 68-70.
MORTON, SAMUEL GEORGE
   1852a. Observations on the antiquity of some races of dogs.
          Proc. Acad. Nat. Sci. Phila. 5: 84-89. 1850.
   1852b. Communications on the races of dogs. Proc. Acad. Nat.
          Sci. Phila. 5: 139-140. 1851.
MORTON, THOMAS
   1637. New English Canaan or New Canaan. 188 pp. Amster-
          dam.
MULTNOMAH COUNTY (OREGON)
   1897. Multnomah County Commissioners' Journal 20: 502.
MULVANY, BARNEY
   1943. The wolves almost got me. Alaska Sportsman 9 (5):
          12-13, 16, 19, illus. May.
MURDOCH, JOHN
   1883. Expedition to Point Barrow, Alaska. 48th Cong., 2nd
          sess., Ex. Doc. 44: 93.
MURIE, ADOLPH
   1940. Ecology of the coyote in the Yellowstone. U. S. Natl.
          Park Service, Fauna Ser. No. 4, Conserv. Bull. 4:
          1-206, illus.

MURPHY, JOHN MORTIMER
1880.   Sporting adventures in the far west. 469 pp., illus. New
        York.
MURRAY, LOUISE WELLS
1908.   A history of Old Tioga and early Athens, Pennsylvania.
        656 pp. Raeder Press, Athens, Pa.
MUSGRAVE, MARK E.
1927.   The mountain lion is just a "fraidy cat." Farm and Fire-
        side 51 (6): 9. June. Springfield, Ohio.
MUSKEEGO
1887.   Wolves in Wisconsin. Forest and Stream 28: 48, Febru-
        ary 10. (20 wolves seen in one pack.)
MYERS, ALBERT COOK
1912.   Narratives of Early Pennsylvania, West New Jersey
        and Delaware, 1630-1707. Letters from Wm. Penn
        to the comm. of the Free Soc. of Traders, 1683. 476
        pp. New York, C. Scribner's Sons.
NASH, C. W.
1908.   Vertebrates of Ontario, sec. 4 (Mammals). P. 95. Dept.
        of Education, Toronto, Canada.
NATIONAL LIVESTOCK HISTORICAL ASSOCIATION
1905.   Prose and poetry of the livestock industry of the United
        States. 3 vols., illus.
NEHRING, A.
1887.   Zur Abstammung der Hunde-Rassen. Zool. Jahr Sys-
        tem. 3: 51-58. November 15.
NELSON, E. W.
1888.   Natural history collections in Alaska between the years
        1877-1881. Arctic Series of Publications, U. S. Army
        Signal Service, No. 3. 337 pp. 1887. Washington.
1916.   The larger North American mammals. Nat. Geog. Mag.
        30 (5): 385-472, with illustrations from paintings by
        Louis Agassiz Fuertes. November. Washington, D. C.
1921.   Lower California and its natural resources. Mem. Nat.
        Acad. Sci. 16 (1): 1-194, illus., 35 pls. Washington.
NELSON, E. W., and GOLDMAN, EDWARD A.
1929.   A new wolf from Mexico. Jour. Mamm. 10 (2): 165-
        166. May 9. New: *Canis nubilus baileyi* (= *Canis
        lupus baileyi*).

NEWBERRY, J. S.
  1857.   Report upon the zoology of the route. Reports expl.
          and surv. RR. route from Miss. River to Pacific
          Ocean, 1854–1855. Vol. 6 (2), pt. 4, 114 pp.
NEWHOUSE, SEWELL
  1865.   Trapper's guide. 118 pp. Oneida Community. Wall-
          ingford, Conn.
  1869.   Trapper's guide. 3rd ed., 215 pp. New York.
NEW YORK (STATE)
  1776–1900. Laws of the State of New York. Bounty legislation.
  1896.   The colonial laws of New York. 5 vols. Albany. Bounty
          legislation.
NICHOL, A. A.
  1936.   Large predator animals. Univ. Ariz. Bull. No. 3: 70.
          Tucson.
NORTON, ARTHUR H.
  1930.   The mammals of Portland, Maine, and vicinity. Proc.
          Portland Soc. Nat. Hist. 4 (pt. 1): 1–151.
NUTTALL, THOMAS
  1821.   Journal of travels into the Arkansas territory during the
          year 1819. 296 pp., illus. Philadelphia.
OGILVIE, WILLIAM (SIR)
  1913.   Early Days on the Yukon. 306 pp., illus. London: John
          Lane, The Bodley Head. New York: John Lane
          Co. Toronto: Bell & Cockburn.
OLIVER, EDMUND H. (REV.)
  1930.   The institutionalizing of the prairies. Trans. Royal Soc.
          Canada, Sec. 2, Ser. 3, vol. 24, pp. 1–21. May 30.
OLSON, SIGURD F.
  1938a. A study in predatory relationship, with particular ref-
          erence to the wolf. Scientific Monthly 46: 323–336.
  1938b. Organization and range of the pack. Ecology 19 (1):
          168–170, illus. January.
ORR, JAMES E.
  1908.   How a pioneer outwitted the wolves. Rod and Gun and
          Motor Sports in Canada 10 (5): 421. October.
ORTON, ALDA
  1942.   Wolves of the Naha. The Alaska Sportsman 8 (1): 8–9,
          28–30, illus. January.

OSBORN, HENRY FAIRFIELD
    1930.   The romance of the woolly mammoth. Natural History
            30 (3): 227-241, illus. May-June.

OSGOOD, WILFRED H.
    1904.   A biological reconnaissance of the base of the Alaska
            peninsula. U. S. Dept. Agr., Bur. Biol. Survey.
            North Amer. Fauna 24: 1-86.

PACKARD, A. S.
    1885.   Origin of the American varieties of the dog. Amer. Nat.
            19 (9): 896-901. September.

PADEREWSKI, IGNACE JAN, and LAWTON, MARY
    1938.   The Paderewski memoirs. 404 pp. New York.

PALMER, L. J.
    1941.   Animal and plant resources of Alaska. U. S. Dept. In-
            terior, Fish and Wildlife Service. Wildlife Leaflet
            176: 1-12. Mimeographed.
    1942.   A survey of available duck foods in some areas in S. E.
            Alaska. Progress Report, pp. 17-18. In files of Fish
            and Wildlife Service, Washington, D. C.

PALMER, T. S.
    1897.   Extermination of noxious animals by bounties. U. S.
            Dept. Agr. Yearbook 1896: 55-68.
    1899.   Report of Acting Chief, Division of Biological Survey.
            In Rept. Sec'y. Agr. 1899, pp. 59-70.
    1912.   Chronology and index of the more important events in
            American game protection, 1776-1911. U. S. Dept.
            Agr., Biol. Survey Bull. 41: 1-62.

PANCOAST, CHARLES EDWARD
    1930.   A Quaker forty-niner—the adventures of Charles Ed-
            ward Pancoast on the American frontier. 402 pp.
            Edited by Anna Paschall Hannum, with a foreword
            by John Bach McMaster. Philadelphia.

PARKER, R. R.
    1926.   The susceptibility of the coyote (Canis lestes) to tula-
            remia. Repts. U. S. Public Health Service 41 (28):
            1407-1410.

PARKER, SAMUEL (REV.)
>   1842.   Journal of an exploring tour beyond the Rocky Moun-
>   tains in the years 1835-37. 3d ed., 408 pp., with a
>   map of Oregon Territory. Ithaca, New York.

PARKINSON, JOHN
>   1640.   Theatrum Botanicum. 1755 pp. 1 vol. in 2. London.

PATTIE, JAMES O.
>   1905.   The personal narrative of James O. Pattie, of Kentucky,
>   during an expedition from St. Louis through the vast
>   regions between that place and the Pacific Ocean, and
>   thence back through the city of Mexico to Vera Cruz,
>   during journeyings of six years. . . . [A reprint of the
>   original edition of 1831] in R. G. Thwaite's Early
>   Western Travels, 1748-1846. . . . vol. 18, 379 pp.,
>   illus. Cleveland.

PATTON, B. S.
>   1914.   Trapping timber wolves. Oregon Sportsman 2 (11):
>   4-9. Portland, Oregon.

PATTON, C. P.
>   1939.   A preliminary list of the mammals of Virginia. Pp. 46,
>   47. Unpubl. MS. to be submitted as thesis for M.S.
>   degree in wildlife management or conservation,
>   V. P. I., Blacksburg, Va.

PAULUS AEGINETA
>   1844-47. The seven books of Paulus Aegineta. Translated from
>   the Greek by Francis Adams. 3 vols. London.

PAYAN, JULES R.
>   1927.   Will wolves take to water? Two more cases for the af-
>   firmative. Rod and Gun 29 (2): 159. July.

PEARCE, STEWART
>   1860.   Annals of Luzerne County, Pennsylvania. 554 pp. J. B.
>   Lippincott & Co., Philadelphia.

PENNANT, THOMAS
>   1793.   History of quadrupeds. 2 vols., 3d ed. London.

PENNSYLVANIA, COMMONWEALTH OF
>   1782.   Laws enacted at the second sitting of the sixth general
>   assembly of the Commonwealth of Pennsylvania. Ch.
>   17: 59.

1819. Acts of General Assembly of the Commonwealth of Pennsylvania. Ch. 79: 114. Harrisburg.

PENNSYLVANIA, STATE OF

1896. The statutes at large of Pennsylvania from 1682 to 1801. Vol. 2, p. 238.

PENNSYLVANIA STATE DEPARTMENT OF AGRICULTURE

1896. Notes on some fur-bearing animals. Report State Dept. Agr. 1896: 327-344. Harrisburg.

PENNYPACKER, SAMUEL W.

1872. Annals of Phoenixville and its vicinity: From the settlement to the year 1771. 295 pp. Philadelphia.

1882. The Pennsylvania Magazine of History and Biography. Hist. Soc. Pa. 6: 312-328. Philadelphia.

PENOBSCOT

1883. Some wolf stories. Forest and Stream 21 (1): 10-11. August 2.

PERKINS, MRS. G. A. (JULIA ANNA SHEPARD)

1870. Early times on the Susquehanna. 287 pp. Malette & Reed, Binghampton.

PETERS, DeWITT CLINTON

1858. Life and adventures of Kit Carson. 534 pp. New York.

PETERSON, WILLIAM J.

1940. Wolves in Iowa. The Iowa Journal of History and Politics 38 (1): 50-93. January.

PICKENS, A. L.

1928. Mammals of upper South Carolina. Jour. Mamm. 9 (2): 155-157. May.

PIERCE, JAMES

1823a. A memoir on the Catskill Mountains. Amer. Jour. Sci. and Arts (Ser. 1) 6: 86-97.

1823b. Notice of the alluvial district of New Jersey. Amer. Jour. Sci. and Arts 6: 237-242.

PIERCE, MILTON P.

1885. Hybrid wolves. Forest and Stream 24: 426-427. June 25.

PIKE, ZEBULON

1932. Zebulon Pike's Arkansaw Journal. 200 pp. Edited by Hart and Hulbert. Denver.

PLUTARCH
    1876.   Lives. A. D. 100. 688 pp. Translated by Arthur Hugh Clough.
POCOCK, R. I.
    1935.   The races of *Canis lupus*. Proc. Zool. Soc. London, pt. 3, pp. 647-686, illus. September.
          General review, with original descriptions of *Canis lupus arctos* and *Canis lupus orion*.
    1937.   Natural History. Mammalia. 1897 ed. 771 pp. Edited by Charles Tate Regan. London.
POCOCK, ROGER S.
    1923.   The wolf trail. 323 pp. New York.
POLICE, ROYAL NORTHWEST MOUNTED
    1919.   Report of the Bathurst Inlet Patrol, 1917-1918. Pp. 13, 40. Ottawa.
PORSILD, ERLING
    1936.   The reindeer industry and the Canadian Eskimo. Geogr. Jour. 88 (1): 1-19, illus. July.
PORTER, J. HAMPDEN
    1903.   Wild beasts. 380 pp., illus. Charles Scribner and Sons, New York.
PREBLE, EDWARD A.
    1902.   A biological investigation of the Hudson Bay region. U. S. Dept. Agr., Bur. Biol. Survey. North Amer. Fauna No. 22, 140 pp. Washington, D. C.
    1908.   A biological investigation of the Athabaska-Mackenzie Region. U. S. Dept. Agr., Bur. Biol. Survey. North Amer. Fauna No. 27, 222 pp. Washington, D. C
    1911.   Report on condition of elk in Jackson Hole, Wyoming, in 1911. U. S. Dept. Agr., Biol. Survey Bull. No. 40, 23 pp., illus. December 21. Washington, D. C.
PRICE, WILLIAM W.
    1893.   Notes on a collection of mammals from Sierra Nevada Mountains. Zoe 4 (4): 315-332. December 21.
QUINN, DAVIS
    1930.   The antelope's S.O.S. 16 pp., 1 map. Emergency Conserv. Comm., New York City, New York.
RAINE, WILLIAM MacLEOD, and BARNES, WILL C.
    1930.   Cattle. 340 pp. New York.

RANDALL, HENRY S.
1858. The life of Thomas Jefferson. 3 vols. Derby and Jackson, New York.
RATHBUN, MARY J.
1918. The Grapsoid crabs of North America. U. S. Natl. Mus. Bull. 97: 1-461. Washington, D. C.
Fiddler crabs being eaten by wolves (*Canis n. rufus*).
RAY, MRS. GEORGE R.
1940. The mad wolf at Fort Churchill. The Beaver, Outfit 271 (2): 30. September, Winnipeg.
RAY, P. H., and MURDOCH, JOHN
1885. Report of The International Polar Expedition to Point Barrow, Alaska. 1 vol. 695 pp. Washington, D. C.
REEKS, HENRY
1870. Notes on the zoology of Newfoundland. The Zoologist (Ser. 2) 5: 2033-2049. March.
RHOADS, SAMUEL N.
1894. A reprint of The North American Zoology by George Ord, pp. 290-361; Appendix 1-52. Taken from Mr. Ord's private, annotated copy. Published by the author. Haddonfield, N. J.
1895. Notes on the mammals of Monroe and Pike Counties, Pennsylvania. Proc. Acad. Nat. Sci. Phila. 1894: 393.
1896. Contributions to the zoology of Tennessee. No. 3, Mammals. Proc. Acad. Nat. Sci. Phila. 1896: 200.
1897a. A contribution to the mammalogy of central Pennsylvania. Proc. Acad. Nat. Sci. Phila., pp. 220-226. April.
1897b. A contribution to the mammalogy of northern New Jersey. Proc. Acad. Nat. Sci. Phila., pp. 23-33.
1899. Snails on the bill of fare. Forest and Stream 53: 206.
1903. Mammals of Pennsylvania and New Jersey. 266 pp. Philadelphia.
RICHARDSON, JOHN
1829. Fauna Boreali Americana. Part 1, pp. XLVI plus 300 pp., illus.
1836. Zoological remarks, appendix, of narrative of the Arctic Land expedition . . . . pp. 492, 493. London.

1839.   The Zoology of Capt. Beechey's voyage of the Blossom
      1825-28. 186 pp., illus. London.
      New: *Canis lupus* var. *fusca*.

RIDER, SIDNEY S.
1904.   The lands of Rhode Island as they were known to
      Caunounicus and Miantunnomu when Roger Wil-
      liams came in 1636. 297 pp., illus. Providence, R. I.

RIGGS, THOMAS, JR.
1920.   Annual report of the Governor of Alaska on Alaska
      game law, 1919. U. S. Dept. Agr., Dept. Circ. 88:
      1-18.

RISTER, CARL COKE
1928.   The southwestern frontier, 1865-1881. 336 pp. Cleve-
      land.

ROBERTS, N. G.
1939.   The tricks of trapping wolves. Forest and Outdoors 35
      (11): 340-341, 1 photo. Montreal.

ROE, F. G.
1939.   From dogs to horses among the western Indian tribes.
      Trans. Royal Society of Canada, Sec. II, Ser. 3, vol.
      33, pp. 209-275.

ROGERS, HARRISON G.
1918.   The Ashley-Smith explorations and the discovery of a
      central route to the Pacific, 1822-1829, with the orig-
      inal journals, edited by Harrison Clifford Dale. 352
      pp. Cleveland.

ROLLINAT, RAYMOND
1929.   Le loup commun. Revue d'Histoire Naturelle, vol. 10,
      pt. 1, nos. 4, 7, 9, pp. 105-129, 209-238, 289-308.

ROMER, ALFRED SHERWOOD
1933.   Man and the vertebrates. 405 pp. Chicago. 3rd Ed.
      1941.

ROOSEVELT, THEODORE
1885.   Hunting trips of a ranchman. 318 pp. The Medora edi-
      tion. New York.
1893.   The wilderness hunter. Pp. 386, 396, 403, 409.
1895.   Hunting in Many Lands. Hunting in the cattle country.
      447 pp. A book of the Boone and Crockett Club.
      New York.

1897. A Layman's Views on Specific Nomenclature. Science (n.s.) 5 (122): 685-688. April 30.

1900. Hunting trips of a ranchman. 296 pp. New York and London.
(This is probably a reprint of the 1885 edition and not so limited as to copies as the Medora edition, which was only 500 copies.)

1903. The winning of the West. 6 vols. Edition de luxe. Philadelphia.

1904. Hunting trips of a ranchman. 348 pp. The Statesman edition. New York.

1905. A wolf hunt in Oklahoma. Scribner's Mag. 38 (5): 513-532.

ROOSEVELT, THEODORE, VAN DYKE, T. S., ELLIOT, D. G., and STONE, A. J.
1902. The deer family. Macmillan Company, New York. Pp. i-ix; 1-334, illus.; 44, 305-307, 319.

ROSS, ALEXANDER
1849. Adventures of the first settlers on the Oregon, or Columbia, River .... 352 pp. London.

1855. The fur hunters of the Far West. 2 vols. London.

1904. Alexander Ross's adventures of the first settlers on the Oregon or Columbia River, 1810-1813. Early Western Travels 7: 332 pp. Edited by Reuben Gold Thwaites. Cleveland.

ROSS, BERNARD ROGAN
1861. A popular treatise on the fur-bearing animals of the Mackenzie River district. Canadian Nat. and Geol. and Proc. Nat. Hist. Soc. Montreal 6: 5-36. Montreal.

ROWE, ROBERT A.
1941. The receding range of the timber wolf in western Oregon. The Murrelet 22 (3): 53-54, illus. December.

1943. A recent record of the timber wolf in western Oregon. The Murrelet 24 (1): 11, January-April.

ROWELL, A. C.
1918. Wolf lore. Outdoor Life 42: 13-15, 92-93.

RUPP, I. DANIEL
　　1843-45. History of Lancaster and York Counties, Pennsylvania. P. 468. Lancaster.
RUSSELL, OSBORNE
　　1921. Journal of a trapper, or, nine years in the Rocky Mountains, 1834-1843. 149 pp. Boise, Idaho.
SABINE, JOSEPH
　　1823. Mammals and birds. Zoological appendix, Sir John Franklin's Narrative of a Journey to the Shores of the Polar Sea . . . . XVI plus 768 pp. London.
　　　　　Described *Canis lupus griseus* and *Canis lupus albus*, both of which were preoccupied names.
SAGARD, GABRIEL (FATHER)
　　1939. The long journey to the country of the Hurons. 411 pp. Edited with introduction and notes by George M. Wrong, and translated into English by H. H. Langton. The Champlain Society, Toronto, Canada. First pub. in French in 1632. 380 pp.
SAGER, ABM.
　　1839. Report of zoologist of geological survey of Ohio. Ohio State Senate No. 13 (1): 1-15. January 12.
SANDOZ, MARI
　　1935. Old Jules. 424 pp. New York.
SANFORD, LAURA G.
　　1862. History of Erie County, Pennsylvania. 347 pp. J. B. Lippincott & Co., Philadelphia.
SAWYER, E. J.
　　1940. American wolves. Western Sportsman 5 (3): 28. August.
SAY, THOMAS
　　1823 *In* Long's Expedition to Rocky Mountains 1819-1820. 2 vols. Vol. 1, 503 pp., vol. 2, 442 pp.
　　　　　New: *Canis nubilus* (= *C. l. nubilus*).
SCHAFF, MORRIS
　　1905. Etna and Kirkersville [Ohio]. 157 pp., 1 map. Boston and New York.
SCHANTZ, VIOLA S.
　　1936. An unusual specimen of red wolf. Jour. Mamm. 17 (4): 415. November.

SCHAUFFLER, BENNETT F.
   1917. Wolving—with complications. Outing 60 (2): 173-
          176. May.
SCHMID, BASTIAN
   1937. Interviewing animals. 223 pp., illus. New York. Trans.
          by Bernard Miall.
SCHOMBURGK, ROBERT
   1829. Traveling and collecting in eastern United States - New
          Jersey, Virginia, etc., 1804-   Okens Isis, Heft:
          1-570.
SCHORGER, A. W.
   1942. Extinct and Endangered Mammals and Birds of the
          Upper Great Lakes Region. Trans. Wis. Acad. Sci.,
          Arts and Letters 34: 23-44. Madison.
SCHREBER, JOHANN CHRISTIAN DANIEL von
   1774-1846. Die säugthiere in abbildungen nach der Natur mit
          beschreibungen. 8 vols., separately paged, illus. Er-
          langen.
              Name Canis lycaon used on plate 8, 1775, refer-
          ence to "loup noir" of Buffon, vol. 3, p. 353, 1776,
          and name again appears in index, p. 585, 1778.
SCHULTZ, JAMES WILLARD
   1919. Rising wolf, the white blackfoot, or Hugh Monroe's
          story of his first year on the plains. 252 pp. New
          York.
SCLATER, P. L.
   1868. On the breeding of mammals in the garden of the
          Zoological Society of London during the past twenty
          years. Proc. Zool. Soc. London. Pp. 623-626. De-
          cember 10.
   1874. On the black wolf of Thibet. Proc. Zool. Soc. London.
          Pp. 654-655, illus. November 17.
SCOTT, H. HAROLD
   1928. Carcinoma of the tonsil in a common wolf (Canis lupus).
          Proc. Zool. Soc. London, pt. 1: 43-47, illus.
SCOTT, W. E.
   1939. Rare and extinct mammals of Wisconsin. Wisconsin
          Conservation Bull. 4 (10): 21-28. October.

1940.   A seventeen-year summary of data on bountied preda-
cious animals. 33 pp., mimeographed. Wisconsin
Department of Conservation. Madison.

SCOTT, WILLIAM BERRYMAN
1913.   A history of land mammals in the Western Hemisphere.
693 pp., illus. Also 1937 ed. 786 pp. New York.

SETON, ERNEST THOMPSON
1907.   The habits of wolves. American Magazine 64 (6): 636-
645, illus. October.
1929.   Lives of game animals. 4 vols., each in 2 pts.
1937.   Great historical animals. Preface, pp. v, ix. New York.

SETTLE, DIONISE
1810.   The second voyage of Master Martin Frobisher, 1577.
Hakluyt 3: 62, new ed. London.

SETTLE, RAYMOND W.
1940.   The march of the mounted riflemen. 380 pp., illus. Arthur H. Clarke Co., Glendale, Calif.

SEWALL, SAMUEL
1868.   The history of Woburn, Middlesex County, Massachusetts, 1640-1860. 657 pp. Wiggin & Lunt, Boston.

SHANTZ, HOMER LeROY, and PIEMEISEL,
ROBERT LOUIS
1917.   Fungus fairy rings in eastern Colorado and their effect
on vegetation. Jour. Agr. Research 9 (5): 191-246,
illus., U. S. Dept. Agr., Washington, D. C. October
29.

SHEFFY, L. F.
1929.   The lobo as a factor in the cattle industry. The Cattle-
man 15 (10): 94-99.

SHELDON, CAROLYN
1936.   The mammals of Lake Kedgemakooge and vicinity,
Nova Scotia. Jour. Mamm. 17 (3): 207-215. August.

SHELDON, CHARLES
1930.   The wilderness of Denali. 412 pp. New York and
London.

SHELFORD, V. E.
1942.   Biological control of rodents and predators. Scientific
Monthly, 55: 331-341. October. Illus.

SHEPARD, ERNEST E.
  1940. Wolves kill foxes. Hunting and Fishing in Canada 6
        (11): 37. Montreal.
SHEPHERD, SAMUEL
  1792-1803. Statutes at large of Virginia. 3 vols. Richmond.
SHIRAS, GEORGE, III
  1921. The wild life of Lake Superior, past and present. Na-
        tional Geographic Magazine 40 (2): 113-204, illus.
        August.
SHOCKWILL, GEORGE ARCHIE
  1898. Wolf children. Lippincott Monthly Magazine, 61: 115-
        125; Philadelphia, January-June.
SHOEMAKER, HENRY WHARTON
  1913. Stories of Pennsylvania animals. Reprinted from Al-
        toona Tribune. Pp. 5-6. Altoona, Pa.
  1914. Black Forest souvenirs. 404 pp. Reading, Pa.
  1915. Wolf days in Pennsylvania. Altoona.
  1917-19. Extinct Pennsylvania animals. 2 vols. Altoona.
SHUFELDT, R. W.
  1897. Chapters on the natural history of the United States.
        472 pp. New York and Philadelphia.
SILVER, JAMES
  1933. Hunting the den of the timber wolf. The Northern
        Sportsman 3 (12): 3-4, 14. April. Munising, Mich.
SIMMS, B. T., McCAPES, A. M., and MUTH, O. H.
  1932. Salmon poisoning—transmission and immunization ex-
        periments. Jour. Amer. Veterinary Medical Assoc.
        81 (n.s.) 34 (1): 26-36. July.
SIMPSON, GEORGE GAYLORD
  1943. Mammals and the nature of continents. Amer. Jour. Sci.
        241 (1): 1-31. January.
SINGER, DANIEL J.
  1914. Big game fields of America, North and South. 368 pp.,
        illus. New York.
SINGH, J. A. L., and ZINGG, ROBERT M.
  1942. Wolf children and feral man. Pp. XLI plus 379, illus.
        Harper & Bros., New York.

SKINNER, MILTON P.
  1924.   The American antelope. Jour. Mamm. 3 (2): 82-105.
          April 15. (Reprinted as separate from Jour. Mamm.
          by Roosevelt Wild Life Exp. Station, Syracuse, New
          York. 32 pp.)
  1927.   Predatory and fur bearing animals of Yellowstone Park.
          Roosevelt Wild Life Bull. 4 (2): 156-281. June.
SLAUGHTER, GERTRUDE (MRS. ELIZABETH TAYLOR)
  1939.   Calabria, the first Italy. 330 pp., illus. Madison, Wis.
SLEEMAN, SIR W. H. (MAJOR GENERAL)
  1888.   Wolves nurturing children in their dens. The Zoologist,
          3d ser., 12: 87-98. London.
SMART, GRAYDON F.
  1931.   A wolf pack howls in his back yard. American Magazine
          111 (2): 81, 129. February.
SMITH, CHARLES HAMILTON
  1846.   Dogs. 2 vols. The Naturalist's Library, vols. 18-19.
          Edinburgh.
SMITH, JAMES
  1870.   An account of the remarkable occurrences in the life and
          travels of Col. James Smith during his captivity with
          the Indians, in the years 1755-59. With an appendix
          of illustrative notes by William M. Darlington. 190
          pp. Cincinnati.
SMITH, JOHN (CAPTAIN)
  1884.   Captain John Smith's works 1608-1631. Edited by Ed-
          ward Arber. Birmingham. CXXXVI plus 948 pp.,
          with map.
              A compilation of the works of Captain John
          Smith.
SMITH, R. W.
  1883.   History of Armstrong County, Pennsylvania. P. 30.
          Waterman, Watkins & Co., Chicago.
SMITH, SAMUEL
  1765.   The history of the colony of Nova-Caesaria or New Jer-
          sey... 573 pp. Burlington, N. J., and Philadelphia, Pa.
SNYDER, L. L.
  1928.   The mammals of the Lake Abitibi region. Univ. of To-
          ronto Studies, Biol. Series No. 32, pp. 7-15.

SOPER, J. DEWEY
    1928. A faunal investigation of southern Baffin Island. Nat. Mus. Canada Bull. 53 (Biol. Ser. 15): 28-76. Ottawa.
    1940. Eskimo dogs of the Canadian Arctic. Canad. Geog. Jour. 20 (2): 101, 103. February. Ottawa.
    1941. History, range, and home life of the northern bison. Ecological Monographs 11: 347-412. October.
    1942. Mammals of Wood Buffalo Park, northern Alberta, and District of Mackenzie. Jour. Mamm. 23 (2): 119-145, illus. May.

SPEELMAN, S. R., and WILLIAMS, J. O.
    1926. Breeds of dogs. U. S. Dept. Agr. Farmers' Bulletin 1491: 1-46, 34 figs. May.

SPEER, OTIS H.
    1939. Wise old wolves. The Alaska Sportsman 5 (2): 25-27. February.
    1944. A foot in a trap—a head in a snare. Alaska Sportsman, 10 (1): 12-13, 28-29, illus. January.

SPERRY, CHARLES C.
    1939. Food habits of peg-leg coyotes. Jour. Mamm. 20 (2): 190-194. May.

STANWELL-FLETCHER, JOHN F.
    1942. Three years in the wolves' wilderness. Natural History 49 (3): 137-147, illus. March. New York.

STANWELL-FLETCHER, JOHN F., and THEODORA C.
    1940. Naturalists in the wilds of British Columbia. The Sci. Monthly 50 (1): 17-32; 50 (2): 128-131.
    1943. Some accounts of the flora and fauna of the Driftwood Valley region of north central British Columbia. British Columbia Prov. Mus., Occas. Papers No. 4, 97 pp., illus.

STEARNS, W. A.
    1883. Notes on the natural history of Labrador. Proc. U. S. Natl. Mus. 6: 111-137.

STEBLER, A. M.
    1944. The status of the wolf in Michigan. Journ. Mammalogy, 25 (1): 37-43.

STEELE, JOHN
  1930.   Across the plains in 1850. 227 pp. Edited with intro-
          duction and notes by Joseph Schaefer, Supt. of State
          Hist. Soc. of Wisconsin. Chicago.
STEFANSSON, VILHJALMUR
  1928.   The standardization of error. 110 pp. London.
STEINEL, ALVIN T.
  1927.   History of Colorado 2 (Ch. 12, The Range Livestock
          Industry): 668. Denver.
STEPHENS, FRANK
  1906.   California mammals. 351 pp. San Diego.
STERLING, E.
  1883.   The old settlers again. Forest and Stream 21 (18): 348.
          November 29.
STEVENSON, PAUL HUSTON
  1939.   Factors in early human emergence. The Scientific
          Monthly 49 (3): 258. September.
STEWART, AGNES
  1928.   The journey to Oregon—a pioneer girl's diary. Intro-
          duction and editing by Claire Warner Churchill. The
          Oreg. Hist. Quart. 29 (1): 83, 85, 88. March.
STEWART, JOSHUA THOMPSON
  1913.   Indiana County, Pennsylvania; her people past and pres-
          ent, embracing a history of the county. 2 vols., paged
          continuously. J. H. Beers & Co., Chicago.
STILES, C. W., and BAKER, EDITH CLARA
  1934.   Key-catalogue of parasites reported for carnivora (cats,
          dogs, bears, etc.) Nat. Inst. of Health, U. S. Treas.
          Dept., Public Health Serv. Bull. 163: 1099-1124.
          Washington, D. C.
STILLMAN, DONALD
  1939.   Rod and gun. New York Herald-Tribune. January 20.
STIMSON, A. M.
  1910.   Facts and problems of rabies. Hygienic Lab., Treasury
          Dept., Public Health and Marine Hospital of U. S.
          Bull. 65. 85 pp., illus.
STOCKWELL, GEORGE ARCHIE
  1898.   Wolf-children. Lippincott's Monthly Magazine 61:
          117-124. January. Philadelphia.

STONE, WITMER, and CRAM, WILLIAM EVERETT
1902. American animals. 318 pp. New York.
STORER, TRACY I.
1931. Early trade values of skins in Montana. Jour. Mamm.
12 (1): 77-78. February.
STRANGE, JAMES BARON (2ND DUKE OF ATHOLE)
1749. Report from the committee appointed to enquire into
the state and condition of the countries adjoining to
Hudson's Bay . . . . Reports of the House of Commons, 1738-1765, 2: 213-266. April 24. London.
STRONG, WM. DUNCAN
1930. Notes on mammals of the Labrador interior. Jour.
Mamm. 11 (1): 1-10. February.
STUART, GRANVILLE
1925. Forty years on the frontier as seen in the journals and
reminiscences of Granville Stuart. 2 vols. Edited by
Paul C. Phillips. Cleveland.
STURGIS, ROBERT S.
1939. The Wichita Mountains wild life refuge. Chicago Nat.
2 (1): 9-20. Chicago Academy of Sciences. Chicago.
SUCKLEY, GEORGE, and GIBBS, GEORGE
1860. Reports of explorations and surveys to ascertain the
most practicable and economical route for a railroad
from the Mississippi River to the Pacific Ocean 1853-
55. 36th Cong., 1st sess., Senate Ex. Doc. No. 56,
vol. 12 (bk. 2, ch. 3, Zoology): 110-113, 139.
SURBER, THADDEUS
1932. The mammals of Minnesota. 84 pp., illus. Bull. Minn.
Dept. Conserv., Div. Game and Fish, St. Paul.
1942. Our wild dogs and cats. The wolves, foxes, and lynxes.
Conservation Volunteer 4 (24): 44-47. September.
St. Paul.
SUTTON, GEORGE MIKSCH, and HAMILTON,
WILLIAM J., JR.
1932. The mammals of Southampton Island. Mem. Carnegie
Mus. 12 (pt. 2, Zoology, sec. 1): 9-111. August 4.
SWANK, JAMES M.
1908. Progressive Pennsylvania. 360 pp. J. B. Lippincott &
Co., Philadelphia.

SWARTH, H. S.
  1922. Birds and mammals of the Stikine River region of northern British Columbia and southeastern Alaska (Alaska, Sergref Island). Univ. Calif. Publ. Zool. 24 (2): 125-314.
  1936. Mammals of the Atlin region, northwestern British Columbia. Jour. Mamm. 17 (4): 398-405. November.

SWEETSER, M. F.
  1876. White Mountains—a handbook for travellers. 436 pp. Boston.

SWIFT, ERNEST
  1941. The biography of a self-made naturalist. Part II. Wisconsin Conservation Bull. 6 (1): 41-52, illus. January. Madison, Wisconsin.

T., N. A.
  1887. Wolves and squirrels in Texas. Forest and Stream 29: 403. December 15.
  1888a. More about Texas wolves. Forest and Stream 29: 504. January 19.
  1888b. The howl of the wolf. Forest and Stream 30: 24. February 2.
  1888c. The ways of wolves. Forest and Stream 30: 45. February 9.

TALBOT, THEODORE
  1931. The journals of Theodore Talbot, 1843 and 1849-52; with the Fremont expedition of 1843 and with the first military company in Oregon territory, 1849-1852. 153 pp. Edited by Charles H. Carey. Portland, Oreg.
  1939. Journals. Ed. by Charles H. Carey. P. 30. Metropolitan Press, Portland, Oreg.

TAYLOR, JOSEPH HENRY
  1891. Twenty years on the trap line. Pp. 70-73. Bismarck, North Dakota, and Avondale, Pennsylvania.

TAYLOR, WALTER P., and SHAW, WILLIAM T.
  1927. Mammals and birds of Mt. Rainier National Park. 249 pp. U. S. Dept. Interior, National Park Service, Washington, D. C.

1929.   Provisional list of land mammals of the state of Washington. Occasional Papers Charles R. Conner Museum, No. 2, 32 pp. December.

TENCH, C. V.
1940.   Yellow gold and brown grizzly. Forest and Outdoors 36 (4): 133-137. April. Montreal.

TEXAS GAME, FISH AND OYSTER COMMISSION
1930.   Fur-bearers and predatory animals. Year Book on Texas Conservation of Wild Life, 1929-30, pp. 21-42.

THACHER, JAMES
1832.   History of the town of Plymouth from its first settlement in 1620 to the year 1832. 382 pp. Boston.

THOMAS, GABRIEL
1912.   The history of west New Jersey, 1698. Narratives of Early Pennsylvania, West New Jersey, and Delaware. P. 348. New York.

THOMPSON, DAVID
1916.   David Thompson's narrative of his explorations in western America, 1784-1812. 582 pp. Edited by J. B. Tyrrell. Toronto.

—————————, and HENRY, ALEXANDER
1897.   New light on the early history of the greater Northwest, 1799-1814. Manuscript journals of Alexander Henry and David Thompson. 3 vols. Edited by Elliott Coues. New York.

THOMPSON, ERNEST E.
1886.   A list of the mammals of Manitoba. Trans. Manitoba Sci. and Hist. Soc. 23: 1-26. May. Toronto.

THOMPSON, ZADOCK
1853.   Natural history of Vermont. 4 pts. in 1 vol. Burlington.

THORNTON, THOMAS (COLONEL)
1806.   A sporting tour through various parts of France in the year 1802. . . . In a series of letters to the Right Hon. Earl of Darlington. To which is prefixed an account of French wolf-hunting. 2 vols. in one. London.

THRASHER, HALSEY (Pseudonym)
1868.   The hunter and trapper. 91 pp. New York.

THWAITES, REUBEN GOLD
    1902.   Daniel Boone. 257 pp. New York.
    1904-07.   Early Western travels 1748-1846. 32 vols. The Ar-
            thur H. Clark Co., Cleveland, Ohio.
TOME, PHILIP
    1928.   Pioneer life; or, Thirty years a hunter. 173 pp. Aurand
            Press, Harrisburg.
TOMKINS, IVAN R.
    1931.   Some late records of the timber wolf in Pennsylvania.
            Jour. Mamm. 12 (2): 165. May.
TOPSELL, EDWARD
    1607.   The historie of fovr-footed beastes. 757 pp. London.
TOWNSEND, JOHN K.
    1839 and 1905.   Narrative of a journey across the Rocky Moun-
            tains to the Columbia River. 352 pp. Philadelphia.
            Also Thwaites Early Western Travels, vol. 21, 336
            pp. 1905. Cleveland.
    1850.   On the giant wolf of North America. Jour. Acad. Nat.
            Sci. Phila. (ser. 2) 2, 334 pp. Philadelphia.
                New: *Lupus gigas* (= *C. l. fuscus*).
TOWNSHEND, FREDERICK TRENCH
    1875.   Wild life in Florida, with a visit to Cuba. 319 pp. Lon-
            don.
TRAUP, NORMAN E.
    1888.   Wolves nurturing children. The Zoologist (3d ser.) 12
            (138): 221. London.
TRAUTMAN, MILTON B.
    1939.   The numerical status of some mammals throughout his-
            toric time in the vicinity of Buckeye Lake, Ohio. Ohio
            Jour. Sci. 39 (3): 133-143. May.
TREMBLEY, HELEN LOUISE, and BISHOP, F. C.
    1940.   Distribution and hosts of some fleas of economic impor-
            tance. Jour. Economic Entomology 33 (4): 701-703.
            September 28.
TRIPPE, T. MARTIN
    1871.   Some differences between western and eastern birds.
            Amer. Nat. 5: 632-636.
                Incidental reference to retirement with advancing
            civilization of buffalo, elk, antelope, deer, and wolf.

TRUE, ALFRED CHARLES
1937. A history of agricultural experimentation and research in the United States, 1607-1925 . . . . U. S. Dept. Agr. Misc. Publ. 251: 1-321. Washington, D. C.

TRUMBULL, BENJAMIN
1818. A complete history of Connecticut 1630-1764. 2 vols. New Haven.

TURNBULL, T.
1913. T. Turnbull's travels from the United States across the plains to California. Edited by Frederick L. Paxon. Proc. Wis. State Hist. Soc. Pp. 151-225.

TURNER, L. M.
1886. Contributions to the natural history of Alaska. Arctic Series of Publications, 226 pp. Signal Service, U. S. Army.

UMFREVILLE, EDWARD
1790. The present state of Hudson's Bay. 230 pp. London.

UNION, COUNTY OF (OREGON)
1885. County Commissioners' Journal C: 526.

UNITED STATES COMMISSIONER OF AGRICULTURE
1863. Condition and prospects of sheep husbandry in the United States. Report for the year 1862. Pp. 2-285. Washington, D. C.

UNITED STATES CONGRESS
1929. Control of predatory animals. 70th Cong., 2nd sess., House Doc. No. 496. 17 pp.
1930. Control of predatory animals. Hearing before the Committee on Agriculture, House of Representatives, 71st Cong., 2nd sess., on H. R. 9599, by Mr. Scott Leavitt, of Montana. April 29 and 30 and May 1. 100 pp.
1936. The western range. Senate Doc. No. 109, 74th Cong., 2nd sess. 620 pp.
1939. Hearings before a sub-committee of the Committee on Indian Affairs, U. S. Senate, 74th Cong., 2nd sess., pt. 36. Alaska (including reindeer): 19,977, 19,981, 19,982, 20,329, 20,334.

UNITED STATES DEPARTMENT OF AGRICULTURE
1899.   Report of the Acting Chief of the Division of Biological
        Survey Work. Rept. of the Sec. of Agr. Pp. 59-70.
1908.   Report of the Secretary of Agriculture to the President,
        1907. Bureau of Biological Survey, U. S. Dept. Agr.
        Yearbook 1907. Pp. 95-101. Washington, D. C.
UNITED STATES GOVERNMENT
1918.   Joint report upon the survey and demarcation of the in-
        ternational boundary between the United States and
        Canada. P. 282. Washington, D. C.
1940.   The status of wildlife in the United States. Report of
        the special committee on the conservation of wildlife
        sources. 76th Cong., 3d sess., Senate Report 1203.
        457 pp.
UNITED STATES HOUSE OF REPRESENTATIVES
1939.   Congressional Record 84 (156): 14,969. 76th Cong.,
        1st sess. August 2.
UNITED STATES SENATE
1907.   Report on work of the Biological Survey. 60th Cong.,
        1st sess., Document No. 132. 29 pp. December 21.
1930.   Control of Predatory Animals (Confidential Report).
        Hearing before the Committee on Agriculture and
        Forestry. U. S. Senate, 71st Congress, 2d sess., Sen-
        ate Report 3483, 28 pp. May 8.
1931.   Control of Predatory Animals. Hearings before the
        Committee on Agriculture and Forestry, U. S. Sen-
        ate, 71st Congress, 2d and 3d sessions, Senate Report
        3483, May 8, 1930, and January 28 and 29, 1931.
        192 pp.
VALLEJO, GUADALUPE
1890.   Ranch and mission days in Alto, California. Century
        Illustrated Monthly Magazine (n.s.) 19: 183-192.
        December.
VAN WAGENEN, J. A.
1907.   Chased by wolves. Sports Afield 39 (3): 245-246. Sep-
        tember.
VICTOR, FRANCES FULLER (MRS.)
1870.   The river of the West. 602 pp. Hartford, Conn., and
        San Francisco, Calif.

VIRGINIA
   1804-1938. Laws. (Bounty legislation.)
   1849.   The Virginia Code (Law). P. 456. (Bounty legislation.)
   1887.   The Code of Virginia (Law), Section 834: 256. (Bounty
           legislation.)
   1930.   The Virginia Code (Law)? Section 2729, Chapter 109.
           (Bounty legislation.)
                (See also Hening, William Waller, 1823.)
WAGGONER, GEORGE A.
   1905.   Stories of old Oregon. 292 pp. Salem.
WAILES, BENJAMIN LEONARD COVINGTON
   1854.   Report on the agriculture and geology of Mississippi.
           371 pp. Philadelphia.
WALKER, THOMAS
   1898.   Journal of Dr. Thomas Walker. Filson Club Publ. No.
           13, 84 pp. Louisville, Ky.
WALL, THOMAS LINCOLN
   1925.   Clearfield County, Pennsylvania, Present and Past.
           (Library ed.) Published by author. 296 pp. Clear-
           field, Pa.
WALLS, GORDON LYNN
   1942.   The Vertebrate Eye and its Adaptive Radiation. Cran-
           brook Institute of Science, Bull. No. 19, 785 pp.,
           illus. August. Bloomfield Hills, Mich.
WARD, HENRY GEORGE
   1828-29. Mexico in 1827. 2 vols. London.
WARDEN, D. B.
   1819.   Statistical, political, and historical account of the United
           States of North America. . . . 3 vols. Edinburgh.
WARREN, EDWARD ROYAL
   1910.   The mammals of Colorado. 300 pp. New York and
           London.
   1927.   The beaver, its work and its ways. Monog. Amer. Soc.
           Mamm. 2: 1-177, illus. Baltimore.
WASHINGTON, GEORGE
   1801.   Letters from his excellency General Washington to Ar-
           thur Young, Esq., London. 172 pp. London.

WATKINS, M. G.
   1885.   Gleanings from the natural history of the ancients. 258
          pp. London.
WATSON, JOHN F.
   1833.   Historic tales of old times. E. Littell and Thomas
          Holden, Philadelphia.
   1844.   Annals of Philadelphia and Pennsylvania. 2 vols. Phila-
          delphia.
WEBB, DAVID K., and STEVENS, JOHN M.
   1934.   Early bounty hunters of Butler County, Pennsylvania.
          27 pp. Publ. privately, Chillicothe, Ohio.
WEBB, JAMES JOSIAH
   1931.   Adventures in the Santa Fe trade. 301 pp. Ed. by Ralph
          P. Bieber. Glendale, California.
WEBB, WM. E.
   1872.   Buffalo land. 503 pp. Chicago.
WEBBER, CHARLES WILKINS
   1875.   Wild scenes and wild hunters; or the romance of sport-
          ing. 610 pp., illus. Philadelphia.
WEBSTER, E. B.
   1920.   The king of the Olympics. 227 pp., illus. Port Angeles,
          Washington.
WHEELER, OLIN D.
   1904.   The trail of Lewis and Clark. 2 vols., illus. G. P. Put-
          nam's Sons, New York and London. Vol. 2: 298,
          323, 362, 367.
WHIPPLE, A. W., EUBANK, T., and TURNER, W. W.
   1856.   Report upon the Indian tribes. U. S. Exec. Doc. 91, 33d
          Cong., 3d sess., Pac. R. R. Repts., vol. 2, 127 pp.
WHITE, BOUCK
   1913.   The call of the carpenter. 355 pp. Doubleday, Page
          & Co., Garden City, New York.
WHITE, DALE
   1944.   Man-sized wolf. Field & Stream, 48 (9): 75, illus.
          January.
WHITE, ELIJAH (DR.)
   1850.   Ten years in Oregon . . . . 430 pp. Compiled by Miss A.
          J. Allen. Ithaca, New York.

WHITE, JIM
   1906. Traps and poison. Hunter, Trader, Trapper, 13 (1): 41-42. October.

WHITE, SAM O., and RHODE, CLARENCE J.
   1939. Report on Alaska-Yukon Boundary Patrol, March 9-April 7, 9 pp. (mimeog.). Alaska Game Commission, Juneau, Alaska. In files of Fish and Wildlife Service, Washington, D. C.

WHITE, WILLIAM
   1853. Records of the Governor and Company of the Massachusetts Bay in New England. Printed by order of the Legislature, Boston, 1853, vol. 1.

WHITEHEAD, CHARLES E.
   1891. The campfires of the Everglades; or wild sports in the South. 298 pp. Edinburgh.

WHITING, A. B.
   1912. Account of a blizzard in 1856. Kansas Hist. Coll. 1911-1912, vol. 12, pp. 118-120.

WHITTAKER, J. S.
   1864. Wayne. [Annual Report of the Wayne County Agricultural Society.] 9th report State Agr. Soc. 1863. Pp. 483-485.

WHITTAKER, M. W.
   1911. Strange adventures with a wolf. Rod and Gun in Canada 12 (11): 1425-1427. April.

WIGRAM, P.
   1896. Supposititious wild man. The Field 87 (2246): 36-37. January 11. London.

WILBERT, M. I.
   1904. Progress in pharmacy. Amer. Jour. Pharmacy 76 (12): 581-591. December.

WILKES, CHARLES
   1845. Narrative of the United States exploring expedition during the years 1838, 1839, 1840, 1841, 1842. 5 vols. and an atlas. Philadelphia.

WILLIAMS, JOHN LEE
   1837. The territory of Florida—civil and natural history. 304 pp. New York.

WILLIAMS, ROGER
   1827.   A key into the language of America. 205 pp. London.
           Reprinted in Collections Rhode Island Hist. Soc. 1:
           17-163. Providence.
WILLIAMS, ROGER D.
   1895.   Hunting in Many Lands. Wolf coursing. 447 pp., illus.
           A book of the Boone and Crockett Club. New
           York.
   1909.   Hunting the gray wolf. Recreation 29 (1): 3-7, illus.
           January.
WILLIAMS, SAMUEL
   1809.   The natural and civil history of Vermont. 2 vols. 2nd
           Ed. Burlington.
WILLIAMS, SAMUEL COLE
   1928.   Early travels in the Tennessee country 1540-1800. 540
           pp. Johnson City, Tennessee.
WILLIAMSON, WILLIAM D.
   1839.   The history of the State of Maine. 2 vols.
WILLIS, A. R.
   1940.   Talking sticks. The Beaver, outfit 271: 50. June. Win-
           nipeg.
WILSON, CLIFFORD
   1937.   The wolves are always after us. Forest and Outdoors
           33 (2): 37-38, 62, illus.
WILSON, GILBERT LIVINGSTONE
   1924.   The horse and the dog in Hidatsa culture. Amer. Mus.
           Nat. Hist. Anthrop. Papers 15 (2): 125-311, illus.
           New York.
WINEMAN, ELVA
   1930.   White wolf, foe of cattlemen, is dead. Montana Wild
           Life 2 (12): 6-7. Helena, Montana.
WINSHIP, GEORGE PARKER
   1896.   The Coronado expedition, 1540-1542. 14th Ann. Rept.
           Bur. Ethnology to Sec. Smithsonian Inst., 1892-1893,
           pp. 329-613, illus. In 2 parts. Washington, D. C.
WOOD, ABRAHAM
   1928.   A letter. Samuel Cole Williams' Early Travels in the
           Tennessee Country. P. 27. Johnson City, Tennessee.

WOOD, NORMAN A.
   1914.   An annotated check-list of Michigan mammals. Univ.
           Mich. Mus. Zool., Occas. Papers 4: 1-13. April 1.
   1922.   The mammals of Washtenaw County, Michigan. Univ.
           Mich. Mus. Zool., Occas. Papers 123: 1-23. July 10.
WOOD, WILLIAM
   1635.   New England's prospect. 83 pp. London.
WOODHOUSE, S. W.
   1852.   The North American jackal—*Canis frustror*. Jour. Acad.
           Nat. Sci. Phila. 2 (2d ser.): 87-88.
   1853.   Report on the natural history of the country passed over
           by the exploring expedition under the command of
           Brevet Capt. L. Sitgreaves' U. S. Topographical En-
           gineers . . . . 32d Cong., 2d sess., Senate Exec. Doc.
           No. 59, 147 pp. Washington, D. C.
   1854.   Report on the natural history of the country passed over
           by the exploring expedition under command of Brevet
           Capt. L. Sitgreaves. 33d Cong., 1st sess., Senate
           Exec. Doc., 198 pp. Washington, D. C.
WRIGHT, GEORGE M.
   1935.   Big game of our national parks. Scientific Monthly 41:
           141-147, illus. August.
——————— DIXON, JOSEPH S., and THOMPSON, BEN H.
   1933   Fauna of the national parks of the United States. A pre-
           liminary survey of faunal relations in national parks.
           U. S. Dept. Interior, contribution of wildlife survey
           fauna series, 1: i-v; 1-157; illus. 44, 47, 49, 88, 94-
           95, 106, 110, 117, 122, 127-130, 139, 143, 145.
WRIGHT, R. M.
   1902.   Personal reminiscences of frontier life in southwest Kan-
           sas. Trans. Kans. State Hist. Soc. 1901-1902, 7: 47-
           83. Topeka.
XENOPHON
   1925.   Scripta Minora. The cavalry commander. 365 B. C.
           English translation by E. C. Marchant, Sub-Rector
           of Lincoln College, Oxford. A volume of the Loeb
           Classical Library. London, William Heinemann.
           463 pp. G. P. Putnam's Sons, New York.

YARHAM, E. R.
   1941.   Canada's fight for the musk oxen. Amer. Forests 47
           (9): 424–425, 448, illus. September.
YEAGER, DORR G.
   1931.   Our wilderness neighbors. 160 pp., illus. Chicago.
YEAGER, LEE E.
   1938.   Otters of the Delta Hardwood Region of Mississippi.
           Jour. Mamm. 19 (2): 195-201. May.
YOUNG, STANLEY P.
   1925.   The old wolf "Three Toes" of Harding County, South
           Dakota. Daily Science News Bull. August 13.
   1930a. Conquering wolfdom and catdom. Southwest Wilds and
           Waters 2 (1): 6-7, 47, illus. Oklahoma City.
   1930b. Hints on wolf and coyote trapping. U. S. Dept. Agr.,
           Bur. Biol. Survey Leaflet 59: 1-8, illus.; also Amer.
           Field 114 (36): 219-220.
   1934.   Our federal predator control work. Trans. 20th Ameri-
           can Game Conference, pp. 172-176.
   1940.   It's "red," but truly American. Western Sportsman 5
           (6): 10-11, 26, illus. Denver. November.
   1941a. The evolution of the steel wolf trap in North America.
           Western Sportsman 6 (3): 10-11, 30-31, illus. Den-
           ver.
   1941b. The return of the musk oxen. American Forests 47 (8):
           368-372, illus. August.
   1941c. Hints on coyote and wolf trapping. U. S. Dept. of the
           Interior, Fish and Wildlife Service Circular No. 2,
           8 pp., illus.
   1942a. Fading trails—a story of endangered wildlife. Pp. XV
           plus 279, illus. Ch. XI, The Wolf. New York.
   1942b. The war on the wolf. American Forests 48 (11): 492-
           495, 526, illus.; 48 (12): 552-555, 572-574, illus.
   1943.   What was the early Indian dog? Amer. Forests, 49 (12):
           571-573, 594, 603; 4 illus. December.
   1944.   What was the early Indian dog? Amer. Forests, 50 (1):
           26-28, 32, 45; 4 illus. January.
ZINGG, ROBERT M.
   1941.   India's wolf children—two human infants reared by
           wolves. Scientific American 164 (3): 135-137, illus.
           March.

PHOTOGRAPHS OF SKULLS OF
NORTH AMERICAN WOLVES

Plate 88. *Canis lupus tundrarum* Miller; male adult; Mead River, near Point Barrow, Alaska. (No. 4053, Colo. Mus. Nat. Hist.) Note relatively large second and third upper premolars. [One-third natural size]

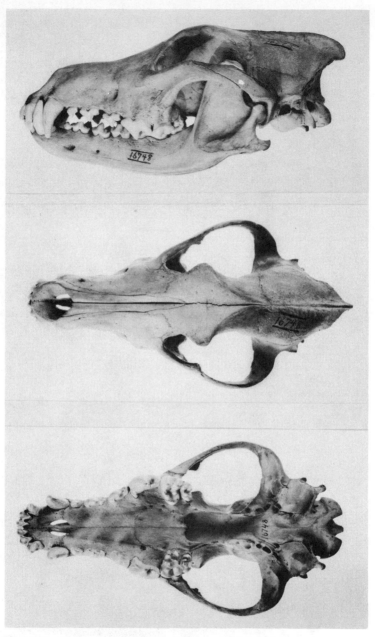

Plate 89. *Canis lupus tundrarum* Miller; type; female adult; Point Barrow, Alaska. (No. 16748, U. S. Nat. Mus.) Note relatively large second and third upper premolars. [One-third natural size]

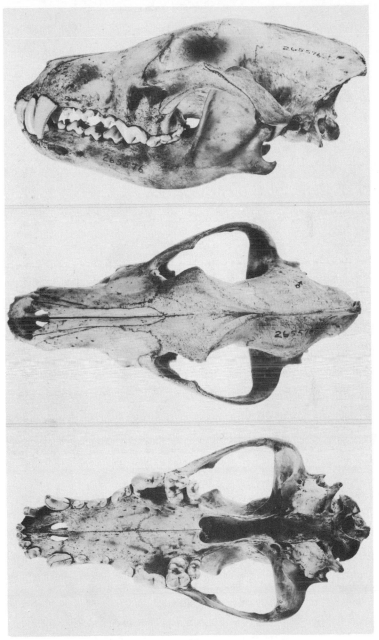

Plate 90. *Canis lupus pambasileus* Elliot; male adult; Big Delta, Tanana River, Alaska. (No. 265576, U. S. Nat. Mus., Biological Surveys collection.) Note large size and tendency toward elongation. [One-third natural size]

591

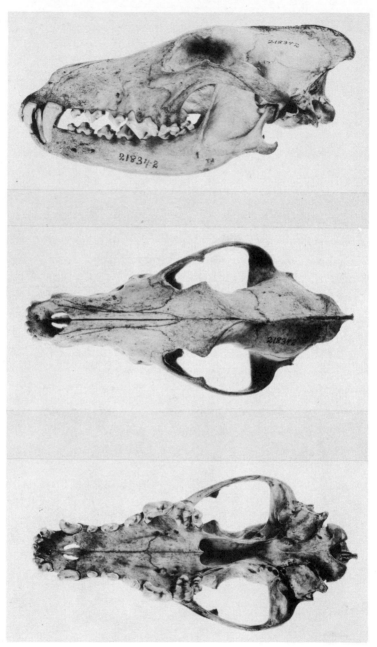

Plate. 91. *Canis lupus pambasileus* Elliot; female adult; Tanana, Alaska.
(No. 218342, U. S. Nat. Mus.) Note large size and tendency toward
elongation. [One-third natural size]

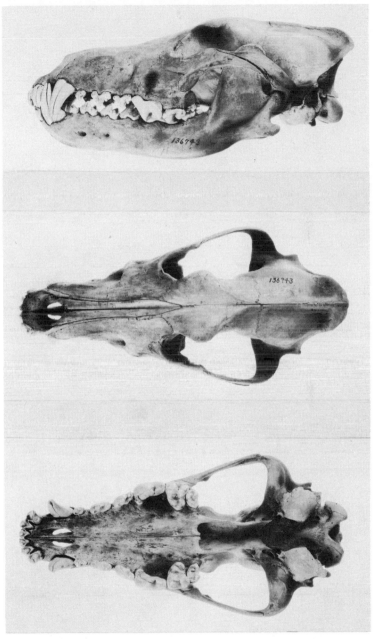

Plate 92. *Canis lupus alces* Goldman; topotype; male subadult; Kachemak
Bay, Alaska. (No. 136743, U. S. Nat. Mus., Biological Surveys collection.) Note large size, slightly spreading zygomata, broad supraoccipital
shield, and relatively small teeth. [One-third natural size]

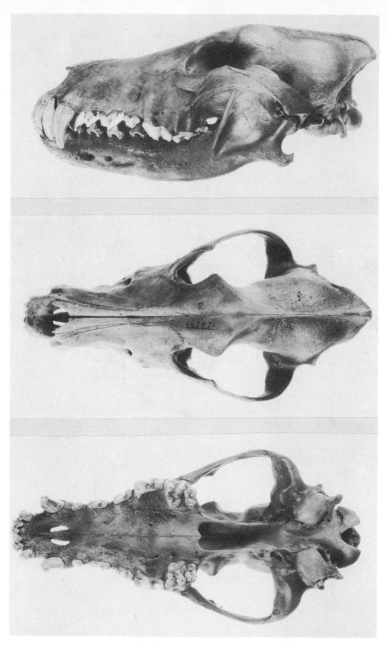

Plate 93. *Canis lupus alces* Goldman; type; female adult; Kachemak Bay, Kenai Peninsula, Alaska. (No. 147471, U. S. Nat. Mus., Biological Surveys collection.) Note large size, slightly spreading zygomata, broad supraoccipital shield, and relatively small teeth. [One-third natural size]

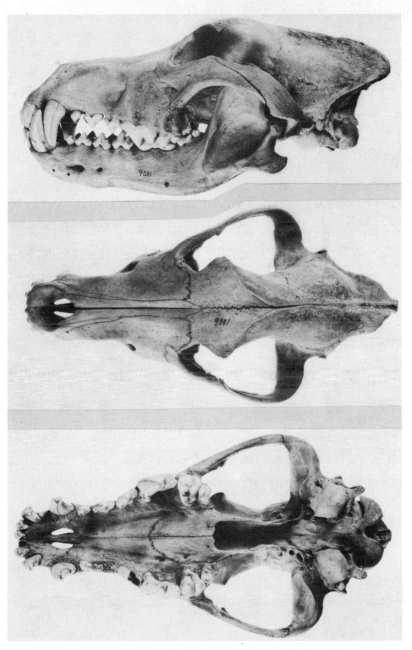

Plate 94. *Canis lupus occidentalis* Richardson; male adult; Simpson, Mackenzie, Canada. (No. 9001, U. S. Nat. Mus.) Note large size and general
massiveness. [One-third natural size]

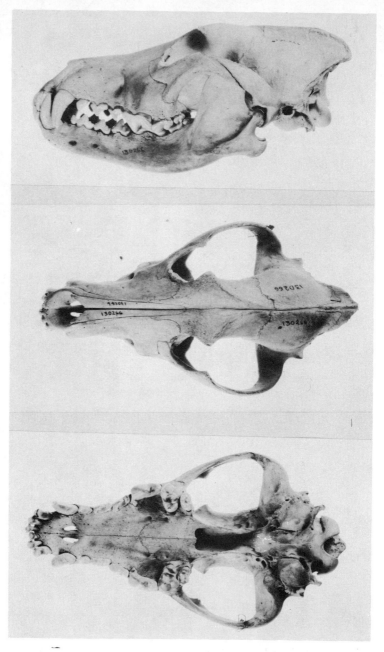

Plate 95. *Canis lupus occidentalis* Richardson; female adult; Wood Buffalo
Park, Alberta, Canada. (No. 130266, Amer. Mus. Nat. Hist.) Note large
size and general massiveness. [One-third natural size]

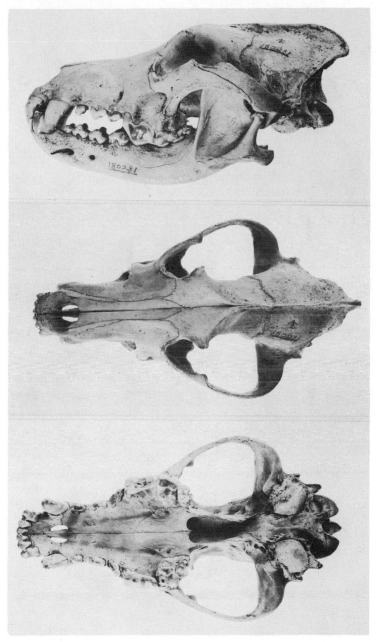

Plate 96. *Canis lupus hudsonicus* Goldman; type; male adult; head of Schultz Lake, Keewatin, Canada. (No. 180281, U. S. Nat. Mus., Biological Surveys collection.) Note medium size, broad postorbital region, and narrow, acutely pointed postorbital processes. [One-third natural size]

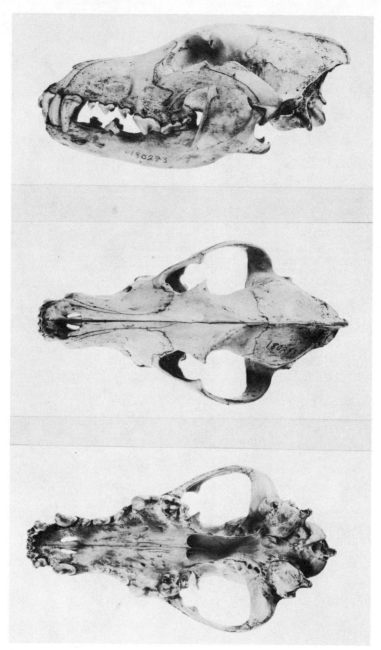

Plate 97. *Canis lupus hudsonicus* Goldman; topotype; female adult; head of Schultz Lake, Keewatin, Canada. (No. 180283, U. S. Nat. Mus., Biological Surveys collection.) Note medium size, broad postorbital region, and narrow, acutely pointed postorbital processes. [One-third natural size]

Plate 98. *Canis lupus arctos* Pocock; male adult; Ellesmere Island, Arctic America. (No. 42119, Amer. Mus. Nat. Hist.) Note narrow, highly arched braincase. [One-third natural size]

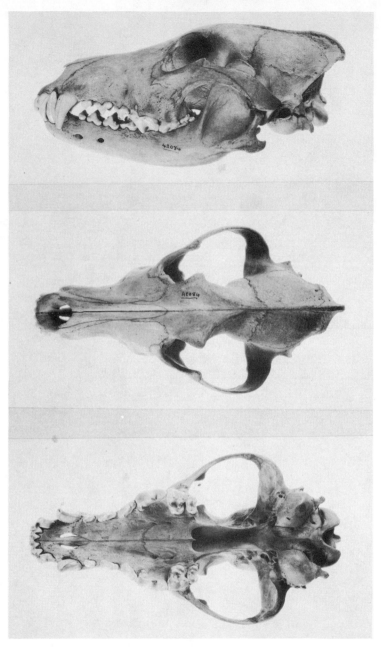

Plate 99. *Canis lupus orion* Pocock; female adult; Greenland, Arctic America. (No. 42084, Amer. Mus. Nat. Hist.) Note smaller size and narrower braincase as compared with mainland wolves. [One-third natural size]

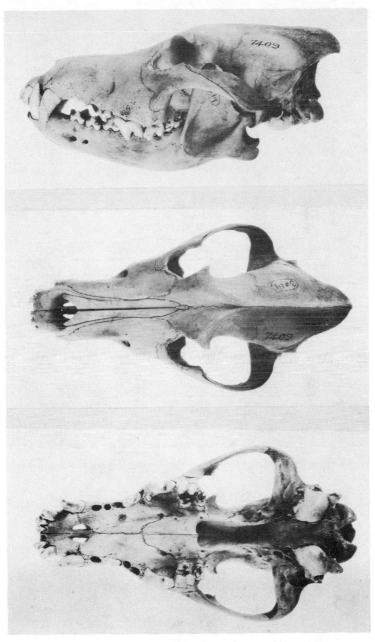

Plate 100. *Canis lupus labradorius* Goldman; male adult; Hopedale, Labrador, Canada. (No. 7409, Mus. Comp. Zool.) Note broad postorbital region. [One-third natural size]

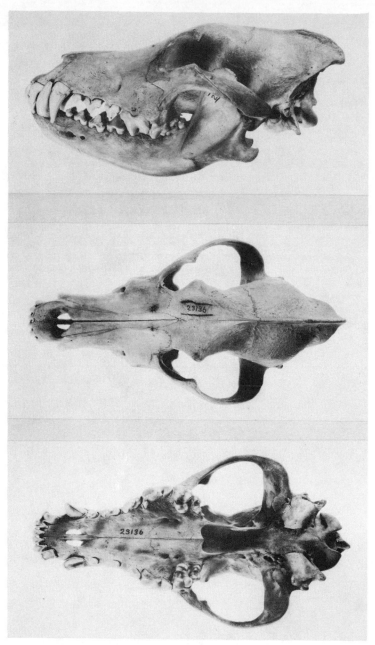

Plate 101. *Canis lupus labradorius* Goldman; type; female adult; Chimo, Quebec, Canada. (No. 23136, U. S. Nat. Mus., Biological Surveys collection.) Note broad postorbital region. [One-third natural size]

Plate 102. *Canis lupus beothucus* Allen and Barbour; probably male, adult; Newfoundland. (No. 264482, U. S. Nat. Mus., Biological Surveys collection.) Note narrow supraoccipital region and obtuse postorbital processes.
[One-third natural size]

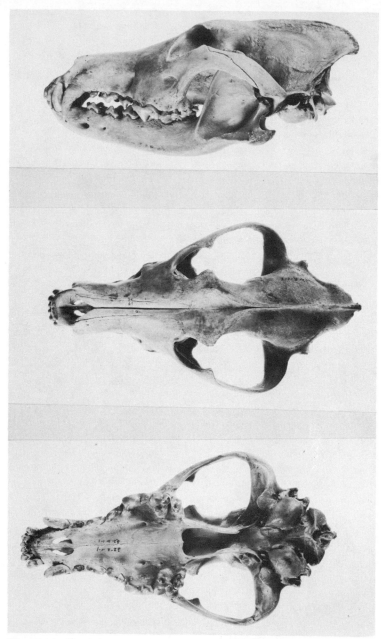

Plate 103. *Canis lupus lycaon* Schreber; male adult; Montebello, Quebec, Canada. (No. 32.2.1.1, Roy. Ont. Mus. Zool.) Note slenderness, especially of rostrum. [One-third natural size]

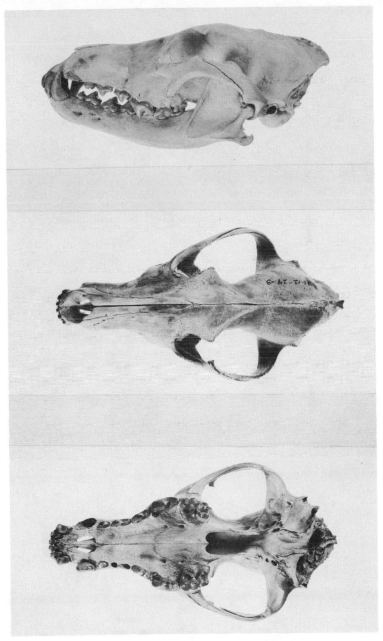

Plate 104. *Canis lupus lycaon* Schreber; female adult; Montebello, Quebec, Canada. No. 31.12.29.3, Roy. Ont. Mus. Zool.) Note slenderness, especially of rostrum. [One-third natural size]

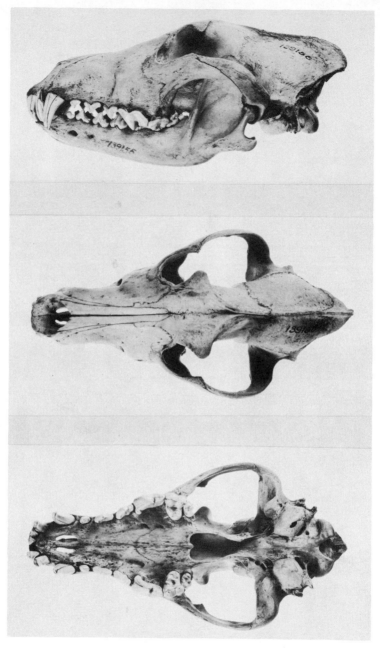

Plate 105. *Canis lupus nubilus* Say; male adult; Gove County, Kansas. (No. 139156, U. S. Nat. Mus., Biological Surveys collection.) Note narrow supraoccipital shield and posterior projection of inion well behind plane of occipital condyles. [One-third natural size]

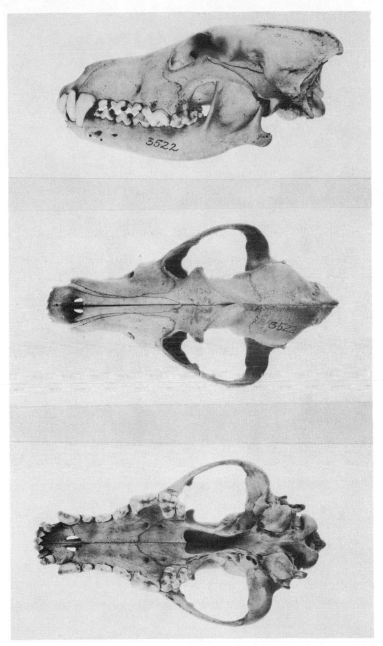

Plate 106. *Canis lupus nubilus* Say; female adult; Platte River Nebraska. (No. 3522/3575, U. S. Nat. Mus.) Note narrow supraoccipital shield and posterior projection of inion well behind plane of occipital condyles. [One-third natural size]

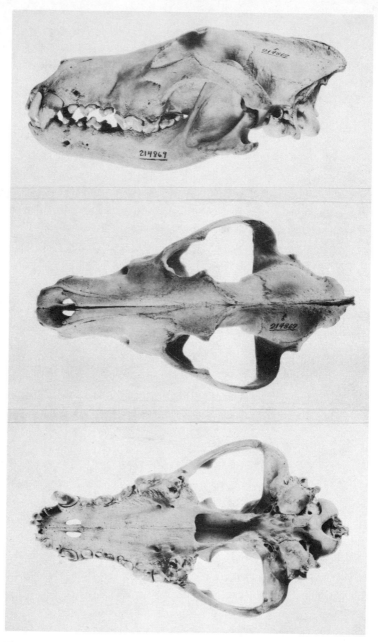

Plate 107. *Canis lupus irremotus* Goldman; type; male adult; Red Lodge, Carbon County, Montana. (No. 214869, U. S. Nat. Mus., Biological Surveys collection.) Note narrow postorbital constriction. [One-third natural size]

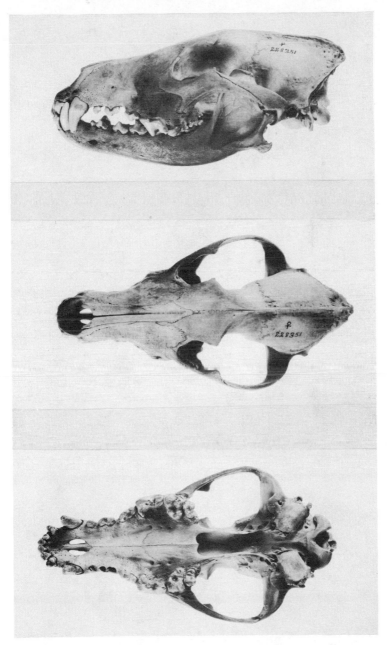

Plate 108. *Canis lupus irremotus* Goldman; female adult; Continental Divide, Montana side, 20 miles east of Leadore, Idaho. (No. 228351, U. S. Nat. Mus., Biological Surveys collection.) Note narrow postorbital constriction. [One-third natural size]

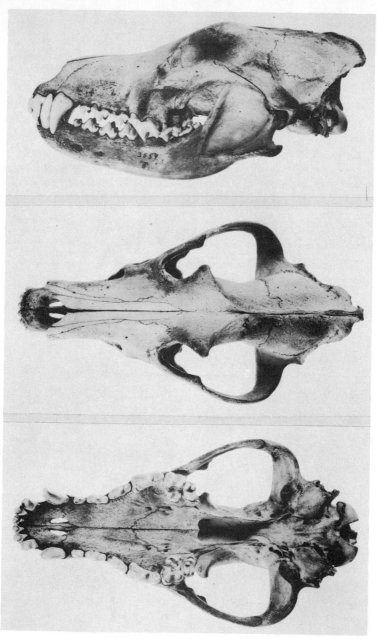

Plate 109. *Canis lupus columbianus* Goldman; type; male adult; Wistaria, north side of Ootsa Lake, Coast District, British Columbia. (No. 3559, Brit. Col. Prov. Mus.) Note large size, broad supraoccipital shield, and narrow carnassials. [One-third natural size]

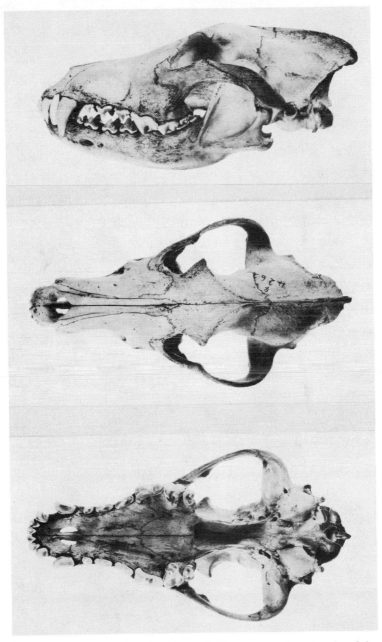

Plate 110. *Canis lupus columbianus* Goldman; topotype; female adult; Wistaria, north side of Ootsa Lake, Coast District, British Columbia. (No. 4262, Brit. Col. Prov. Mus.) Note large size, broad supraoccipital shield, and narrow carnassials. [One-third natural size]

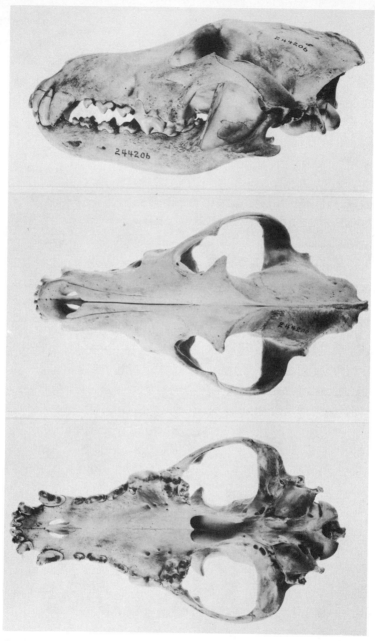

Plate 111. *Canis lupus ligoni* Goldman; male adult; Wrangell, Alaska. (No. 244206, U. S. Nat. Mus., Biological Surveys collection.) Note smaller size, compared with neighboring mainland races. [One-third natural size]

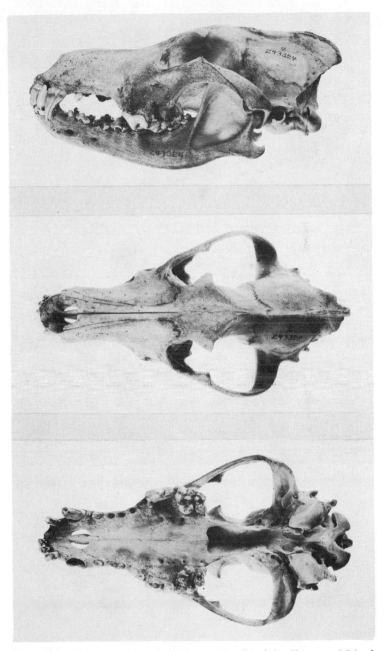

Plate 112. *Canis lupus ligoni* Goldman; female adult; Kupreanof Island, Alaska. No. 243324, U. S. Nat. Mus., Biological Surveys collection.) Note smaller size, compared with neighboring mainland races. [One-third natural size]

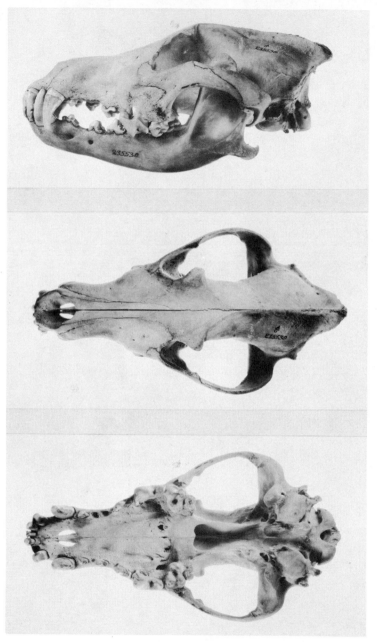

Plate 113. *Canis lupus fuscus* Richardson; male adult; Cascadia, Oregon. (No. 235530, U. S. Nat. Mus., Biological Surveys collection.) Note nasals ending posteriorly in same transverse plane as maxillae, instead of extending beyond this plane as in other races. [One-third natural size]

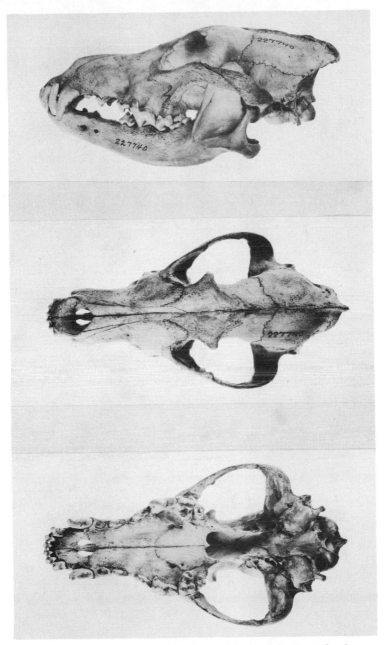

Plate 114. *Canis lupus fuscus* Richardson; female adult; Estacada, Oregon.
(No. 227740, U. S. Nat. Mus., Biological Surveys collection.) Note nasals
ending posteriorly in same transverse plane as maxillae, instead of extending
beyond this plane as in other races. [One-third natural size]

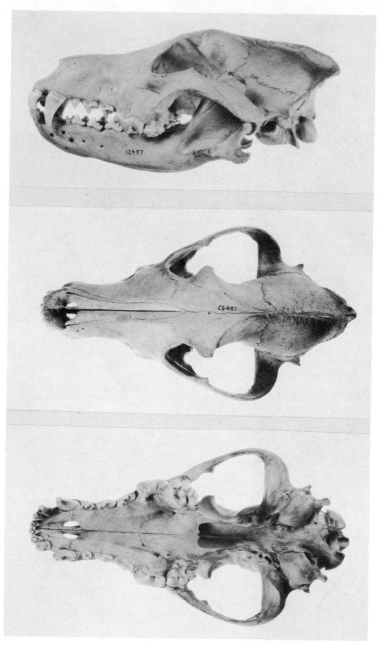

Plate 115. *Canis lupus crassodon* Hall; topotype; male adult; Tahsis Canal, Nootka Sound, Vancouver Island, British Columbia, Canada. (No. 12457, Mus. Vert. Zool.) Note heavy dentition, and form of upper carnassial with outer side longer than inner side. [One-third natural size]

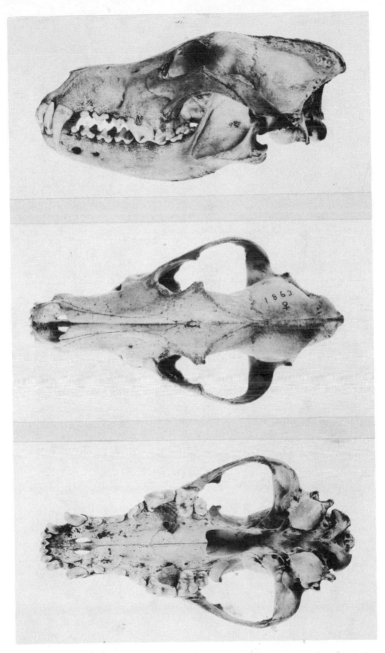

Plate 116. *Canis lupus crassodon* Hall; female adult; Alberni, British Columbia, Canada. (No. 1862, Brit. Col. Prov. Mus.) Note heavy dentition and form of upper carnassial with outer side longer than inner side. [One-third natural size]

Plate 117. *Canis lupus youngi* Goldman; type; male adult; Harts Draw,
20 miles northwest of Monticello, Utah. (No. 224001, U. S. Nat. Mus.,
Biological Surveys collection.) Note large size, wide supraoccipital shield,
and slight posterior projection of inion. [One-third natural size]

Plate 118. *Canis lupus youngi* Goldman; female adult; Glade Park (Black Ridge), Mesa County, Colorado. (No. 223710, U. S. Nat. Mus., Biological Surveys collection.) Note large size, wide supraoccipital shield, and slight posterior projection of inion. [One-third natural size]

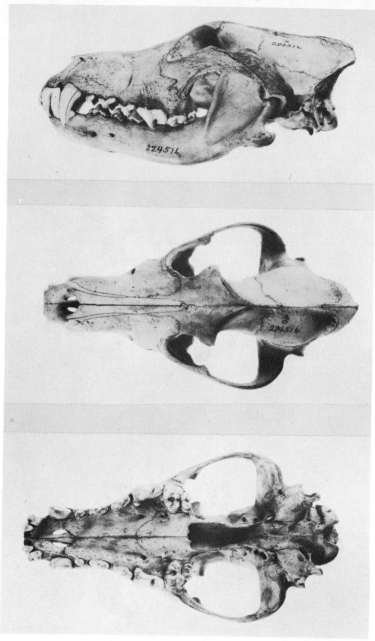

Plate 119. *Canis lupus mogollonensis* Goldman; male adult; Chloride, New Mexico. (No. 224516, U. S. Nat. Mus., Biological Surveys collection.) Note medium size (between *youngi* and *baileyi*). [One-third natural size]

Plate 120. *Canis lupus mogollonensis* Goldman; female adult; Chloride, New Mexico. (No. 224167, U. S. Nat. Mus., Biological Surveys collection.) Note medium size (between *youngi* and *baileyi*). [One-third natural size]

621

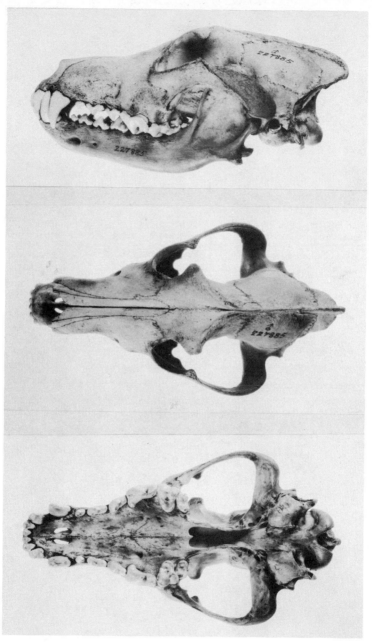

Plate 121. *Canis lupus monstrabilis* Goldman; male adult; Ozona (25 miles west), Texas. (No. 227885, U. S. Nat. Mus., Biological Surveys collection.) Note high arch of braincase. [One-third natural size]

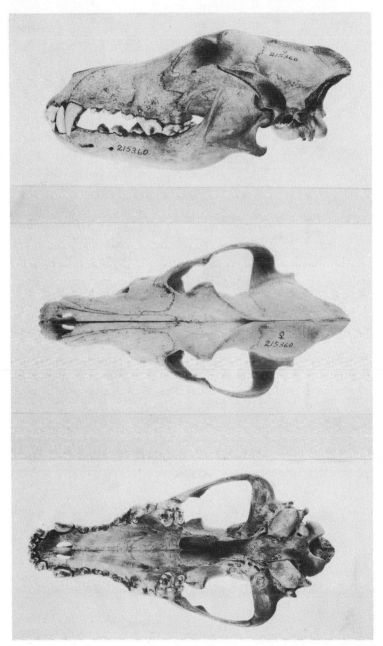

Plate 122. *Canis lupus monstrabilis* Goldman; female adult; Rankin (18 miles southeast), Texas. (No. 215360, U. S. Nat. Mus., Biological Surveys collection.) Note high arch of braincase. [One-third natural size]

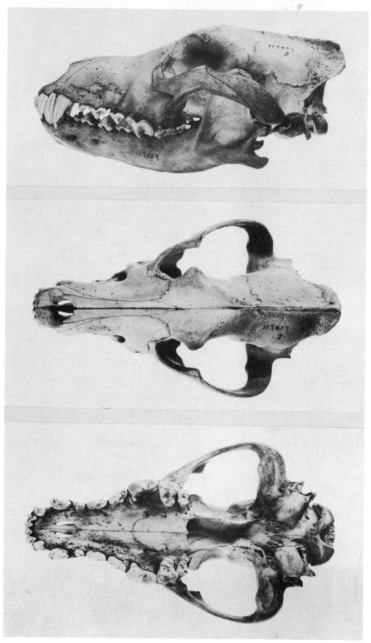

Plate 123. *Canis lupus baileyi* Nelson and Goldman; topotype; male adult;
Colonia Garcia, Chihuahua, Mexico. (No. 117059, U. S. Nat. Mus. Biological Surveys collection.) Note small size, slender rostrum, and widely
spreading zygomata. [One-third natural size]

624

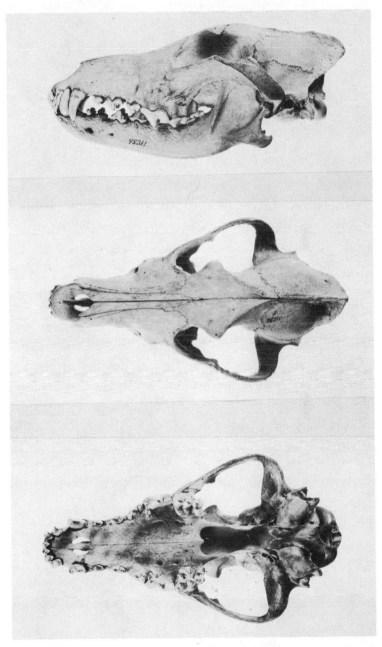

Plate 124. *Canis lupus baileyi* Nelson and Goldman; topotype; female adult; Colonia Garcia, Chihuahua, Mexico. (No. 98311, U. S. Nat. Mus., Biological Surveys collection.) Note small size, slender rostrum, and widely spreading zygomata. [One-third natural size]

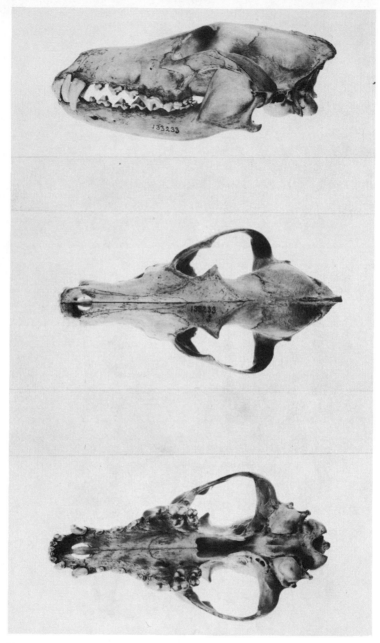

Plate 125. *Canis niger rufus* Audubon and Bachman; male adult; Red Fork, Oklahoma. (No. 133233, U. S. Nat. Mus., Biological Surveys collection.) Note small size and general resemblance to *Canis latrans;* orbits more strongly bowed outward; rostrum deeper. [One-third natural size]

Plate 126. *Canis niger rufus* Audubon and Bachman; female adult; Llano
(seven miles northwest), Texas. (No. 214852, U. S. Nat. Mus., Biological
Surveys collection.) Note small size and general resemblance to *Canis
latrans*; orbits more strongly bowed outward; rostrum deeper. [One-third
natural size]

Plate 127. *Canis niger gregoryi* Goldman; male adult; Winn Parish, Louisiana. (No. 265475, U. S. Nat. Mus., Biological Surveys collection.) Note slender proportions and slight elevation of braincase. [One-third natural size]

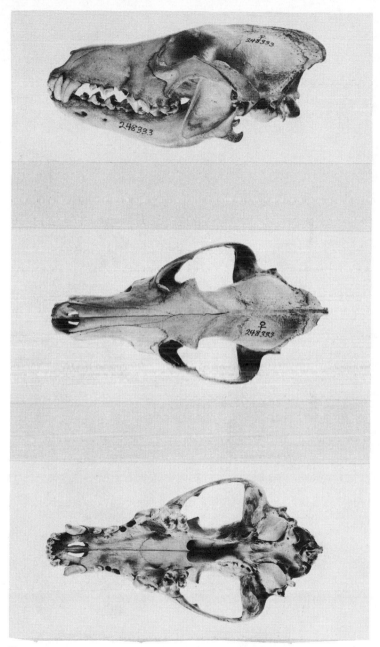

Plate 128. *Canis niger gregoryi* Goldman; female adult; Sabine River, Beauregard Parish, Louisiana. (No. 248333, U. S. Nat. Mus., Biological Surveys collection.) Note slender proportions and slight elevation of braincase. [One-third natural size]

629

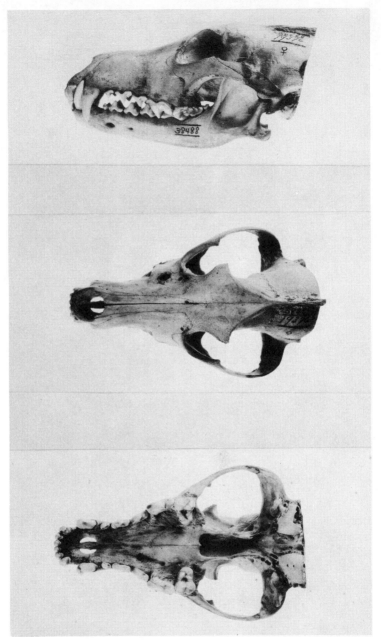

Plate 129. *Canis niger niger* Miller; female adult; Horse Landing, St. Johns River, about 12 miles south of Palatka, Florida. (No. 38488/19376 U. S. Nat. Mus.) Note large teeth. [One-third natural size]

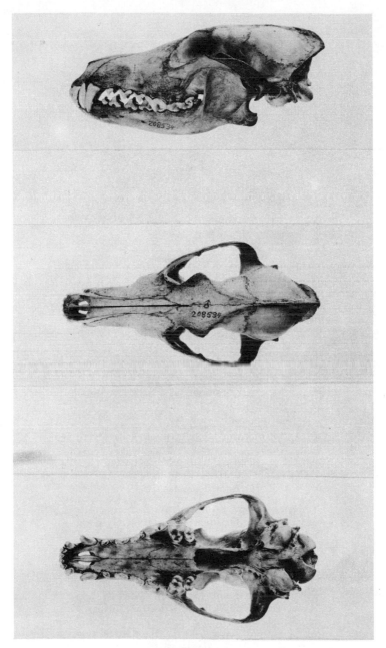

Plate 130. *Canis latrans texensis* Bailey; male adult; San Angelo, Texas. (No. 208534, U. S. Nat. Mus., Biological Surveys collection.) Note similarity to *Canis niger rufus*. [One-third natural size]

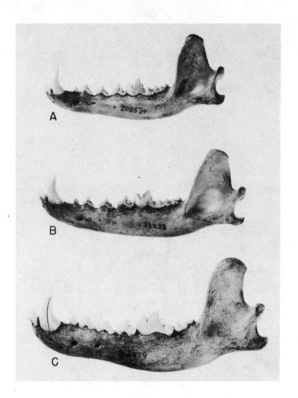

Plate 131. A. *Canis latrans texensis* Bailey; male adult; San Angelo, Texas. (No. 208534, U. S. Nat. Mus., Biological Surveys collection.) Note small size and deeply cleft crowns of cheek teeth. [One-third natural size]

B. *Canis niger rufus* Audubon and Bachman; male adult; Redfork, Oklahoma. (No. 133233, U. S. Nat. Mus., Biological Surveys collection.) Note resemblance to *Canis latrans texensis*; size larger. [One-third natural size]

C. *Canis lupus pambasileus* Elliot; male adult; Toklat River, Mount McKinley National Park, Alaska. (No. 266379, U. S. Nat. Mus., Biological Surveys collection.) Note large size and shallowly cleft crowns of cheek teeth. [One-third natural size]

INDEX

[Principal page references to a species in **boldface** type; synonyms in *italics*]

634

A CATALOGUE OF SELECTED DOVER BOOKS
IN ALL FIELDS OF INTEREST

A CATALOGUE OF SELECTED DOVER BOOKS
IN ALL FIELDS OF INTEREST

AMERICA'S OLD MASTERS, James T. Flexner. Four men emerged unexpectedly from provincial 18th century America to leadership in European art: Benjamin West, J. S. Copley, C. R. Peale, Gilbert Stuart. Brilliant coverage of lives and contributions. Revised, 1967 edition. 69 plates. 365pp. of text.

21806-6 Paperbound $3.00

FIRST FLOWERS OF OUR WILDERNESS: AMERICAN PAINTING, THE COLONIAL PERIOD, James T. Flexner. Painters, and regional painting traditions from earliest Colonial times up to the emergence of Copley, West and Peale Sr., Foster, Gustavus Hesselius, Feke, John Smibert and many anonymous painters in the primitive manner. Engaging presentation, with 162 illustrations. xxii + 368pp.

22180-6 Paperbound $3.50

THE LIGHT OF DISTANT SKIES: AMERICAN PAINTING, 1760-1835, James T. Flexner. The great generation of early American painters goes to Europe to learn and to teach: West, Copley, Gilbert Stuart and others. Allston, Trumbull, Morse; also contemporary American painters—primitives, derivatives, academics—who remained in America. 102 illustrations. xiii + 306pp. 22179-2 Paperbound $3.00

A HISTORY OF THE RISE AND PROGRESS OF THE ARTS OF DESIGN IN THE UNITED STATES, William Dunlap. Much the richest mine of information on early American painters, sculptors, architects, engravers, miniaturists, etc. The only source of information for scores of artists, the major primary source for many others. Unabridged reprint of rare original 1834 edition, with new introduction by James T. Flexner. and 394 new illustrations. Edited by Rita Weiss. 6⅝ x 9⅝.

21695-0, 21696-9, 21697-7 Three volumes, Paperbound $13.50

EPOCHS OF CHINESE AND JAPANESE ART, Ernest F. Fenollosa. From primitive Chinese art to the 20th century, thorough history, explanation of every important art period and form, including Japanese woodcuts; main stress on China and Japan, but Tibet, Korea also included. Still unexcelled for its detailed, rich coverage of cultural background, aesthetic elements, diffusion studies, particularly of the historical period. 2nd, 1913 edition. 242 illustrations. lii + 439pp. of text.

20364-6, 20365-4 Two volumes, Paperbound $6.00

THE GENTLE ART OF MAKING ENEMIES, James A. M. Whistler. Greatest wit of his day deflates Oscar Wilde, Ruskin, Swinburne; strikes back at inane critics, exhibitions, art journalism; aesthetics of impressionist revolution in most striking form. Highly readable classic by great painter. Reproduction of edition designed by Whistler. Introduction by Alfred Werner. xxxvi + 334pp.

21875-9 Paperbound $2.50

DESIGN BY ACCIDENT; A BOOK OF "ACCIDENTAL EFFECTS" FOR ARTISTS AND DESIGNERS, James F. O'Brien. Create your own unique, striking, imaginative effects by "controlled accident" interaction of materials: paints and lacquers, oil and water based paints, splatter, crackling materials, shatter, similar items. Everything you do will be different; first book on this limitless art, so useful to both fine artist and commercial artist. Full instructions. 192 plates showing "accidents," 8 in color. viii + 215pp. 8⅜ x 11¼. 21942-9 Paperbound $3.50

THE BOOK OF SIGNS, Rudolf Koch. Famed German type designer draws 493 beautiful symbols: religious, mystical, alchemical, imperial, property marks, runes, etc. Remarkable fusion of traditional and modern. Good for suggestions of timelessness, smartness, modernity. Text. vi + 104pp. 6⅛ x 9¼.
20162-7 Paperbound $1.25

HISTORY OF INDIAN AND INDONESIAN ART, Ananda K. Coomaraswamy. An unabridged republication of one of the finest books by a great scholar in Eastern art. Rich in descriptive material, history, social backgrounds; Sunga reliefs, Rajput paintings, Gupta temples, Burmese frescoes, textiles, jewelry, sculpture, etc. 400 photos. viii + 423pp. 6⅜ x 9¾. 21436-2 Paperbound $4.00

PRIMITIVE ART, Franz Boas. America's foremost anthropologist surveys textiles, ceramics, woodcarving, basketry, metalwork, etc.; patterns, technology, creation of symbols, style origins. All areas of world, but very full on Northwest Coast Indians. More than 350 illustrations of baskets, boxes, totem poles, weapons, etc. 378 pp.
20025-6 Paperbound $3.00

THE GENTLEMAN AND CABINET MAKER'S DIRECTOR, Thomas Chippendale. Full reprint (third edition, 1762) of most influential furniture book of all time, by master cabinetmaker. 200 plates, illustrating chairs, sofas, mirrors, tables, cabinets, plus 24 photographs of surviving pieces. Biographical introduction by N. Bienenstock. vi + 249pp. 9⅞ x 12¾. 21601-2 Paperbound $4.00

AMERICAN ANTIQUE FURNITURE, Edgar G. Miller, Jr. The basic coverage of all American furniture before 1840. Individual chapters cover type of furniture—clocks, tables, sideboards, etc.—chronologically, with inexhaustible wealth of data. More than 2100 photographs, all identified, commented on. Essential to all early American collectors. Introduction by H. E. Keyes. vi + 1106pp. 7⅞ x 10¾.
21599-7, 21600-4 Two volumes, Paperbound $11.00

PENNSYLVANIA DUTCH AMERICAN FOLK ART, Henry J. Kauffman. 279 photos, 28 drawings of tulipware, Fraktur script, painted tinware, toys, flowered furniture, quilts, samplers, hex signs, house interiors, etc. Full descriptive text. Excellent for tourist, rewarding for designer, collector. Map. 146pp. 7⅞ x 10¾.
21205-X Paperbound $2.50

EARLY NEW ENGLAND GRAVESTONE RUBBINGS, Edmund V. Gillon, Jr. 43 photographs, 226 carefully reproduced rubbings show heavily symbolic, sometimes macabre early gravestones, up to early 19th century. Remarkable early American primitive art, occasionally strikingly beautiful; always powerful. Text. xxvi + 207pp. 8⅜ x 11¼. 21380-3 Paperbound $3.50

THE ARCHITECTURE OF COUNTRY HOUSES, Andrew J. Downing. Together with Vaux's *Villas and Cottages* this is the basic book for Hudson River Gothic architecture of the middle Victorian period. Full, sound discussions of general aspects of housing, architecture, style, decoration, furnishing, together with scores of detailed house plans, illustrations of specific buildings, accompanied by full text. Perhaps the most influential single American architectural book. 1850 edition. Introduction by J. Stewart Johnson. 321 figures, 34 architectural designs. xvi + 560pp.
22003-6 Paperbound $4.00

LOST EXAMPLES OF COLONIAL ARCHITECTURE, John Mead Howells. Full-page photographs of buildings that have disappeared or been so altered as to be denatured, including many designed by major early American architects. 245 plates. xvii + 248pp. 7⅞ x 10¾.
21143-6 Paperbound $3.50

DOMESTIC ARCHITECTURE OF THE AMERICAN COLONIES AND OF THE EARLY REPUBLIC, Fiske Kimball. Foremost architect and restorer of Williamsburg and Monticello covers nearly 200 homes between 1620-1825. Architectural details, construction, style features, special fixtures, floor plans, etc. Generally considered finest work in its area. 219 illustrations of houses, doorways, windows, capital mantels. xx + 314pp. 7⅞ x 10¾.
21743-4 Paperbound $4.00

EARLY AMERICAN ROOMS: 1650-1858, edited by Russell Hawes Kettell. Tour of 12 rooms, each representative of a different era in American history and each furnished, decorated, designed and occupied in the style of the era. 72 plans and elevations, 8-page color section, etc., show fabrics, wall papers, arrangements, etc. Full descriptive text. xvii + 200pp. of text. 8⅜ x 11¼.
21633-0 Paperbound $5.00

THE FITZWILLIAM VIRGINAL BOOK, edited by J. Fuller Maitland and W. B. Squire. Full modern printing of famous early 17th-century ms. volume of 300 works by Morley, Byrd, Bull, Gibbons, etc. For piano or other modern keyboard instrument; easy to read format. xxxvi + 938pp. 8⅜ x 11.
21068-5, 21069-3 Two volumes, Paperbound $10.00

KEYBOARD MUSIC, Johann Sebastian Bach. Bach Gesellschaft edition. A rich selection of Bach's masterpieces for the harpsichord: the six English Suites, six French Suites, the six Partitas (Clavierübung part I), the Goldberg Variations (Clavierübung part IV), the fifteen Two-Part Inventions and the fifteen Three-Part Sinfonias. Clearly reproduced on large sheets with ample margins; eminently playable. vi + 312pp. 8⅛ x 11.
22360-4 Paperbound $5.00

THE MUSIC OF BACH: AN INTRODUCTION, Charles Sanford Terry. A fine, nontechnical introduction to Bach's music, both instrumental and vocal. Covers organ music, chamber music, passion music, other types. Analyzes themes, developments, innovations. x + 114pp.
21075-8 Paperbound $1.25

BEETHOVEN AND HIS NINE SYMPHONIES, Sir George Grove. Noted British musicologist provides best history, analysis, commentary on symphonies. Very thorough, rigorously accurate; necessary to both advanced student and amateur music lover. 436 musical passages. vii + 407 pp.
20334-4 Paperbound $2.75

AGAINST THE GRAIN (A REBOURS), Joris K. Huysmans.· Filled with weird images, evidences of a bizarre imagination, exotic experiments with hallucinatory drugs, rich tastes and smells and the diversions of its sybarite hero Duc Jean des Esseintes, this classic novel pushed 19th-century literary decadence to its limits. Full unabridged edition. Do not confuse this with abridged editions generally sold. Introduction by Havelock Ellis. xlix + 206pp. 22190-3 Paperbound $2.00

VARIORUM SHAKESPEARE: HAMLET. Edited by Horace H. Furness; a landmark of American scholarship. Exhaustive footnotes and appendices treat all doubtful words and phrases, as well as suggested critical emendations throughout the play's history. First volume contains editor's own text, collated with all Quartos and Folios. Second volume contains full first Quarto, translations of Shakespeare's sources (Belleforest, and Saxo Grammaticus), Der Bestrafte Brudermord, and many essays on critical and historical points of interest by major authorities of past and present. Includes details of staging and costuming over the years. By far the best edition available for serious students of Shakespeare. Total of xx + 905pp. 21004-9, 21005-7, 2 volumes, Paperbound $7.00

A LIFE OF WILLIAM SHAKESPEARE, Sir Sidney Lee. This is the standard life of Shakespeare, summarizing everything known about Shakespeare and his plays. Incredibly rich in material, broad in coverage, clear and judicious, it has served thousands as the best introduction to Shakespeare. 1931 edition. 9 plates. xxix + 792pp. (USO) 21967-4 Paperbound $3.75

MASTERS OF THE DRAMA, John Gassner. Most comprehensive history of the drama in print, covering every tradition from Greeks to modern Europe and America, including India, Far East, etc. Covers more than 800 dramatists, 2000 plays, with biographical material, plot summaries, theatre history, criticism, etc. "Best of its kind in English," *New Republic*. 77 illustrations. xxii + 890pp. 20100-7 Clothbound $8.50

THE EVOLUTION OF THE ENGLISH LANGUAGE, George McKnight. The growth of English, from the 14th century to the present. Unusual, non technical account presents basic information in very interesting form: sound shifts, change in grammar and syntax, vocabulary growth, similar topics. Abundantly illustrated with quotations. Formerly *Modern English in the Making*. xii + 590pp. 21932-1 Paperbound $3.50

AN ETYMOLOGICAL DICTIONARY OF MODERN ENGLISH, Ernest Weekley. Fullest, richest work of its sort, by foremost British lexicographer. Detailed word histories, including many colloquial and archaic words; extensive quotations. Do not confuse this with the Concise Etymological Dictionary, which is much abridged. Total of xxvii + 830pp. 6½ x 9¼. 21873-2, 21874-0 Two volumes, Paperbound $6.00

FLATLAND: A ROMANCE OF MANY DIMENSIONS, E. A. Abbott. Classic of science-fiction explores ramifications of life in a two-dimensional world, and what happens when a three-dimensional being intrudes. Amusing reading, but also useful as introduction to thought about hyperspace. Introduction by Banesh Hoffmann. 16 illustrations. xx + 103pp. 20001-9 Paperbound $1.00

POEMS OF ANNE BRADSTREET, edited with an introduction by Robert Hutchinson. A new selection of poems by America's first poet and perhaps the first significant woman poet in the English language. 48 poems display her development in works of considerable variety—love poems, domestic poems, religious meditations, formal elegies, "quaternions," etc. Notes, bibliography. viii + 222pp.
22160-1 Paperbound $2.00

THREE GOTHIC NOVELS: THE CASTLE OF OTRANTO BY HORACE WALPOLE; VATHEK BY WILLIAM BECKFORD; THE VAMPYRE BY JOHN POLIDORI, WITH FRAGMENT OF A NOVEL BY LORD BYRON, edited by E. F. Bleiler. The first Gothic novel, by Walpole; the finest Oriental tale in English, by Beckford; powerful Romantic supernatural story in versions by Polidori and Byron. All extremely important in history of literature; all still exciting, packed with supernatural thrills, ghosts, haunted castles, magic, etc. xl + 291pp.
21232-7 Paperbound $2.50

THE BEST TALES OF HOFFMANN, E. T. A. Hoffmann. 10 of Hoffmann's most important stories, in modern re-editings of standard translations: Nutcracker and the King of Mice, Signor Formica, Automata, The Sandman, Rath Krespel, The Golden Flowerpot, Master Martin the Cooper, The Mines of Falun, The King's Betrothed, A New Year's Eve Adventure. 7 illustrations by Hoffmann. Edited by E. F. Bleiler. xxxix + 419pp. 21793-0 Paperbound $3.00

GHOST AND HORROR STORIES OF AMBROSE BIERCE, Ambrose Bierce. 23 strikingly modern stories of the horrors latent in the human mind: The Eyes of the Panther, The Damned Thing, An Occurrence at Owl Creek Bridge, An Inhabitant of Carcosa, etc., plus the dream-essay, Visions of the Night. Edited by E. F. Bleiler. xxii + 199pp. 20767-6 Paperbound $1.50

BEST GHOST STORIES OF J. S. LEFANU, J. Sheridan LeFanu. Finest stories by Victorian master often considered greatest supernatural writer of all. Carmilla, Green Tea, The Haunted Baronet, The Familiar, and 12 others. Most never before available in the U. S. A. Edited by E. F. Bleiler. 8 illustrations from Victorian publications. xvii + 467pp. 20415-4 Paperbound $3.00

MATHEMATICAL FOUNDATIONS OF INFORMATION THEORY, A. I. Khinchin. Comprehensive introduction to work of Shannon, McMillan, Feinstein and Khinchin, placing these investigations on a rigorous mathematical basis. Covers entropy concept in probability theory, uniqueness theorem, Shannon's inequality, ergodic sources, the E property, martingale concept, noise, Feinstein's fundamental lemma, Shanon's first and second theorems. Translated by R. A. Silverman and M. D. Friedman. iii + 120pp. 60434-9 Paperbound $1.75

SEVEN SCIENCE FICTION NOVELS, H. G. Wells. The standard collection of the great novels. Complete, unabridged. *First Men in the Moon, Island of Dr. Moreau, War of the Worlds, Food of the Gods, Invisible Man, Time Machine, In the Days of the Comet.* Not only science fiction fans, but every educated person owes it to himself to read these novels. 1015pp. 20264-X Clothbound $5.00

EAST O' THE SUN AND WEST O' THE MOON, George W. Dasent. Considered the best of all translations of these Norwegian folk tales, this collection has been enjoyed by generations of children (and folklorists too). Includes True and Untrue, Why the Sea is Salt, East O' the Sun and West O' the Moon, Why the Bear is Stumpy-Tailed, Boots and the Troll, The Cock and the Hen, Rich Peter the Pedlar, and 52 more. The only edition with all 59 tales. 77 illustrations by Erik Werenskiold and Theodor Kittelsen. xv + 418pp. 22521-6 Paperbound $3.50

GOOPS AND HOW TO BE THEM, Gelett Burgess. Classic of tongue-in-cheek humor, masquerading as etiquette book. 87 verses, twice as many cartoons, show mischievous Goops as they demonstrate to children virtues of table manners, neatness, courtesy, etc. Favorite for generations. viii + 88pp. 6½ x 9¼.
22233-0 Paperbound $1.25

ALICE'S ADVENTURES UNDER GROUND, Lewis Carroll. The first version, quite different from the final Alice in Wonderland, printed out by Carroll himself with his own illustrations. Complete facsimile of the "million dollar" manuscript Carroll gave to Alice Liddell in 1864. Introduction by Martin Gardner. viii + 96pp. Title and dedication pages in color. 21482-6 Paperbound $1.25

THE BROWNIES, THEIR BOOK, Palmer Cox. Small as mice, cunning as foxes, exuberant and full of mischief, the Brownies go to the zoo, toy shop, seashore, circus, etc., in 24 verse adventures and 266 illustrations. Long a favorite, since their first appearance in St. Nicholas Magazine. xi + 144pp. 6⅝ x 9¼.
21265-3 Paperbound $1.75

SONGS OF CHILDHOOD, Walter De La Mare. Published (under the pseudonym Walter Ramal) when De La Mare was only 29, this charming collection has long been a favorite children's book. A facsimile of the first edition in paper, the 47 poems capture the simplicity of the nursery rhyme and the ballad, including such lyrics as I Met Eve, Tartary, The Silver Penny. vii + 106pp. 21972-0 Paperbound $1.25

THE COMPLETE NONSENSE OF EDWARD LEAR, Edward Lear. The finest 19th-century humorist-cartoonist in full: all nonsense limericks, zany alphabets, Owl and Pussycat, songs, nonsense botany, and more than 500 illustrations by Lear himself. Edited by Holbrook Jackson. xxix + 287pp. (USO) 20167-8 Paperbound $2.00

BILLY WHISKERS: THE AUTOBIOGRAPHY OF A GOAT, Frances Trego Montgomery. A favorite of children since the early 20th century, here are the escapades of that rambunctious, irresistible and mischievous goat—Billy Whiskers. Much in the spirit of Peck's Bad Boy, this is a book that children never tire of reading or hearing. All the original familiar illustrations by W. H. Fry are included: 6 color plates, 18 black and white drawings. 159pp. 22345-0 Paperbound $2.00

MOTHER GOOSE MELODIES. Faithful republication of the fabulously rare Munroe and Francis "copyright 1833" Boston edition—the most important Mother Goose collection, usually referred to as the "original." Familiar rhymes plus many rare ones, with wonderful old woodcut illustrations. Edited by E. F. Bleiler. 128pp. 4½ x 6⅜. 22577-1 Paperbound $1.25

TWO LITTLE SAVAGES; BEING THE ADVENTURES OF TWO BOYS WHO LIVED AS INDIANS AND WHAT THEY LEARNED, Ernest Thompson Seton. Great classic of nature and boyhood provides a vast range of woodlore in most palatable form, a genuinely entertaining story. Two farm boys build a teepee in woods and live in it for a month, working out Indian solutions to living problems, star lore, birds and animals, plants, etc. 293 illustrations. vii + 286pp.
20985-7 Paperbound $2.50

PETER PIPER'S PRACTICAL PRINCIPLES OF PLAIN & PERFECT PRONUNCIATION. Alliterative jingles and tongue-twisters of surprising charm, that made their first appearance in America about 1830. Republished in full with the spirited woodcut illustrations from this earliest American edition. 32pp. $4\frac{1}{2}$ x $6\frac{3}{8}$.
22560-7 Paperbound $1.00

SCIENCE EXPERIMENTS AND AMUSEMENTS FOR CHILDREN, Charles Vivian. 73 easy experiments, requiring only materials found at home or easily available, such as candles, coins, steel wool, etc.; illustrate basic phenomena like vacuum, simple chemical reaction, etc. All safe. Modern, well-planned. Formerly *Science Games for Children*. 102 photos, numerous drawings. 96pp. $6\frac{1}{8}$ x $9\frac{1}{4}$.
21856-2 Paperbound $1.25

AN INTRODUCTION TO CHESS MOVES AND TACTICS SIMPLY EXPLAINED, Leonard Barden. Informal intermediate introduction, quite strong in explaining reasons for moves. Covers basic material, tactics, important openings, traps, positional play in middle game, end game. Attempts to isolate patterns and recurrent configurations. Formerly *Chess*. 58 figures. 102pp. (USO) 21210-6 Paperbound $1.25

LASKER'S MANUAL OF CHESS, Dr. Emanuel Lasker. Lasker was not only one of the five great World Champions, he was also one of the ablest expositors, theorists, and analysts. In many ways, his Manual, permeated with his philosophy of battle, filled with keen insights, is one of the greatest works ever written on chess. Filled with analyzed games by the great players. A single-volume library that will profit almost any chess player, beginner or master. 308 diagrams. xli x 349pp.
20640-8 Paperbound $2.75

THE MASTER BOOK OF MATHEMATICAL RECREATIONS, Fred Schuh. In opinion of many the finest work ever prepared on mathematical puzzles, stunts, recreations; exhaustively thorough explanations of mathematics involved, analysis of effects, citation of puzzles and games. Mathematics involved is elementary. Translated by F. Göbel. 194 figures. xxiv + 430pp.
22134-2 Paperbound $3.00

MATHEMATICS, MAGIC AND MYSTERY, Martin Gardner. Puzzle editor for Scientific American explains mathematics behind various mystifying tricks: card tricks, stage "mind reading," coin and match tricks, counting out games, geometric dissections, etc. Probability sets, theory of numbers clearly explained. Also provides more than 400 tricks, guaranteed to work, that you can do. 135 illustrations. xii + 176pp.
20338-2 Paperbound $1.50

How to Know the Wild Flowers, Mrs. William Starr Dana. This is the classical book of American wildflowers (of the Eastern and Central United States), used by hundreds of thousands. Covers over 500 species, arranged in extremely easy to use color and season groups. Full descriptions, much plant lore. This Dover edition is the fullest ever compiled, with tables of nomenclature changes. 174 full-page plates by M. Satterlee. xii + 418pp. 20332-8 Paperbound $2.75

Our Plant Friends and Foes, William Atherton DuPuy. History, economic importance, essential botanical information and peculiarities of 25 common forms of plant life are provided in this book in an entertaining and charming style. Covers food plants (potatoes, apples, beans, wheat, almonds, bananas, etc.), flowers (lily, tulip, etc.), trees (pine, oak, elm, etc.), weeds, poisonous mushrooms and vines, gourds, citrus fruits, cotton, the cactus family, and much more. 108 illustrations. xiv + 290pp. 22272-1 Paperbound $2.50

How to Know the Ferns, Frances T. Parsons. Classic survey of Eastern and Central ferns, arranged according to clear, simple identification key. Excellent introduction to greatly neglected nature area. 57 illustrations and 42 plates. xvi + 215pp. 20740-4 Paperbound $2.00

Manual of the Trees of North America, Charles S. Sargent. America's foremost dendrologist provides the definitive coverage of North American trees and tree-like shrubs. 717 species fully described and illustrated: exact distribution, down to township; full botanical description; economic importance; description of subspecies and races; habitat, growth data; similar material. Necessary to every serious student of tree-life. Nomenclature revised to present. Over 100 locating keys. 783 illustrations. lii + 934pp. 20277-1, 20278-X Two volumes, Paperbound $6.00

Our Northern Shrubs, Harriet L. Keeler. Fine non-technical reference work identifying more than 225 important shrubs of Eastern and Central United States and Canada. Full text covering botanical description, habitat, plant lore, is paralleled with 205 full-page photographs of flowering or fruiting plants. Nomenclature revised by Edward G. Voss. One of few works concerned with shrubs. 205 plates, 35 drawings. xxviii + 521pp. 21989-5 Paperbound $3.75

The Mushroom Handbook, Louis C. C. Krieger. Still the best popular handbook: full descriptions of 259 species, cross references to another 200. Extremely thorough text enables you to identify, know all about any mushroom you are likely to meet in eastern and central U. S. A.: habitat, luminescence, poisonous qualities, use, folklore, etc. 32 color plates show over 50 mushrooms, also 126 other illustrations. Finding keys. vii + 560pp. 21861-9 Paperbound $3.95

Handbook of Birds of Eastern North America, Frank M. Chapman. Still much the best single-volume guide to the birds of Eastern and Central United States. Very full coverage of 675 species, with descriptions, life habits, distribution, similar data. All descriptions keyed to two-page color chart. With this single volume the average birdwatcher needs no other books. 1931 revised edition. 195 illustrations. xxxvi + 581pp. 21489-3 Paperbound $5.00

AMERICAN FOOD AND GAME FISHES, David S. Jordan and Barton W. Evermann. Definitive source of information, detailed and accurate enough to enable the sportsman and nature lover to identify conclusively some 1,000 species and sub-species of North American fish, sought for food or sport. Coverage of range, physiology, habits, life history, food value. Best methods of capture, interest to the angler, advice on bait, fly-fishing, etc. 338 drawings and photographs. 1 + 574pp. 6⅝ x 9⅜.
22383-1 Paperbound $4.50

THE FROG BOOK, Mary C. Dickerson. Complete with extensive finding keys, over 300 photographs, and an introduction to the general biology of frogs and toads, this is the classic non-technical study of Northeastern and Central species. 58 species; 290 photographs and 16 color plates. xvii + 253pp.
21973-9 Paperbound $4.00

THE MOTH BOOK: A GUIDE TO THE MOTHS OF NORTH AMERICA, William J. Holland. Classical study, eagerly sought after and used for the past 60 years. Clear identification manual to more than 2,000 different moths, largest manual in existence. General information about moths, capturing, mounting, classifying, etc., followed by species by species descriptions. 263 illustrations plus 48 color plates show almost every species, full size. 1968 edition, preface, nomenclature changes by A. E. Brower. xxiv + 479pp. of text. 6½ x 9¼.
21948-8 Paperbound $5.00

THE SEA-BEACH AT EBB-TIDE, Augusta Foote Arnold. Interested amateur can identify hundreds of marine plants and animals on coasts of North America; marine algae; seaweeds; squids; hermit crabs; horse shoe crabs; shrimps; corals; sea anemones; etc. Species descriptions cover: structure; food; reproductive cycle; size; shape; color; habitat; etc. Over 600 drawings. 85 plates. xii + 490pp.
21949-6 Paperbound $3.50

COMMON BIRD SONGS, Donald J. Borror. 33⅓ 12-inch record presents songs of 60 important birds of the eastern United States. A thorough, serious record which provides several examples for each bird, showing different types of song, individual variations, etc. Inestimable identification aid for birdwatcher. 32-page booklet gives text about birds and songs, with illustration for each bird.
21829-5 Record, book, album. Monaural. $2.75

FADS AND FALLACIES IN THE NAME OF SCIENCE, Martin Gardner. Fair, witty appraisal of cranks and quacks of science: Atlantis, Lemuria, hollow earth, flat earth, Velikovsky, orgone energy, Dianetics, flying saucers, Bridey Murphy, food fads, medical fads, perpetual motion, etc. Formerly "In the Name of Science." x + 363pp.
20394-8 Paperbound $2.00

HOAXES, Curtis D. MacDougall. Exhaustive, unbelievably rich account of great hoaxes: Locke's moon hoax, Shakespearean forgeries, sea serpents, Loch Ness monster, Cardiff giant, John Wilkes Booth's mummy, Disumbrationist school of art, dozens more; also journalism, psychology of hoaxing. 54 illustrations. xi + 338pp.
20465-0 Paperbound $2.75

THE PRINCIPLES OF PSYCHOLOGY, William James. The famous long course, complete and unabridged. Stream of thought, time perception, memory, experimental methods—these are only some of the concerns of a work that was years ahead of its time and still valid, interesting, useful. 94 figures. Total of xviii + 1391pp.
20381-6, 20382-4 Two volumes, Paperbound $8.00

THE STRANGE STORY OF THE QUANTUM, Banesh Hoffmann. Non-mathematical but thorough explanation of work of Planck, Einstein, Bohr, Pauli, de Broglie, Schrödinger, Heisenberg, Dirac, Feynman, etc. No technical background needed. "Of books attempting such an account, this is the best," Henry Margenau, Yale. 40-page "Postscript 1959." xii + 285pp. 20518-5 Paperbound $2.00

THE RISE OF THE NEW PHYSICS, A. d'Abro. Most thorough explanation in print of central core of mathematical physics, both classical and modern; from Newton to Dirac and Heisenberg. Both history and exposition; philosophy of science, causality, explanations of higher mathematics, analytical mechanics, electromagnetism, thermodynamics, phase rule, special and general relativity, matrices. No higher mathematics needed to follow exposition, though treatment is elementary to intermediate in level. Recommended to serious student who wishes verbal understanding. 97 illustrations. xvii + 982pp. 20003-5, 20004-3 Two volumes, Paperbound $6.00

GREAT IDEAS OF OPERATIONS RESEARCH, Jagjit Singh. Easily followed non-technical explanation of mathematical tools, aims, results: statistics, linear programming, game theory, queueing theory, Monte Carlo simulation, etc. Uses only elementary mathematics. Many case studies, several analyzed in detail. Clarity, breadth make this excellent for specialist in another field who wishes background. 41 figures. x + 228pp. 21886-4 Paperbound $2.50

GREAT IDEAS OF MODERN MATHEMATICS: THEIR NATURE AND USE, Jagjit Singh. Internationally famous expositor, winner of Unesco's Kalinga Award for science popularization explains verbally such topics as differential equations, matrices, groups, sets, transformations, mathematical logic and other important modern mathematics, as well as use in physics, astrophysics, and similar fields. Superb exposition for layman, scientist in other areas. viii + 312pp.
20587-8 Paperbound $2.50

GREAT IDEAS IN INFORMATION THEORY, LANGUAGE AND CYBERNETICS, Jagjit Singh. The analog and digital computers, how they work, how they are like and unlike the human brain, the men who developed them, their future applications, computer terminology. An essential book for today, even for readers with little math. Some mathematical demonstrations included for more advanced readers. 118 figures. Tables. ix + 338pp. 21694-2 Paperbound $2.50

CHANCE, LUCK AND STATISTICS, Horace C. Levinson. Non-mathematical presentation of fundamentals of probability theory and science of statistics and their applications. Games of chance, betting odds, misuse of statistics, normal and skew distributions, birth rates, stock speculation, insurance. Enlarged edition. Formerly "The Science of Chance." xiii + 357pp. 21007-3 Paperbound $2.50

PLANETS, STARS AND GALAXIES: DESCRIPTIVE ASTRONOMY FOR BEGINNERS, A. E. Fanning. Comprehensive introductory survey of astronomy: the sun, solar system, stars, galaxies, universe, cosmology; up-to-date, including quasars, radio stars, etc. Preface by Prof. Donald Menzel. 24pp. of photographs. 189pp. 5¼ x 8¼.
21680-2 Paperbound $1.75

TEACH YOURSELF CALCULUS, P. Abbott. With a good background in algebra and trig, you can teach yourself calculus with this book. Simple, straightforward introduction to functions of all kinds, integration, differentiation, series, etc. "Students who are beginning to study calculus method will derive great help from this book." Faraday House Journal. 308pp.
20683-1 Clothbound $2.50

TEACH YOURSELF TRIGONOMETRY, P. Abbott. Geometrical foundations, indices and logarithms, ratios, angles, circular measure, etc. are presented in this sound, easy-to-use text. Excellent for the beginner or as a brush up, this text carries the student through the solution of triangles. 204pp.
20682-3 Clothbound $2.50

BASIC MACHINES AND HOW THEY WORK, U. S. Bureau of Naval Personnel. Originally used in U.S. Naval training schools, this book clearly explains the operation of a progression of machines, from the simplest—lever, wheel and axle, inclined plane, wedge, screw—to the most complex—typewriter, internal combustion engine, computer mechanism. Utilizing an approach that requires only an elementary understanding of mathematics, these explanations build logically upon each other and are assisted by over 200 drawings and diagrams. Perfect as a technical school manual or as a self-teaching aid to the layman. 204 figures. Preface. Index. vii + 161pp. 6½ x 9¼.
21709-4 Paperbound $2.50

THE FRIENDLY STARS, Martha Evans Martin. Classic has taught naked-eye observation of stars, planets to hundreds of thousands, still not surpassed for charm, lucidity, adequacy. Completely updated by Professor Donald H. Menzel, Harvard Observatory. 25 illustrations. 16 x 30 chart. x + 147pp.
21099-5 Paperbound $1.50

MUSIC OF THE SPHERES: THE MATERIAL UNIVERSE FROM ATOM TO QUASAR, SIMPLY EXPLAINED, Guy Murchie. Extremely broad, brilliantly written popular account begins with the solar system and reaches to dividing line between matter and nonmatter; latest understandings presented with exceptional clarity. Volume One: Planets, stars, galaxies, cosmology, geology, celestial mechanics, latest astronomical discoveries; Volume Two: Matter, atoms, waves, radiation, relativity, chemical action, heat, nuclear energy, quantum theory, music, light, color, probability, antimatter, antigravity, and similar topics. 319 figures. 1967 (second) edition. Total of xx + 644pp.
21809-0, 21810-4 Two volumes, Paperbound $5.50

OLD-TIME SCHOOLS AND SCHOOL BOOKS, Clifton Johnson. Illustrations and rhymes from early primers, abundant quotations from early textbooks, many anecdotes of school life enliven this study of elementary schools from Puritans to middle 19th century. Introduction by Carl Withers. 234 illustrations. xxxiii + 381pp.
21031-6 Paperbound $3.50

THE PHILOSOPHY OF THE UPANISHADS, Paul Deussen. Clear, detailed statement of upanishadic system of thought, generally considered among best available. History of these works, full exposition of system emergent from them, parallel concepts in the West. Translated by A. S. Geden. xiv + 429pp.

21616-0 Paperbound $3.50

LANGUAGE, TRUTH AND LOGIC, Alfred J. Ayer. Famous, remarkably clear introduction to the Vienna and Cambridge schools of Logical Positivism; function of philosophy, elimination of metaphysical thought, nature of analysis, similar topics. "Wish I had written it myself," Bertrand Russell. 2nd, 1946 edition. 160pp.

20010-8 Paperbound $1.50

THE GUIDE FOR THE PERPLEXED, Moses Maimonides. Great classic of medieval Judaism, major attempt to reconcile revealed religion (Pentateuch, commentaries) and Aristotelian philosophy. Enormously important in all Western thought. Unabridged Friedländer translation. 50-page introduction. lix + 414pp.

(USO) 20351-4 Paperbound $3.50

OCCULT AND SUPERNATURAL PHENOMENA, D. H. Rawcliffe. Full, serious study of the most persistent delusions of mankind: crystal gazing, mediumistic trance, stigmata, lycanthropy, fire walking, dowsing, telepathy, ghosts, ESP, etc., and their relation to common forms of abnormal psychology. Formerly *Illusions and Delusions of the Supernatural and the Occult*. iii + 551pp. 20503-7 Paperbound $3.50

THE EGYPTIAN BOOK OF THE DEAD: THE PAPYRUS OF ANI, E. A. Wallis Budge. Full hieroglyphic text, interlinear transliteration of sounds, word for word translation, then smooth, connected translation; Theban recension. Basic work in Ancient Egyptian civilization; now even more significant than ever for historical importance, dilation of consciousness, etc. clvi + 377pp. 6½ x 9¼.

21866-X Paperbound $3.95

PSYCHOLOGY OF MUSIC, Carl E. Seashore. Basic, thorough survey of everything known about psychology of music up to 1940's; essential reading for psychologists, musicologists. Physical acoustics; auditory apparatus; relationship of physical sound to perceived sound; role of the mind in sorting, altering, suppressing, creating sound sensations; musical learning, testing for ability, absolute pitch, other topics. Records of Caruso, Menuhin analyzed. 88 figures. xix + 408pp.

21851-1 Paperbound $3.50

THE I CHING (THE BOOK OF CHANGES), translated by James Legge. Complete translated text plus appendices by Confucius, of perhaps the most penetrating divination book ever compiled. Indispensable to all study of early Oriental civilizations. 3 plates. xxiii + 448pp. 21062-6 Paperbound $3.00

THE UPANISHADS, translated by Max Müller. Twelve classical upanishads: Chandogya, Kena, Aitareya, Kaushitaki, Isa, Katha, Mundaka, Taittiriyaka, Brhadaranyaka, Svetasvatara, Prasna, Maitriyana. 160-page introduction, analysis by Prof. Müller. Total of 670pp. 20992-X, 20993-8 Two volumes, Paperbound $6.50

JIM WHITEWOLF: THE LIFE OF A KIOWA APACHE INDIAN, Charles S. Brant, editor. Spans transition between native life and acculturation period, 1880 on. Kiowa culture, personal life pattern, religion and the supernatural, the Ghost Dance, breakdown in the White Man's world, similar material. 1 map. xii + 144pp.
22015-X Paperbound $1.75

THE NATIVE TRIBES OF CENTRAL AUSTRALIA, Baldwin Spencer and F. J. Gillen. Basic book in anthropology, devoted to full coverage of the Arunta and Warramunga tribes; the source for knowledge about kinship systems, material and social culture, religion, etc. Still unsurpassed. 121 photographs, 89 drawings. xviii + 669pp.
21775-2 Paperbound $5.00

MALAY MAGIC, Walter W. Skeat. Classic (1900); still the definitive work on the folklore and popular religion of the Malay peninsula. Describes marriage rites, birth spirits and ceremonies, medicine, dances, games, war and weapons, etc. Extensive quotes from original sources, many magic charms translated into English. 35 illustrations. Preface by Charles Otto Blagden. xxiv + 685pp.
21760-4 Paperbound $4.00

HEAVENS ON EARTH: UTOPIAN COMMUNITIES IN AMERICA, 1680-1880, Mark Holloway. The finest nontechnical account of American utopias, from the early Woman in the Wilderness, Ephrata, Rappites to the enormous mid 19th-century efflorescence; Shakers, New Harmony, Equity Stores, Fourier's Phalanxes, Oneida, Amana, Fruitlands, etc. "Entertaining and very instructive." *Times Literary Supplement*. 15 illustrations. 246pp.
21593-8 Paperbound $2.00

LONDON LABOUR AND THE LONDON POOR, Henry Mayhew. Earliest (c. 1850) sociological study in English, describing myriad subcultures of London poor. Particularly remarkable for the thousands of pages of direct testimony taken from the lips of London prostitutes, thieves, beggars, street sellers, chimney-sweepers, street-musicians, "mudlarks," "pure-finders," rag-gatherers, "running-patterers," dock laborers, cab-men, and hundreds of others, quoted directly in this massive work. An extraordinarily vital picture of London emerges. 110 illustrations. Total of lxxvi + 1951pp. 6⅝ x 10.
21934-8, 21935-6, 21936-4, 21937-2 Four volumes, Paperbound $16.00

HISTORY OF THE LATER ROMAN EMPIRE, J. B. Bury. Eloquent, detailed reconstruction of Western and Byzantine Roman Empire by a major historian, from the death of Theodosius I (395 A.D.) to the death of Justinian (565). Extensive quotations from contemporary sources; full coverage of important Roman and foreign figures of the time. xxxiv + 965pp. 20398-0, 20399-9 Two volumes, Paperbound $7.00

AN INTELLECTUAL AND CULTURAL HISTORY OF THE WESTERN WORLD, Harry Elmer Barnes. Monumental study, tracing the development of the accomplishments that make up human culture. Every aspect of man's achievement surveyed from its origins in the Paleolithic to the present day (1964); social structures, ideas, economic systems, art, literature, technology, mathematics, the sciences, medicine, religion, jurisprudence, etc. Evaluations of the contributions of scores of great men. 1964 edition, revised and edited by scholars in the many fields represented. Total of xxix + 1381pp. 21275-0, 21276-9, 21277-7 Three volumes, Paperbound $10.50

ADVENTURES OF AN AFRICAN SLAVER, Theodore Canot. Edited by Brantz Mayer. A detailed portrayal of slavery and the slave trade, 1820-1840. Canot, an established trader along the African coast, describes the slave economy of the African kingdoms, the treatment of captured negroes, the extensive journeys in the interior to gather slaves, slave revolts and their suppression, harems, bribes, and much more. Full and unabridged republication of 1854 edition. Introduction by Malcom Cowley. 16 illustrations. xvii + 448pp. 22456-2 Paperbound $3.50

MY BONDAGE AND MY FREEDOM, Frederick Douglass. Born and brought up in slavery, Douglass witnessed its horrors and experienced its cruelties, but went on to become one of the most outspoken forces in the American anti-slavery movement. Considered the best of his autobiographies, this book graphically describes the in-human treatment of slaves, its effects on slave owners and slave families, and how Douglass's determination led him to a new life. Unaltered reprint of 1st (1855) edition. xxxii + 464pp. 22457-0 Paperbound $2.50

THE INDIANS' BOOK, recorded and edited by Natalie Curtis. Lore, music, narratives, dozens of drawings by Indians themselves from an authoritative and important survey of native culture among Plains, Southwestern, Lake and Pueblo Indians. Standard work in popular ethnomusicology. 149 songs in full notation. 23 draw-ings, 23 photos. xxxi + 584pp. 6⅝ x 9⅜. 21939-9 Paperbound $4.50

DICTIONARY OF AMERICAN PORTRAITS, edited by Hayward and Blanche Cirker. 4024 portraits of 4000 most important Americans, colonial days to 1905 (with a few important categories, like Presidents, to present). Pioneers, explorers, colonial figures, U. S. officials, politicians, writers, military and naval men, scientists, inven-tors, manufacturers, jurists, actors, historians, educators, notorious figures, Indian chiefs, etc. All authentic contemporary likenesses. The only work of its kind in existence; supplements all biographical sources for libraries. Indispensable to any-one working with American history. 8,000-item classified index, finding lists, other aids. xiv + 756pp. 9¼ x 12¾. 21823-6 Clothbound $30.00

TRITTON'S GUIDE TO BETTER WINE AND BEER MAKING FOR BEGINNERS, S. M. Tritton. All you need to know to make family-sized quantities of over 100 types of grape, fruit, herb and vegetable wines; as well as beers, mead, cider, etc. Com-plete recipes, advice as to equipment, procedures such as fermenting, bottling, and storing wines. Recipes given in British, U. S., and metric measures. Accompanying booklet lists sources in U. S. A. where ingredients may be bought, and additional information. 11 illustrations. 157pp. 5⅝ x 8⅛. (USO) 22090-7 Clothbound $3.50

GARDENING WITH HERBS FOR FLAVOR AND FRAGRANCE, Helen M. Fox. How to grow herbs in your own garden, how to use them in your cooking (over 55 recipes included), legends and myths associated with each species, uses in medicine, per-fumes, etc.—these are elements of one of the few books written especially for Amer-ican herb fanciers. Guides you step-by-step from soil preparation to harvesting and storage for each type of herb. 12 drawings by Louise Mansfield. xiv + 334pp. 22540-2 Paperbound $2.50

INCIDENTS OF TRAVEL IN YUCATAN, John L. Stephens. Classic (1843) exploration of jungles of Yucatan, looking for evidences of Maya civilization. Stephens found many ruins; comments on travel adventures, Mexican and Indian culture. 127 striking illustrations by F. Catherwood. Total of 669 pp.
20926-1, 20927-X Two volumes, Paperbound $5.00

INCIDENTS OF TRAVEL IN CENTRAL AMERICA, CHIAPAS, AND YUCATAN, John L. Stephens. An exciting travel journal and an important classic of archeology. Narrative relates his almost single-handed discovery of the Mayan culture, and exploration of the ruined cities of Copan, Palenque, Utatlan and others; the monuments they dug from the earth, the temples buried in the jungle, the customs of poverty-stricken Indians living a stone's throw from the ruined palaces. 115 drawings by F. Catherwood. Portrait of Stephens. xii + 812pp.
22404-X, 22405-8 Two volumes, Paperbound $6.00

A NEW VOYAGE ROUND THE WORLD, William Dampier. Late 17-century naturalist joined the pirates of the Spanish Main to gather information; remarkably vivid account of buccaneers, pirates; detailed, accurate account of botany, zoology, ethnography of lands visited. Probably the most important early English voyage, enormous implications for British exploration, trade, colonial policy. Also most interesting reading. Argonaut edition, introduction by Sir Albert Gray. New introduction by Percy Adams. 6 plates, 7 illustrations. xlvii + 376pp. 6½ x 9¼.
21900-3 Paperbound $3.00

INTERNATIONAL AIRLINE PHRASE BOOK IN SIX LANGUAGES, Joseph W. Bátor. Important phrases and sentences in English paralleled with French, German, Portuguese, Italian, Spanish equivalents, covering all possible airport-travel situations; created for airline personnel as well as tourist by Language Chief, Pan American Airlines. xiv + 204pp.
22017-6 Paperbound $2.00

STAGE COACH AND TAVERN DAYS, Alice Morse Earle. Detailed, lively account of the early days of taverns; their uses and importance in the social, political and military life; furnishings and decorations; locations; food and drink; tavern signs, etc. Second half covers every aspect of early travel; the roads, coaches, drivers, etc. Nostalgic, charming, packed with fascinating material. 157 illustrations, mostly photographs. xiv + 449pp.
22518-6 Paperbound $4.00

NORSE DISCOVERIES AND EXPLORATIONS IN NORTH AMERICA, Hjalmar R. Holand. The perplexing Kensington Stone, found in Minnesota at the end of the 19th century. Is it a record of a Scandinavian expedition to North America in the 14th century? Or is it one of the most successful hoaxes in history. A scientific detective investigation. Formerly *Westward from Vinland*. 31 photographs, 17 figures. x + 354pp.
22014-1 Paperbound $2.75

A BOOK OF OLD MAPS, compiled and edited by Emerson D. Fite and Archibald Freeman. 74 old maps offer an unusual survey of the discovery, settlement and growth of America down to the close of the Revolutionary war: maps showing Norse settlements in Greenland, the explorations of Columbus, Verrazano, Cabot, Champlain, Joliet, Drake, Hudson, etc., campaigns of Revolutionary war battles, and much more. Each map is accompanied by a brief historical essay. xvi + 299pp.
11 x 13¾.
22084-2 Paperbound $6.00

DESIGN BY ACCIDENT; A BOOK OF "ACCIDENTAL EFFECTS" FOR ARTISTS AND DESIGNERS, James F. O'Brien. Create your own unique, striking, imaginative effects by "controlled accident" interaction of materials: paints and lacquers, oil and water based paints, splatter, crackling materials, shatter, similar items. Everything you do will be different; first book on this limitless art, so useful to both fine artist and commercial artist. Full instructions. 192 plates showing "accidents," 8 in color. viii + 215pp. 8⅜ x 11¼. 21942-9 Paperbound $3.50

THE BOOK OF SIGNS, Rudolf Koch. Famed German type designer draws 493 beautiful symbols: religious, mystical, alchemical, imperial, property marks, runes, etc. Remarkable fusion of traditional and modern. Good for suggestions of timelessness, smartness, modernity. Text. vi + 104pp. 6⅛ x 9¼. 20162-7 Paperbound $1.25

HISTORY OF INDIAN AND INDONESIAN ART, Ananda K. Coomaraswamy. An unabridged republication of one of the finest books by a great scholar in Eastern art. Rich in descriptive material, history, social backgrounds; Sunga reliefs, Rajput paintings, Gupta temples, Burmese frescoes, textiles, jewelry, sculpture, etc. 400 photos. viii + 423pp. 6⅜ x 9¾. 21436-2 Paperbound $4.00

PRIMITIVE ART, Franz Boas. America's foremost anthropologist surveys textiles, ceramics, woodcarving, basketry, metalwork, etc.; patterns, technology, creation of symbols, style origins. All areas of world, but very full on Northwest Coast Indians. More than 350 illustrations of baskets, boxes, totem poles, weapons, etc. 378 pp. 20025-6 Paperbound $3.00

THE GENTLEMAN AND CABINET MAKER'S DIRECTOR, Thomas Chippendale. Full reprint (third edition, 1762) of most influential furniture book of all time, by master cabinetmaker. 200 plates, illustrating chairs, sofas, mirrors, tables, cabinets, plus 24 photographs of surviving pieces. Biographical introduction by N. Bienenstock. vi + 249pp. 9⅞ x 12¾. 21601-2 Paperbound $4.00

AMERICAN ANTIQUE FURNITURE, Edgar G. Miller, Jr. The basic coverage of all American furniture before 1840. Individual chapters cover type of furniture—clocks, tables, sideboards, etc.—chronologically, with inexhaustible wealth of data. More than 2100 photographs, all identified, commented on. Essential to all early American collectors. Introduction by H. E. Keyes. vi + 1106pp. 7⅞ x 10¾. 21599-7, 21600-4 Two volumes, Paperbound $11.00

PENNSYLVANIA DUTCH AMERICAN FOLK ART, Henry J. Kauffman. 279 photos, 28 drawings of tulipware, Fraktur script, painted tinware, toys, flowered furniture, quilts, samplers, hex signs, house interiors, etc. Full descriptive text. Excellent for tourist, rewarding for designer, collector. Map. 146pp. 7⅞ x 10¾. 21205-X Paperbound $2.50

EARLY NEW ENGLAND GRAVESTONE RUBBINGS, Edmund V. Gillon, Jr. 43 photographs, 226 carefully reproduced rubbings show heavily symbolic, sometimes macabre early gravestones, up to early 19th century. Remarkable early American primitive art, occasionally strikingly beautiful; always powerful. Text. xxvi + 207pp. 8⅜ x 11¼. 21380-3 Paperbound $3.50

A HISTORY OF COSTUME, Carl Köhler. Definitive history, based on surviving pieces of clothing primarily, and paintings, statues, etc. secondarily. Highly readable text, supplemented by 594 illustrations of costumes of the ancient Mediterranean peoples, Greece and Rome, the Teutonic prehistoric period; costumes of the Middle Ages, Renaissance, Baroque, 18th and 19th centuries. Clear, measured patterns are provided for many clothing articles. Approach is practical throughout. Enlarged by Emma von Sichart. 464pp. 21030-8 Paperbound $3.50

ORIENTAL RUGS, ANTIQUE AND MODERN, Walter A. Hawley. A complete and authoritative treatise on the Oriental rug—where they are made, by whom and how, designs and symbols, characteristics in detail of the six major groups, how to distinguish them and how to buy them. Detailed technical data is provided on periods, weaves, warps, wefts, textures, sides, ends and knots, although no technical background is required for an understanding. 11 color plates, 80 halftones, 4 maps. vi + 320pp. 6⅛ x 9⅛. 22366-3 Paperbound $5.00

TEN BOOKS ON ARCHITECTURE, Vitruvius. By any standards the most important book on architecture ever written. Early Roman discussion of aesthetics of building, construction methods, orders, sites, and every other aspect of architecture has inspired, instructed architecture for about 2,000 years. Stands behind Palladio, Michelangelo, Bramante, Wren, countless others. Definitive Morris H. Morgan translation. 68 illustrations. xii + 331pp. 20645-9 Paperbound $3.50

THE FOUR BOOKS OF ARCHITECTURE, Andrea Palladio. Translated into every major Western European language in the two centuries following its publication in 1570, this has been one of the most influential books in the history of architecture. Complete reprint of the 1738 Isaac Ware edition. New introduction by Adolf Placzek, Columbia Univ. 216 plates. xxii + 110pp. of text. 9½ x 12¾. 21308-0 Clothbound $10.00

STICKS AND STONES: A STUDY OF AMERICAN ARCHITECTURE AND CIVILIZATION, Lewis Mumford.One of the great classics of American cultural history. American architecture from the medieval-inspired earliest forms to the early 20th century; evolution of structure and style, and reciprocal influences on environment. 21 photographic illustrations. 238pp. 20202-X Paperbound $2.00

THE AMERICAN BUILDER'S COMPANION, Asher Benjamin. The most widely used early 19th century architectural style and source book, for colonial up into Greek Revival periods. Extensive development of geometry of carpentering, construction of sashes, frames, doors, stairs; plans and elevations of domestic and other buildings. Hundreds of thousands of houses were built according to this book, now invaluable to historians, architects, restorers, etc. 1827 edition. 59 plates. 114pp. 7⅞ x 10¾. 22236-5 Paperbound $3.50

DUTCH HOUSES IN THE HUDSON VALLEY BEFORE 1776, Helen Wilkinson Reynolds. The standard survey of the Dutch colonial house and outbuildings, with constructional features, decoration, and local history associated with individual homesteads. Introduction by Franklin D. Roosevelt. Map. 150 illustrations. 469pp. 6⅝ x 9¼. 21469-9 Paperbound $4.00

JOHANN SEBASTIAN BACH, Philipp Spitta. One of the great classics of musicology, this definitive analysis of Bach's music (and life) has never been surpassed. Lucid, nontechnical analyses of hundreds of pieces (30 pages devoted to St. Matthew Passion, 26 to B Minor Mass). Also includes major analysis of 18th-century music. 450 musical examples. 40-page musical supplement. Total of xx + 1799pp.
(EUK) 22278-0, 22279-9 Two volumes, Clothbound $15.00

MOZART AND HIS PIANO CONCERTOS, Cuthbert Girdlestone. The only full-length study of an important area of Mozart's creativity. Provides detailed analyses of all 23 concertos, traces inspirational sources. 417 musical examples. Second edition. 509pp.
(USO) 21271-8 Paperbound $3.50

THE PERFECT WAGNERITE: A COMMENTARY ON THE NIBLUNG'S RING, George Bernard Shaw. Brilliant and still relevant criticism in remarkable essays on Wagner's Ring cycle, Shaw's ideas on political and social ideology behind the plots, role of Leitmotifs, vocal requisites, etc. Prefaces. xxi + 136pp.
21707-8 Paperbound $1.50

DON GIOVANNI, W. A. Mozart. Complete libretto, modern English translation; biographies of composer and librettist; accounts of early performances and critical reaction. Lavishly illustrated. All the material you need to understand and appreciate this great work. Dover Opera Guide and Libretto Series; translated and introduced by Ellen Bleiler. 92 illustrations. 209pp.
21134-7 Paperbound $1.50

HIGH FIDELITY SYSTEMS: A LAYMAN'S GUIDE, Roy F. Allison. All the basic information you need for setting up your own audio system: high fidelity and stereo record players, tape records, F.M. Connections, adjusting tone arm, cartridge, checking needle alignment, positioning speakers, phasing speakers, adjusting hums, trouble-shooting, maintenance, and similar topics. Enlarged 1965 edition. More than 50 charts, diagrams, photos. iv + 91pp.   21514-8 Paperbound $1.25

REPRODUCTION OF SOUND, Edgar Villchur. Thorough coverage for laymen of high fidelity systems, reproducing systems in general, needles, amplifiers, preamps, loudspeakers, feedback, explaining physical background. "A rare talent for making technicalities vividly comprehensible," R. Darrell, *High Fidelity.* 69 figures. iv + 92pp.
21515-6 Paperbound $1.00

HEAR ME TALKIN' TO YA: THE STORY OF JAZZ AS TOLD BY THE MEN WHO MADE IT, Nat Shapiro and Nat Hentoff. Louis Armstrong, Fats Waller, Jo Jones, Clarence Williams, Billy Holiday, Duke Ellington, Jelly Roll Morton and dozens of other jazz greats tell how it was in Chicago's South Side, New Orleans, depression Harlem and the modern West Coast as jazz was born and grew. xvi + 429pp.
21726-4 Paperbound $2.50

FABLES OF AESOP, translated by Sir Roger L'Estrange. A reproduction of the very rare 1931 Paris edition; a selection of the most interesting fables, together with 50 imaginative drawings by Alexander Calder. v + 128pp. 6½x9¼.
21780-9 Paperbound $1.25

MATHEMATICAL PUZZLES FOR BEGINNERS AND ENTHUSIASTS, Geoffrey Mott-Smith. 189 puzzles from easy to difficult—involving arithmetic, logic, algebra, properties of digits, probability, etc.—for enjoyment and mental stimulus. Explanation of mathematical principles behind the puzzles. 135 illustrations. viii + 248pp.
20198-8 Paperbound $1.75

PAPER FOLDING FOR BEGINNERS, William D. Murray and Francis J. Rigney. Easiest book on the market, clearest instructions on making interesting, beautiful origami. Sail boats, cups, roosters, frogs that move legs, bonbon boxes, standing birds, etc. 40 projects; more than 275 diagrams and photographs. 94pp.
20713-7 Paperbound $1.00

TRICKS AND GAMES ON THE POOL TABLE, Fred Herrmann. 79 tricks and games—some solitaires, some for two or more players, some competitive games—to entertain you between formal games. Mystifying shots and throws, unusual caroms, tricks involving such props as cork, coins, a hat, etc. Formerly *Fun on the Pool Table*. 77 figures. 95pp.
21814-7 Paperbound $1.00

HAND SHADOWS TO BE THROWN UPON THE WALL: A SERIES OF NOVEL AND AMUSING FIGURES FORMED BY THE HAND, Henry Bursill. Delightful picturebook from great-grandfather's day shows how to make 18 different hand shadows: a bird that flies, duck that quacks, dog that wags his tail, camel, goose, deer, boy, turtle, etc. Only book of its sort. vi + 33pp. 6½ x 9¼. 21779-5 Paperbound $1.00

WHITTLING AND WOODCARVING, E. J. Tangerman. 18th printing of best book on market. "If you can cut a potato you can carve" toys and puzzles, chains, chessmen, caricatures, masks, frames, woodcut blocks, surface patterns, much more. Information on tools, woods, techniques. Also goes into serious wood sculpture from Middle Ages to present, East and West. 464 photos, figures. x + 293pp.
20965-2 Paperbound $2.00

HISTORY OF PHILOSOPHY, Julián Marias. Possibly the clearest, most easily followed, best planned, most useful one-volume history of philosophy on the market; neither skimpy nor overfull. Full details on system of every major philosopher and dozens of less important thinkers from pre-Socratics up to Existentialism and later. Strong on many European figures usually omitted. Has gone through dozens of editions in Europe. 1966 edition, translated by Stanley Appelbaum and Clarence Strowbridge. xviii + 505pp.
21739-6 Paperbound $3.00

YOGA: A SCIENTIFIC EVALUATION, Kovoor T. Behanan. Scientific but non-technical study of physiological results of yoga exercises; done under auspices of Yale U. Relations to Indian thought, to psychoanalysis, etc. 16 photos. xxiii + 270pp.
20505-3 Paperbound $2.50

Prices subject to change without notice.
Available at your book dealer or write for free catalogue to Dept. GI, Dover Publications, Inc., 180 Varick St., N. Y., N. Y. 10014. Dover publishes more than 150 books each year on science, elementary and advanced mathematics, biology, music, art, literary history, social sciences and other areas.